A UNIFYING
Essays of

Edited by
DAVID W. HERON

INFLUENCE
Raynard Coe Swank

With a foreword by
LAWRENCE CLARK POWELL

and an appreciation by
J. PERIAM DANTON

The Scarecrow Press, Inc.
Metuchen, N.J., & London
1981

Library of Congress Cataloging in Publication Data

Swank, Raynard Coe, 1912-
   A unifying influence.

   Includes bibliographical references.
   1. Library science--Addresses, essays, lectures.
I. Heron, David W., 1942- .   II. Title.
Z665.S89   020   80-28595
ISBN 0-8108-1407-2

Copyright © 1981 by Raynard Coe Swank

Manufactured in the United States of America

Contents

Foreword by Lawrence Clark Powell		v
An Appreciation by J. Periam Danton		ix
Preface by David W. Heron		xiii
1.	Subject Catalogs, Classification, or Bibliographies? (1944)	1
2.	The Cost of Keeping Books (1955)	29
3.	The Educational Function of the University Library (1952)	41
4.	Sight and Sound in the World of Books (1953)	55
5.	Too Much and Too Little (1959)	65
6.	The Help We Give (1960)	81
7.	Librarians and Librarianship (with Melville J. Ruggles) (1962)	91
8.	Six Items for Export (1963)	107
9.	Documentation and Information Science in the Core Library School Curriculum (1967)	119
10.	Interlibrary Cooperation, Interlibrary Communications, and Information Networks (1971)	129
11.	Cataloging Cost Factors (1956)	155
12.	Subject Cataloging in the Subject-Departmentalized Library (1951)	177

13. The Pacific Northwest Bibliographic Center (1960)   191

14. A Dream in Action: 211
    The California Library Network Plan (1974)

Foreword

Ours was not a personal friendship though not because of any incompatability, but rather from the infrequent conjunction of our professional orbits. We held each other in mutual esteem and given the chance we could have enjoyed the friendship that is possible between temperamental opposites. When our careers did meet, Ray Swank brought assets foreign to me-- patience, analytical judgment, and experience in the conduct of day-to-day library operations. I was the gainer.

I remember our first meeting. It was about thirty-five years ago in Margot and Richard Archer's backyard near the Clark Library. Archer had come from Chicago to be my bibliographical assistant as we both embarked on our professional careers. Ray was in town to assist Lowell Martin in a survey of the Los Angeles Public Library. He and Archer had been Ph. D. candidates at the Graduate Library School. All I recall is that we ate well and talked books. I liked Ray. How could I have not? He let me talk.

There is one of the qualities on which Ray has built his distinguished career: He is a good listener. Wherever his work took him, he listened first and then talked. I had good reason to appreciate this quality when our paths next crossed sometime in the 1950s. The UCLA Library Acquisitions Department was in trouble. Bob Vosper had gone to Kansas and I missed his help in administering a library that was growing rapidly on all fronts.

Aware of Ray Swank's success in technical matters at Minnesota, Oregon, and Stanford, I asked him to come for a week and tell us what to do about the backlog of orders and arrivals and the low morale of the department. He spent most of the week in Acquisitions in his shirt sleeves, going from desk to desk--there were twenty-five or thirty in all-- sitting down, asking questions and listening and saying little. He met also with the heads of the other departments and branches and with faculty book chairmen.

At the end of the week Ray spent the night with us in
Malibu, and after dinner he and I sat by a driftwood fire and
I listened to his account of the week's work and what he
recommended be done. The next morning I called the entire
Acquisitions staff into my office (Provost Clarence Dykstra
once asked how it was that the littlest administrator had the
largest office) and invited Ray to tell them what he had told
me the night before. It took all morning, and when he was
through and had responded to their questions and comments,
they applauded. Major changes were called for in assignments, checking, ordering and receiving. What at the beginning of the week had been an apprehensive, insecure staff
had been won over by Ray's forthright, humane, and reasonable approach, so that they were willing to adjust to his
recommendations.

In the 1960s when we had both become library school
deans, I again profited from Ray's sagacity as he served as
director of the statewide Library Research Institute and as a
member of the University Library Council. He and Don
Coney were two of the finest colleagues of my entire career.

Soon after the beginning of my Arizona incarnation, I
called again on Ray Swank in 1972 to do what needed doing
when I saw that the task was beyond my competence. It was
to conduct a survey of the troubled University of Arizona library system. Aided by Page Ackerman and Melvin Voigt,
Ray commuted from Berkeley at a sacrifice to his own teaching program. Again I witnessed his going about, asking,
listening, probing, and then putting it all together in a report
that is still serving, eight years later, as a blueprint for the
development program led by David Laird.

The papers collected here reflect Ray Swank's many
professional achievements at home and abroad. No one in our
time has given more devoted and effective service to the American Library Association's boards and committees, to library
administration and education in California, and to his students
and colleagues for whom he has been a great good listener
and teller. To have been his grateful and admiring associate
these many years gives me a sense of reward gained from
few friendships.

May we meet again now in our sweet retirement, this
time in front of a mesquite fire here where Fay and I are

Foreword

living out our lives on the Sonoran desert. Again I'll be glad to do the listening.

                                  Lawrence Clark Powell

Bajada of the
Santa Catalinas
Tucson

An Appreciation

Raynard Swank was born in Butler, Ohio, and was graduated from Wooster College (1934), and the Western Reserve School of Library Science (1937). He received his Ph. D. from Chicago (1944). In 1937 he joined the staff of the University of Colorado Library, thus beginning a westward trek that brought him eventually to Palo Alto and Berkeley.

After four years at Colorado there were two as catalog librarian and library school faculty member at the University of Minnesota, and two as Librarian of the University of Oregon. It was while at Eugene that Ray was invited to make a survey of the Stanford University libraries, then in exceedingly bad shape. The excellent document he produced led to his appointment as Director of Libraries at Stanford in 1948. There he remained until 1962, with a two-year leave of absence, 1959-1961, to serve as Director of ALA's International Relations Office. Ray revolutionized the library system at Palo Alto and made it one of the best-run and most respected academic libraries in the State.

I hardly knew Ray personally before his Stanford days, but beginning then our paths crossed with increasing frequency, both socially and professionally. As they did, I came more and more to like the quiet, judicious person Ray is.

In the spring of 1960, after I had announced my resignation from the deanship of the Berkeley School of Librarianship, and indicated that I preferred not to be on the search committee for my successor, then-Chancellor Glenn Seaborg called to ask me to give him, informally, my personal recommendation for the new dean. Of course, I had speculated some on the matter but after Seaborg's call I weighed it in dead earnest. I reviewed the faculties of the principal library schools and the top management of the major university libraries. I finally gave the Chancellor Ray's name. I wasn't conversant with the later developments then until I returned from a year's sabbatical leave in late summer, 1961--to find Acting Dean LeRoy Merritt still on the bridge! I had another call from the Chancellor's office and learned that Ray had been approached three times and had three times declined. Did I have any new ideas? I inferred that a quick answer was wanted. I went into another huddle with myself. In the meantime, I'd had at least one conversation with Ray.

I can't now say whether I sensed that Ray's answers to the Chancellor had not been absolutely final and irrevocable ones, or whether the wish was simply father to the thought. At any rate, I was more than ever convinced that Ray was the best person for the position and that we might still get him. So I told the Chancellor that I was unwilling to offer another name until I was absolutely certain it was unavoidable. My response wasn't received with much enthusiasm. Ray did, of course, eventually accept Berkeley's invitation and assumed the Deanship in 1962.

During his eight-year tenure he engineered a thoroughgoing revision of the curriculum, substantially strengthened the faculty, served on a number of national and local committees, published <u>Soviet Libraries and Librarianship</u>, and was a consultant to the Universities of the Philippines, Singapore, and Malaysia and the Chinese University of Hong Kong. The diversity and breadth of his interests, and his convictions and commitments are attested by the papers in this volume. Upon his retirement from the Deanship, in 1970, I wrote a short piece about Ray for <u>The Calibrarian</u>, the newsletter of the UCLA and Berkeley library schools' Alumni Association. I feel now as I did then, and repeat a few lines for the wider readership this volume will have:

> ... many would feel that his most signal achievements were the establishment and development of the Institute of Library Research and the securing of South Hall for the School. It seems pretty clear to this observer that neither would have come to pass without Ray's determination, unswerving conviction, and persistent, almost Herculean effort. Very few know how exceedingly close we came to losing South Hall entirely to other, more politically powerful interests on the campus. The building was our last chance for an adequate home reasonably close to the University Library. Had we lost South Hall, we would have lost for the foreseeable future any hope of growth and development in faculty, student body, library and Institute. It would not be inappropriate for South Hall, like Sir Christopher

An Appreciation

Wren's Saint Paul's Cathedral, to bear a plaque with the words 'Si monumentum requaerit, circumspice.' (That the Institute was later lost does not detract from the credit due Ray for its establishment.)

It is said that there's no better way to know a man than to be his tent or camp mate. Though I've never camped with Ray, I had a comparable experience; he and I were roommates for six weeks during a South East Asian survey for the Ford Foundation, and I vividly remember many pleasures--and a few pains--shared with this excellent companion and fellow-traveler.

I remember also two other things of more professional concern. No matter what kind of library or aspect of librarianship we were looking at, Ray never failed to be genuinely interested; he thus quickly established a rapport with and won the confidence of the local librarians. He also proved to be, as he still is, a master at presenting even the severest criticism or disapproval in a way that didn't hurt, or damage amour propre.

I don't believe that Ray's retirement is anything but nominal, and for this I am personally grateful.

J. Periam Danton
Professor Emeritus

School of Library and Information Studies
University of California, Berkeley

Preface

Since Ray Swank decided, one day in 1936, that the piano and clarinet were not his ultimate vocation, he has done a lot of things, and seen most of the world. In these last forty-four years he has had an important influence on the institutions and on the profession to which he has chosen to lend his commanding presence.

These essays reflect some of the ways in which he has changed libraries and librarianship, some of his most important professional accomplishments. They reflect his early and continuing gift for bibliography, his understanding of the workings of university libraries--and of the people who use them and make them work--an appreciation, ahead of his time, of the phenomena which gave rise to the McLuhan cult, and his breadth of vision. They reflect his internationalism and his interest in cooperative communities of libraries. They may not do justice to his eight years as dean of the U. C. library school, which he moved from the Doe Library attic into splendid old South Hall, and which flourished there under his regime.

His Stanford and Berkeley years are those which Perry Danton and Larry Powell recall so well. My own awareness of Ray Swank began in the same era, but was different. They were his peers, each a few years his senior; I was an apprentice. One of the great things about Ray Swank is that his apprentices and students, along with the thousand or so people who worked under his direction (as well as his peers) have tended to become his devoted friends.

My apprenticeship started in 1955, when Elmer Grieder went off to teach library science in Turkey. Ray was in the middle of a four-year term on the ALA Executive Board (a time-consuming responsibility) and needed a temporary assistant. Larry Powell sent me up from UCLA for an interview, and in August 1955 I was ensconced in Elmer's little office, learning how to squeeze student wages out of unspent salaries and how to recruit librarians without offering more than the Old Timers were getting.

As apprentices do, I learned from making mistakes, but when I needed advice or direction Ray was there to give it (unless he was in Chicago) patiently and judiciously. Diffidently (he is more of a listener than a talker) he shared some of the things he knows about universities and libraries, about library associations, about books, about music both sacred and profane, about written exposition, and also about how to skin a catfish.

He learned how to skin a catfish and how to catalog a book during the Great Depression. During and after his undergraduate years at the College of Wooster (which has since given him an honorary doctorate) he played church organ and, whenever the dance band was working, played clarinet and tenor saxophone. This musical career, in the depths of the Depression, didn't seem to be going anywhere, although he continued to play church organ for many more years.

He applied for jobs in a cigar store, in a pipe organ factory, and at the Cleveland Public Library. He recalls that his explorations of Ohio history had led him to a number of libraries throughout the state, and to the notion that he might like to be a librarian. Linda Eastman, director of the Cleveland Library, was cordial but had no job to offer. She suggested that he apply to the Western Reserve Library School. He did, and in 1936 he was admitted.

He emerged in the summer of 1937 with a BS in LS degree, some doubts about his new profession, and no job. Late that fall Ralph Ellsworth offered him--sight unseen--a position in the University of Colorado Library. In those days one accepted promptly. There were also the Rocky Mountains to be climbed.

There followed four halcyon years as a junior librarian. Ellsworth turned him loose on the catalog, in which he replaced ALA subject headings with Library of Congress headings; when that was done he organized a new central serial-record file for the University of Colorado Libraries. After that he brought together the library's government documents in a new documents department, using the Superintendent of Documents scheme to arrange federal publications and devising a parallel system for state, local, and foreign documents.

Preface

After four years with Ralph Ellsworth at Colorado, he knew that he was a librarian. Armed with a fellowship which Ellsworth had helped to get, he moved his wife Lel and baby son Damon to Chicago, where he became a doctoral candidate at the Graduate Library School.

His dissertation, accepted by the University of Chicago in 1944, was Organization of Library Materials for Research in English Literature, a comparison of subject catalogs, classification, and published bibliographies as means of access to library collections. An abbreviated version of the thesis was published in Library Quarterly articles during the following year. (One of these articles is here included.)

After two years spent reorganizing the University of Minnesota Library's catalog department and teaching cataloging in the library school, he became director, in the summer of 1946, of the University of Oregon Library. The following winter he was invited to join Louis Round Wilson in surveying the Stanford University Libraries.

Nathan Van Patten retired as director of Stanford's libraries in 1947, and in 1948 Ray succeeded him.

The next fourteen years at Stanford's libraries became the Swank era, a period of steady progress, but not a period of spectacular change. Stanford was a comfortable and friendly place, poor but honest, with an academic tradition able to accommodate both Thorstein Veblen and Herbert Hoover. "The Farm" was a more appropriate epithet for it in the fifties than since.

The Library needed a new building, which the University couldn't afford. Finally in the late fifties plans were made for an undergraduate library, which was finished in 1966. Book funds in the fifties were hard to come by, and Stanford library salaries were among the lowest in the west. Still the Stanford libraries staff was stable, loyal, and fond of Ray Swank.

During this time Ray was prominent in the affairs of the American Library Association as well as those of the Association of Research Libraries. At the University of Oregon he had become fascinated by the potentialities of audio-visual materials both as teaching aids and as primary sources for historical and sociological research. Stanford, however, showed little interest. For two terms he chaired the ALA Audio-Visual Board, and also the California Library Association's Audio-Visual Committee, as well as founded the state's cooperative public library film circuits, formed to share the cost of film purchase.

In 1953 he was elected to the ALA Executive Board for a four-year term, and a year later became a member of the first committee to deal with the Association's tendency to over-organize. The next year he chaired a committee charged with deciding whether ALA should move to Washington. The committee said yes; the membership--as it has done periodically--voted no.

Four years on the ALA Executive Board (which has four regular meetings of several days each during the year, and occasional special meetings) often causes former Board members to disappear from the Association once their terms are up. Ray Swank did not succumb to this syndrome, although he did cut back to three committees for a couple of years after ending his Board term. He was nominated for, and narrowly defeated in the next year's election for the ALA presidency, and at the same time became involved in ALA's international relations activities, in which he has been active ever since.

In 1959 he took a temporary leave of absence from Stanford to become Director of ALA's International Relations Office. After two years of globe-trotting he began a six year term on the International Relations Committee--the first year as chairman--and as a member of the U.S. National Commission for Unesco.

The Stanford ties were loosened somewhat by all this internationalism ("How ya gonna keep 'em down on the farm...."); when the University of California asked him a fourth time to become dean of the Library School at Berkeley--with some persuasion from Perry Danton and from his old Colorado friend and Graduate Library School classmate LeRoy Merritt--he accepted.

In those Stanford years, when the weather was good, Ray would pack up his three youngest and I my two--all of an age, more or less--and go over the coast range to camp, usually at San Mateo County or Portola State parks--leaving our spouses at home to enjoy their luxurious solitude.

Camped, on one of these outings, on Pescadero Creek, the kids caught two catfish, a very small perch, and a sim-

Preface   xvii

ilarly small crayfish. Preparing them was relatively simple, except for the catfish, which had to be skinned, and Ray demonstrated his familiarity with this tedious process, a skill acquired in his youth in Ohio. After dinner, on these occasions, the children blew up their air mattresses and retired; Ray and I then began the evening recorder recital, inspired by an occasional sip of bourbon whiskey, and sat talking by the fire. We have camped, even recently, complete with recorders (time has not dulled our duet rendition of Du, Du Liegst Mir im Herzen); the kids now grown but still campers, occasionally come along.

In the sixties Ray Swank was fully occupied with running the library school, although he kept his international bag packed, and travelled occasionally to Asia or South America. Although the school's most conspicuous problem was space, and the acquisition of South Hall his most conspicuous achievement, Ray recalls that curriculum revision-- the introduction of Information Science to the curriculum-- was his most urgent objective. Not only did the school and the profession gain from the Victorian splendor of the University's oldest and most centrally located building, but the computer, during the Swank era, became an instrument of librarianship in both the School and the Library Research Institute.

He devoted the decade of the Seventies to teaching, principally of library management, interlibrary cooperation, and comparative librarianship, and continued as an international consultant.

It is fitting that a couple of months after his retirement he should be off again to the Western Pacific, representing the University of California at the Manila Conference of the International Federation of Library Associations.

Across oceans, national boundaries, and the smaller, tighter barriers which academicians sometimes erect around themselves and their domains, Ray Swank's inquisitive mind, goodwill, and easy humor have been at work in this last half-century--a unifying influence among the world's libraries.

                                                David W. Heron

Hoover Institution Library
Stanford University

1. Subject Catalogs, Classifications, or Bibliographies?
A Review of Critical Discussions, 1876-1942

In recent years librarians have increasingly questioned the efficiency of library cataloging and especially shelf classification as devices for guiding readers to materials on particular subjects. This wholesome interrogation has led to many fruitful suggestions both for improving the general catalog and classification and for reducing their cost. On the other hand, it has led at least a few librarians to reconsider the possibility that subject bibliographies may be in the long run more effective and economical than either catalogs or classifications--the possibility that, if the field of bibliography were more fully developed and exploited, subject catalogs and classifications could be greatly modified or perhaps abandoned entirely.

This suggestion is by no means a new one. The bibliography vs. cataloging controversy is one of traditional import. Many times during the past century catalog-minded librarians have believed, or wished to believe, that the issue was finally dead. But the arguments favoring bibliography have reappeared again and again to disturb new generations of librarians. By now their history is long and interesting.

This paper reviews briefly a part of that history. It recounts the important critical discussions from 1876 to 1942 in which subject cataloging and classification, as contrasted with bibliography, were challenged and defended. Since these controversies related largely to American cataloging practice, attention is limited to discussions in American library literature, with the addition of certain English discussions which bore directly or indirectly upon American practice. The plan of the paper is, first, to notice chronologically the outstanding controversies and controversialists and, second,

---

Reprinted from The Library Quarterly, 14 (October 1944), pp. 316-32, by permission of the University of Chicago Press. Copyright © 1944 by The University of Chicago Press.

to summarize the principal arguments on both sides of the question.

The Outstanding Controversies

In 1876, when Charles A. Cutter first published his Rules for a Printed Dictionary Catalogue[1] and Melvil Dewey his decimal classification,[2] the broad lines of modern library policy were already well established. Even then the energies of American librarians were being expended largely in one activity: the systematic recataloging and reclassification, according to new principles, of all library accumulations up to that time. This was the "librarian's work" which John Fisk of Harvard University enthusiastically described in a current issue of the Atlantic Monthly.[3]

Fisk's article touched off the first controversy which falls within the limits of this account. It was read by interested members of the Harvard faculty, one of whom, Dr. Hermann A. Hagen, wrote a vigorous reply in the Nation.[4] In his opinion the proper function of the library catalog was "to show whether a given book is in the library and where it is placed"--a function which required no such catalog as Mr. Fisk described. The subject approach to books could be handled adequately only through bibliography. Any program to construct elaborate subject catalogs would not only fail to achieve its goal but would become an incumbrance, "a mountainous obstacle," to the compilation of bibliographies which were even then urgently needed.

Dr. Hagen's arguments drew a reply from Cutter.[5] Of all members of the library profession, Cutter had perhaps the least good to say for bibliographies. To him they were little better than nothing; therefore, a subject catalog was indispensable to the reader. Justin Winsor, librarian of the Boston Public Library and president of the newly organized American Library Association, joined Cutter in defense of the subject catalog.[6] Hagen then received support from one of his Harvard colleagues, Alexander Agassiz, the son of Louis Agassiz.[7] About that time it was prematurely announced that the subject catalog of the Harvard College Library was to be discontinued, whereupon Winsor wrote a longer and more careful statement of his views.[8] In this, he emphasized that Hagen represented the traditional European attitude toward libraries--an attitude from which American librarians had now happily revolted. A reversion to subject bibliographies,

Subject Catalogs, ... ? 3

as Hagen suggested, would be a long step backward in library service, especially to the inexperienced student and layman, who must have "the advantages of the catalogue to open to them the methods of research and independent learning."

Hagen's letter was little more than a disturbing incident in the progress of library affairs. Among librarians themselves, a more important question of the day was the relative values of subject cataloging and classification. Dewey's idea of minute subject classification of books on the library shelves had so caught the imagination of many librarians that even the subject catalog had been relegated to a position of secondary importance. Thus when two English librarians, Benjamin Wheatley and Eiríkr Magnússon, expressed their belief in 1877 that minute shelf classification was not needed, provided a library was fully cataloged, [9] they were immediately challenged. [10] One concluded that both the catalog and the classification were "desirable if they could be obtained, but, if the latter only, then let us have it by all means."

Shortly after this discussion, Cutter took occasion to state in his usual concise manner the advantages of catalogs over classifications. [11] Other librarians had no use whatever for shelf arrangements. Among these was Frederic Vinton, librarian at the College of New Jersey. [12] To him, shelf classification was time wasted, labor lost. Indeed, any library without a modern subject catalog--he seemed oblivious to the possibilities of bibliography--was useless for purposes of research. Without it, great resources "sleep in dishonorable dust, awaiting resurrection at the call of intelligent librarians."

In these discussions no exclusive decision was reached; indeed, none was sought. The acceptance of both subject cataloging and classification, with their respective advantages and disadvantages, seemed already assured. Yet the two camps remained more or less separate. In cataloging, the time had already come when innovations were relatively few, when progress tended to follow the lines already laid down. [13] It was a time for promotion rather than for invention. Critical discussions persisted in some quarters only on the question of classed versus dictionary catalogs. [14] Classification, on the other hand, was still in its formative stages. Cutter was now at work on his expansive classification, and Schwartz was vigorously promoting his alphabetical scheme. Logical or alphabetical classification?--this debate was now at its height, the balance tipped in favor of the logical. [15]

It was ten years after Hagen's letter before another champion for bibliographies appeared--William I. Fletcher, the librarian of Amherst College and chairman of the A. L. A. Committee on Cooperation. Fletcher had been associated with Poole in compiling the Index to Periodical Literature, which had just been published.[16] In the course of that great co-operative undertaking, young Fletcher had evolved ideas for which he fought all the rest of his life. In 1886 he wrote:

> It is to the great credit of our American librarians ... that we have such admirable catalogues of so many libraries. But our library system is but passing out of its infancy. The demands of the past are but a shadow of what is to come, and already this system of elaborate cataloguing, repeating itself in scores, even in hundreds, of libraries, is breaking down of its own weight. The only question now is, How can it be replaced with something more elastic, less expensive, and capable of meeting the needs of the twentieth century, when our libraries will be numbered by the thousands, and the volumes in scores of them by the millions?
> Co-operation furnishes the clue.[17]

And by co-operation Fletcher did not mean the co-operative production of dictionary catalogs but of printed bibliographies and indexes, like Poole's Index, which would serve "equally for one library or another" and which would replace the subject catalogs of individual libraries.

At the A. L. A. conference a few months later, Fletcher read a paper in which he severely denounced minute shelf classification.[18] Again he spoke eloquently for the need of analytical bibliographies and indexes, without which a more progressive library service was impossible. Even analytical cataloging was not enough. "Bibliography would be the watchword of the future," while classification, owing to its obvious and irreparable deficiencies, would be relegated to a subordinate place in library administration.

> I have attempted to show that in improving the bibliographical resources of our libraries, and laying the chief stress on them as guides to readers, we are on the solid ground of experience and an orderly development of our library system. But this Will-o'-the-wisp of close classification dances

over the quagmires of inexperience, uncertainty, and extravagance.... [It] will prove to be a delusion.[19]

The discussion which followed the reading of this paper was confused and bitter.[20] Dewey and Biscoe, in particular, attempted an impromptu defense of close classification, although neither seemed to grasp the import of Fletcher's arguments. Cutter, apparently, was not present at the meeting; but at his first opportunity he again put in his word for library catalogs and classifications.[21] With this, the close classifiers felt satisfied, and the elaboration of the great schemes continued. Fletcher, however, was not yet finished. As a counterblow to the close classifiers, he eventually constructed his own classification--a simple, unpretentious list of broad headings which he offered as a way of escape for librarians who shrank from the intricacies and difficulties of the more elaborate schemes.[22] This unfortunate effort roused only the scorn of his colleagues, who simply pointed out how much less perfect was Fletcher's scheme than the great Dewey and Cutter schemes which it was supposed to replace.[23] Fletcher's principal contention that no shelf classification--neither his nor any other--could in practice possess any real value whatever, except administrative, had completely miscarried.

Fletcher lost his cause, but he never lost faith in his arguments. All his life he worked persistently to strip shelf classification of its "artificial and factitious value" and to effect the co-operative production by the library profession of analytical indexes and bibliographies which would gradually render subject cataloging unnecessary.[24] He won his point in connection with the analysis of periodicals; but for other types of materials the majority of librarians saw no reason for abandoning the development of subject catalogs and classifications.

The logic of Fletcher's arguments nevertheless continued to disturb a few librarians, especially those who minimized the values of shelf classification. In 1889 W. E. Foster attempted to redefine the relations of subject cataloging and bibliography.[25] After drawing a sharp line between the needs of the specialist and the layman, he concluded that bibliographies were more useful to the former and that catalogs were more useful to the latter. A year later there appeared an article by Charles H. Hull, the assistant librarian at Cornell University, which is still the best statement in library literature of the case against subject cataloging as contrasted with bibliography.[26] This closely reasoned article took the point of view that

> bibliographies are not perfect. Judged by an ideal standard, the most complete collection of them will be found sadly deficient. But the best subject catalogues, judged by the same standard, will be found still more deficient....

Having answered one by one the various objections which had been raised to the use of bibliographies and having pointed out the disadvantages of subject catalogs, Hull concluded that there was no need for a subject catalog other than a careful and complete index of the library's bibliographies and reference lists--an index which should include analytical entries for important lists buried in general works, periodicals, etc.

No one answered Hull directly, not even Cutter. But Cutter's feelings were explicit in a paragraph which he published a month or so later in the Library Journal.[27] About the same time, George W. Cole published his notable article on "The Future of Cataloguing,"[28] in which he expressed the following convictions:

> A collection of books, no matter what may be its size, is not of necessity a library. Not until it has been arranged, and systematically and thoroughly catalogued, is it worthy to be dignified by that name....
> The labor necessary to make a carefully prepared catalogue is of necessity great; ... but it is one which every librarian must face. He has no right to shirk it, trusting that special bibliographies and indexes may be brought out, perhaps by this generation, perhaps by the next, and which, when provided, will still be clumsy tools for his constituency. No, rather give us more and better catalogues.

At an A. L. A. meeting several years later, Cole expressed the prevailing opinion that "the success of any library, other things being equal, depends entirely upon the excellence of its catalogue";[29] and at the same meeting Emily Wade, of the San Francisco Public Library, stated that "it is by means of the catalogue that the books in a library are expected to accomplish the purpose for which they were cre-

Subject Catalogs, ...? 7

ated."[30] There was little room for bibliography in the plans of these librarians.

While American librarians were thus aggressively developing library service through subject catalogs and classifications, the English for the most part remained wary. By 1890 a few English librarians had adopted American practice,[31] but the majority was not yet convinced of its lasting value. In 1896 Frank Campbell, of the British Museum, published a highly original book, The Theory of National and International Bibliography,[32] in which he attacked several assumptions which underlie modern cataloging and classification. He advocated the development of special bibliographies based upon the work of a government bureau which would assume responsibility for the initial registering, cataloging, and indexing of the whole of the national literature. This book, however, appears to have had no appreciable effect upon the trends of the day, either in England or in America. By 1900 the English had gone further toward accepting American practice. Thus, twenty-three years after the Hagen-Cutter dispute in America, another of the same nature became possible in England.

The occasion for this English dispute was the British Museum's announced intention of publishing a subject catalog. Presently there appeared in the London Times an article signed "A Scholar" which claimed that such a catalog, in view of the constantly increasing number of bibliographies, would be superfluous--a waste of public money and of the time of public servants.[33] Like Hagen, Fletcher, and Hull before him, the "Scholar" counted out the advantages of bibliographies and the disadvantages of catalogs. His challenge was quickly accepted, and for some weeks the debate reeled back and forth in the Times, with neither faction quite meeting the arguments of the other.[34] It was James Duff Brown who finally ended the controversy with an angry statement in the Library World:

> The correspondence which has been going on in the Times since October 15th, on "The Proposed Subject-Index to the Library of the British Museum," proves conclusively the amazing fact that there are scholars and readers in these progressive days who yearn for the darkness and exclusiveness in which men of the type of the late Augustus de Morgan would have Public Libraries managed. According to these gentlemen the British

Museum, and all similar Public Libraries, should
be browsing places for a few selfish students, or
those professional searchers who make a profit out
of the difficulties which have been allowed to grow
up in certain libraries, because of bad and insufficient catalogues.... The "Scholar" ... has only
a very vague idea of what a subject-index is, while
his ideas on the subject of bibliographies are grotesque in the extreme.... Bibliographies are about
the least satisfactory aids upon which anyone could
rely.... A simple subject-catalogue ... which
even a school boy could use and understand, is
immeasurably superior to any series of bibliographies, however complete or extensive, which could
be collected.[35]

Brown then counted out the disadvantages of bibliographies
and the advantages of catalogs. He left no one in doubt about
the finality of his decision.

Back in the United States events were now taking shape
rapidly. The standardization of card sizes, accomplished
about 1890, had opened the way to centralized cataloging.
By 1900 the analytical cards printed by the A. L. A. were already flowing into catalogs throughout the country. In 1901
the Library of Congress began distributing its printed cards
on a commercial scale. But also in 1901 the A. L. A. 's Index to General Literature was published. This was the latest
step in Fletcher's scheme of transferring the functions of the
library catalog to printed indexes. The ensuing conflict was
reflected in papers and discussions presented before the College and Reference Section of the A. L. A. at the 1902 conference.[36] Fletcher was present at this meeting. After
hearing his scheme denounced from several quarters, he
quietly called attention to the fact that such a transfer was
already going on. "How many people here, " he asked, "are
writing index cards for current periodicals and putting them
into their card catalogs?" No reply. "How many people
here are making as many analytical cards now as they did
before the 'A. L. A. Index' and the 'Annual Literary Index'
came into existence?" Still no reply. He continued:

Why not? That illustrates the situation. If
Poole's Index, which was the first of our great
co-operative bibliographical undertakings, has made
such cataloging unnecessary, why will not other
such undertakings make a great deal more cataloging work unnecessary?

Subject Catalogs, ...? 9

Still no answer. This was perhaps the clearest victory that Fletcher had yet won. Even so, it was still denied to him in principle. The analysis of certain types of materials in the library catalog had indeed already ceased, but there was no intention of pursuing Fletcher's plan to its logical conclusion. A concession had been granted to a necessary evil, and that was all.

Throughout many of the discussions reported thus far, the champions of bibliography were thinking in terms of the more or less exhaustive needs of the scholar or specialist, while the defenders of the subject catalog were thinking, though not exclusively, of the needs of the general reader. A few librarians, however, especially those most keenly aware of the educational responsibility of the library, were dissatisfied with the catalog, as contrasted with selective bibliography, as a guide for the general reader. Between 1895 and 1905 several pleas were heard from English librarians for selected lists of best books on important subjects. [37] Although these statements involved serious criticism of the values of library catalogs, they did not appear to rouse the antagonism of the cataloger.

In 1904 and 1905 the case for and against subject catalogs was again reviewed by two prominent American librarians. Frank L. Tolman, reference librarian at the University of Chicago, after analyzing the relations of bibliographies and catalogs, concluded that subject cataloging was less a kind of bibliography in its own right than a necessarily imperfect attempt to imitate true bibliography. [38] He enumerated various ways in which bibliographies were superior. About the same time, though not in answer to Tolman, J. C. M. Hanson, of the Library of Congress, gave authoritative expression to the cataloger's point of view. [39] The university library at Vienna was about to recatalog its collections, and advice had been sought of the Library of Congress. Hanson had been delegated to answer. The question was: "Which class of subject indexes is to be most recommended --catalogs or bibliographies?" His answer was clear and cool.

> My conclusion ... would be that while a subject catalog might possibly be dispensed with by a specialist who is thoroughly familiar with his subject, it will nevertheless prove also to him a convenience and an economy of sufficient value to justify its compilation. To the ordinary user of the li-

brary who cannot lay claim to special knowledge, and to the specialist when his investigations carry him into fields which are not strictly within his particular domain, it is a prime necessity.

With Hanson's work on the L. C. catalog, the development of modern subject cataloging reached a climax. Similarly, the new L. C. classification marked a climax in the development of minute shelf arrangements. By now these two forms of bibliographical organization were firmly entrenched in library theory and practice. An occasional writer still proposed the use of published bibliographies in place of subject catalogs and classifications, [40] but for many years to come there was little open discussion of this problem among librarians.

Nevertheless, around the turn of the century there were several important developments in the field of bibliography--developments which occurred for the most part outside the field of librarianship. Owing to a sharp increase of scholarly research and publication, [41] demands were renewed for the expansion and integration of library services through forms of bibliographical organization which were not restricted to the resources of individual libraries. This resulted in the production of numerous scholarly bibliographies, ranging from informal bibliographical manuals on special subjects to such grandiose projects as the International Catalogue of Scientific Literature. [42] Another significant result of those demands was the organization of the great bibliographical societies: the Bibliographical Society of London in 1894, the International Institute of Bibliography (Brussels) in 1895, the Institut de Bibliographie (Paris) in 1899, and the Bibliographical Society of America in 1904.

These developments not only were extraneous to the library program but also encouraged the tendency to define bibliography and librarianship as separete, even though related, fields. Thus E. C. Richardson wrote in 1904:

> The foundation in connection with this conference of an American Bibliographical Society is in itself a distinct contribution to the conception of what belongs to a conference of librarians. It marks off the field of pure bibliography from that section of the field of applied bibliography which belongs to the librarian.... With pure bibliography the librarian, as librarian, has nothing to do, although

as student or book-lover he may be deeply interested in it ..., but it is not the characteristic business of the librarian nor the proper business of a library association.[43]

During the first two decades of the twentieth century, bibliography and library cataloging thus developed more or less independently. As libraries grew larger and more complex, so also did the comprehensive dictionary catalog. By 1915 an early cry for simplification of the catalog was heard,[44] and by 1921 the possibility of substituting bibliographies for subject catalogs was again openly discussed.[45] In that same year A. C. Coolidge expressed his conviction that the modern subject catalog possessed little value for college faculties and students:

> There is one truth which may be painful to our pride but which we shall do well to accept without wincing. The subject cards of the catalog are for the general public and will seldom be of much service to the specialist save for casual convenience.... The idea that the library catalog can add much to his information is apt to strike him as ridiculous.... I am convinced that the great majority of my colleagues in the faculty regard the subject portion of the catalog as little more than a means and often not the best means for the undergraduate to find material for writing theses, and certainly not as of particular value to themselves. They know and it is their business to know and keep up with the bibliographical aids in their own field....[46]

Coolidge argued strongly against the now traditional object of trying to make an exhaustive catalog which would satisfy the principal needs of all library readers. Three years later the possibility of narrowing the objects of the catalog and of compromising its functions with those of bibliographies received attention at the A.L.A. Cataloger's Round Table meeting at Saratoga Springs.[47] This notable meeting, which popularized the term "selective" cataloging and which was dominated by the ideas of T. F. Currier, head cataloger at the Harvard College Library, signalized a growing realization among some librarians that if the catalog could not be all things to all readers, it was time to consider how and in what degree it could be some things to some readers. In terms of readers, Currier believed that a deliberately selective subject catalog should be constructed primarily for the undergraduate, the novice, or the general reader, while the more exhaustive and exacting needs of the specialist or scholar should be left to special bibliographies and the shelf classification. In terms of books, he pointed out various categories of materials which could be omitted from the subject catalog, either because they were not needed by the novice or because they were adequately treated in published tools.

The significance of this movement toward selective cataloging, however, lay more in a change of attitude toward the catalog than in actual modifications effected in the tool itself. The modern subject catalog has never become selective in any real sense of the word. Yet librarians since that time have been more ready to acknowledge its limitations and to admit that for some purposes bibliographies may be superior. Thus the way was again open for a thorough re-examination of the values and relations of subject cataloging, classification, and bibliography.

The history of our problem during the last twenty years is too familiar to require detailed notice here. Several important trends may be mentioned, however, in order to complete the picture. During this period various writers reviewed from one angle or another the problems of classification in general and the limitations of shelf classification in particular, usually without reference to the comparative values of other tools.[48] On the other hand, a number of writers extolled the values of bibliographies, especially to research, also without reference to the comparative values of other tools.[49] A substantial body of librarians, however, wrote directly about the relations of subject bibliographies and catalogs, with conclusions more or less favorable to a greater emphasis on bibliographies.[50] Some argued that librarians, even catalogers, should assume more responsibility for the production of subject bibliographies,[51] while others declared that the subject approach to books, through whatever kind of tool, is outside the proper scope of librarianship.[52] But all agreed that librarians, in making their catalogs, should take into fuller account the potentialities--indeed, the actualities--of subject bibliographies, whether or not they consider it their business to make the bibliographies.

The remarkable growth in those years of union catalogs or co-operative finding-lists also struck deeply into our problem, since the usefulness of such lists obviously depends upon the exploitation of subject tools which are not limited to

Subject Catalogs, ...? 13

the resources of single libraries. As long as a person selects the books he wants from the catalog of one library, it is apparent that he can have no use for a finding-list of books in other libraries. The question arose, then, whether the union author catalog--in fact, the whole movement toward the integration and co-ordination of library services and resources --should be implemented by developing entirely new union subject catalogs analogous to the present library catalog or by developing further the field of subject bibliography. Both sides of this far-reaching question--the implications of which do not yet seem to be fully realized--have had their champions in recent years. [53]

Meanwhile, the majority of librarians have held fast to the conviction that the subject catalog and classification are fundamental to efficient library service and that recourse to subject bibliographies is feasible only after the greater potentialities of the library tools have been exploited. The major concern of the library profession thus was--and still is--not the production of bibliographies which might be better and more economical than the library tools but the production of better and more economical catalogs and classifications. To this end much effort was expended during these years on co-operative and centralized cataloging and classification, recataloging and reclassification, simplified cataloging, and the divided catalog. A revival of the classed catalog was even suggested. These and other activities involved no fundamental changes in the nature and purpose of the library tools or in their relations to bibliographies. Although the analysis of certain forms of library materials--for example, periodicals, essays, plays, short stories, and government documents-- was conceded to the printed index, [54] no important concessions were made from the point of view of subject fields or the needs of well-defined groups of readers. Still, the subject catalog and classification were conceived as indispensable general tools which may be supplemented at times by special bibliographies but which should never be supplanted by them.

The problem of today, then, differs little from that of 1876, except in size and complexity. For essentially the same purpose--to guide the reader to books on particular subjects--two separate programs continue to be developed, the one by the librarian and the other chiefly by the scholar, with no planned economy between them; and the relative merits of these two programs continue to be debated, still without even the promise of a reasonable compromise.

Summary of the Arguments

During these sixty-eight years the same arguments for and against a greater reliance on subject bibliographies were repeated ad infinitum and ad nauseam. Although the force of particular arguments varied from time to time as the problem was reviewed in different contexts, the basic issues changed little after 1876. The purpose of the following section is to summarize the more significant and persistent of these arguments on both sides of the question.

The crux of the whole controversy can be stated briefly: which kind of bibliographical organization reveals most conveniently and economically the materials needed by the reader on particular subjects? The answer to this question involves a variety of factors: the degree of completeness or selectivity required, the generality and modernity of the classifications used, the amount of analysis undertaken, and many others. With regard to each of these factors, the arguments for and against subject catalogs and classifications, as contrasted with bibliographies, are presented below. Whenever possible, actual statements by outstanding controversialists have been paraphrased.

Completeness

The cataloger. --The desire of most readers, when they are in a library, is to know what books the library has on a given topic, not what books exist. They neither want nor expect absolute completeness, but they do expect a library to place at their fingertips a good working collection on the subjects in which they are interested. If a library does this, as a good library should, then the catalog and classification are the most direct and convenient tools for their purposes. Bibliographies are superfluous. If they contain materials frequently needed by the reader, those materials should be in the library and therefore on the shelves and in the catalog. If they include useless materials or if they fail to include useful materials which are already in the library, they are a nuisance. In special cases of exhaustive research, when the resources of no single library are adequate, bibliographies may be helpful, but a union subject catalog would be more helpful. Such cases, however, are the exception, not the rule.

The bibliographer. --The librarian both underestimates the quantity and quality of scholarly needs and overestimates

Subject Catalogs, ... ? 15

the ability of any single library to satisfy those needs. No
scholar, if his work is to be of any value, can afford to
stop at even the greatest libraries, without first determining
what relation the materials in those libraries bear to those
which are not there. To do this, he must know what materials exist on his topic. No catalog or classification can
tell him that; he must use bibliographies. And if he must
use bibliographies anyway, why bother with subject catalogs
and classifications, which by definition are incomplete bibliographies? Even when the need is less exacting, there is
no excuse for passing off on the reader whatever materials
may be close at hand. The ideal of the complete, self-sufficient library is a snare and a delusion. There never was
and never will be any library which can be depended upon to
have even a good working collection of materials on all subjects. This explains the whole movement toward the integration of library resources and services, toward union findinglists, interlibrary loans, etc. If this movement is right,
then the subject catalog and classification are wrong. In the
interests of better scholarship, the serious reader should be
taught to use bibliographies. Union subject catalogs would
be better than catalogs of individual libraries, but they would
still fall short of the ideal of bibliography.

Selectivity

The cataloger. --If the library catalog is to serve the general
reader only, and if the library contains materials of no value
to that reader, then selective subject cataloging is desirable.
Special collections of selected books may also be provided.
Ideally, though, the library itself should be weeded of obsolete materials and only the best materials added. In that
case, the catalog and classification would automatically be
selective.

The bibliographer. --Most libraries, and thus their
catalogs and classifications, are no more selective for desultory purposes than complete for scholarly purposes. Selective cataloging has barely touched the problem. Good,
bad, and indifferent books are entered indiscriminately in the
library tools. The novice can only choose at random; and
the older and larger the library, the greater his risk, in
this lottery, of drawing a misleading or obsolete work. This
is an injury to the reader. For educational purposes there
is no substitute for brief, annotated reading lists on topics
of current interest. Again, the reader's needs cannot be identified with the books in any one library--no more, no less.

General versus Special Classifications

The cataloger. --Efficiency requires the use of a single comprehensive subject scheme, the same for all books and all readers--a simple, logical, consistent scheme which reflects the natural order of things and which can be learned and remembered even by a schoolboy. The library catalog and classification provide such schemes. They are designed to give the best service to the largest number of readers. Bibliographies, on the other hand, employ an endless variety of arrangements which can be mastered only with difficulty by the specialist and never by the average reader. They are unsystematic, inconsistent, and unco-ordinated; they overlap in every direction. Each is a law to itself and can serve only the peculiar needs of a very small group of readers. To require the general public to labor through such complex apparatus is to deny it library service altogether.

The bibliographer. --There is neither a natural order of things nor an average reader. Subjects and their relations are ideas in the minds of people, and every person has a different point of view. Each has his special interest around which the whole universe revolves, and the shape and proportions of that universe change as the reader shifts his point of view. Any attempt to generalize the mental frames and categories of all readers in a single universal scheme, like the L. C. classification, is a tremendous oversimplification of the realities involved. Such a scheme may succeed in offering a little help to everybody, but it cannot succeed in offering much to anybody. The special bibliography is more particularized. It sets out to do a better job for a comparatively few readers whose needs are fairly homogeneous. It selects a subject and develops it independently. Inconsistencies and overlappings with other subjects do not matter; neither does the logical unity of the whole. Whereas the universal scheme is rigid, unresponsive, and impersonal, the special bibliography is flexible, sensitive, and intimate. Whereas the former lacks any specific object, the latter is clearly focused on a definite need. If the reader can be handed an appropriate special bibliography, he will not be confused; he will be enlightened. He will be glad to acquaint himself with its peculiarities, since those peculiarities will be the essence of his problem.

Modernity of Classifications

The cataloger. --Owing to the changing order of knowledge, the headings and arrangements in printed bibliographies quickly become obsolete. Once published they cannot be changed. Card catalogs and shelf arrangements can be revised as needed; new headings can be added, old ones dropped, and the relations among headings modified.

The bibliographer. --The library tools can be modified, yes, but only in a minor way and within a fixed conceptual pattern. At intervals which represent shocking frequency in the life of a library, complete recataloging and reclassification become necessary. New bibliographies in rapidly changing fields are not burdened by tradition or precedent. Each can make a fresh start. Moreover, the new bibliography does not destroy the old, and the old is never obsolete for studies in cultural history. Bibliographies thus preserve the past, are more responsive to the present, and are better prepared for the future. The single, over-all classification, through gradual revision, can only obscure the past, compromise the present, and look forward to abandoning both in the near future.

Amount of Analysis

The cataloger. --It is granted, of course, that no analysis is possible on the library shelves, but the subject catalog provides all that is needed for most purposes. The larger the library, the less analysis is needed, since books are more likely to be available on all subjects. In exceptional cases, when more material is needed, analytical bibliographies may be used to supplement the catalog. The analysis of certain forms of materials--for example, periodicals--should always be left, for the sake of economy, to printed indexes.

The bibliographer. --For lack of analysis the shelf classification is hopeless, and the subject catalog does not even scratch the surface of the problem. Under any given subject the catalog reveals only a small portion of the materials in the library, and often the least desirable portion, especially under minute subjects. It stops short of periodicals, transactions, proceedings, collections, chapters in general works, and other bibliographically dependent materials and leaves only the monographs. More and more, the most valuable materials for both the scholar and the layman are published in periodicals and other composite works. Thus, more and more, the catalog omits the grain and leaves the chaff. As long as it deals mainly with independent title-pages, or with whole books, it reflects the accidents of publication more than the intellectual content of the library. Many bibliographies do no better, but the good special bibliography endeavors to bring together the useful materials on a subject, regardless of where, or how, or in what relation they were published. In doing so, it is likely to reveal more and better materials, even among those owned by the library, than the library's own catalog. The catalog could, of course, be more analytical; but to compete with the special bibliography, it would need elaboration beyond the wildest dreams of the modern cataloger.

Entries for Current Materials

The cataloger. --As new books appear on various subjects, they can be inserted on the shelves and in the card catalog without inconvenience or delay. The library tools are therefore always up to date. The published bibliography, on the other hand, is out of date before it reaches the printer's hands. Supplements, if issued at all, are slow and inconvenient. The current bibliography in periodical form is suitable for some purposes but not for general library use. There is no substitute for having all the books on a subject, including the very latest, brought together in one arrangement.

The bibliographer. --The materials which are most in need of up-to-the-minute treatment (especially scientific materials) appear in journals, transactions, and other composite works which are not revealed by the library tools either soon or late. Thus the reader must still use the admittedly inconvenient supplements and cumulations of current bibliography. No practicable substitute has yet been found for them. In less active fields the librarian sometimes overestimates the value of the latest book, wherefore the problem may not be so crucial as he thinks. Whenever a substantial body of new data has accumulated--and this is not often for a great many subjects--there is time enough to incorporate it in new editions of the standard bibliographies.

Subject Coverage

The cataloger. --The general subject catalog and classification are indispensable because adequate bibliographies on many

Subject Catalogs, ... ?   19

subjects do not exist, and many that do exist are not available in the library. The claim that they exist and are available on all subjects is sheer absurdity. Moreover, the library cannot wait for them to be compiled, perhaps by this generation, perhaps by the next. The catalog and classification are needed now to assure the reader of satisfactory service in all fields.

The bibliographer.--There are more bibliographies than one might think, and some fields are superbly covered. Even so, it must be admitted that the reader will sometimes fail to find a bibliography on his subject. But it is just as possible that he will fail to find what he wants in the catalog or classification, either because the library has no books on that subject or because those tools do not reveal them. Indeed, if the claim that good bibliographies exist on every subject is sheer absurdity, so also is the assumption that good results on every subject can be obtained from the library tools. Where bibliographies are needed, the lack of them is no argument for making catalogs and classifications; it is an argument for making bibliographies--a job at which librarians, if they wished, could be more helpful.

Cost

The cataloger.--The charge is made that subject cataloging and classification are too expensive. They are expensive, but the results justify the cost. They are a great economy in the end. In answer to the charge that librarians could buy more books if they spent less on cataloging, it need only be pointed out that a smaller collection well cataloged and classified is more valuable and serviceable than a larger one without those benefits. Much can still be done, however, to reduce cataloging costs as the tools themselves are perfected and simplified and as co-operative and centralized processes are further developed.

The bibliographer.--The compilation of separate catalogs and minute classifications for each of thousands of libraries is an extravagance which, if continued, is likely to bankrupt the profession, despite efforts at co-operation. Bibliographies are less costly of labor and time and through publication serve a wider public. If even a fraction of the money now spent on subject catalogs and classifications were diverted to support an organized bibliographical program, an array of bibliographies could soon be produced which would surpass any catalog or classification yet conceived. Such bibliographies could be works of true scholarship compiled by experts in special fields, critical and analytical, and designed to fit the needs of well-defined groups of readers. The economy and practicability of printed tools has long been demonstrated by the periodical indexes.

Competence of the Compiler

The cataloger. --The assumption that the subject specialist is more competent in bibliographical matters than the library cataloger is false. The cataloger is given the best possible training for his work. The specialist may know his subject field more thoroughly, but he is less familiar with the technical aspects of bibliographical work. To achieve adequate subject competence, the cataloger in large libraries often specializes in particular fields.

The bibliographer. --The modern library cataloger is not competent to produce a good bibliographical tool, as the subject catalog demonstrates. A really good bibliography bears the marks of long and extensive research by a scholar who is thoroughly acquainted with the publications on his subject and with the uses to which they are put. The technical skills of the cataloger are of distinctly secondary importance.

Accuracy

The cataloger. --Bibliographies are frequently inaccurate, owing to the careless and inefficient methods of their compilers. No sooner is a bibliography off the press than dozens of imperfections are discovered in it.

The bibliographer. --Bibliographies are likely to be more accurate than the catalog, since they are, or should be, the work of specialists. Minor technical errors do, of course, appear; but they are nothing when compared with the conceptual blunders perpetrated in the library catalog.

Process of Compilation

The bibliographer. --The process of cataloging and classification is the reverse of what it should be. The cataloger be-

Subject Catalogs, ...?

gins with a book and asks what subjects are related to it. The bibliographer begins with a subject and asks what books are related to it. The former produces a classified library; the latter, a reading list. Of the two, the bibliographer takes the reader's point of view, is more realistic and purposeful, and produces better results.

The cataloger. --(No answer to the above argument has been noted by this writer.)

Difficulty of Use

The cataloger. --The process of using bibliographies is slow and exasperating. First, one must ascertain if the library has a bibliography on his subject; second, he must find the bibliography; and then he must still find out if the library has the books listed in the bibliography. The reader scorns this indirection. The subject catalog takes him to the circulation desk in one step; and if he uses the shelf classification, the books are already at his fingertips.

The bibliographer. --Bibliographies are less direct than the subject catalog and classification, but they produce so much better results that they should be used anyway. If the stakes are high enough to justify the existence of our great modern libraries, then it is not too much to ask--perhaps, even to insist--that readers take a little longer to get better service from them. Serious readers might think so too, once they were educated to the possibilities.

Amount of Use

The cataloger. --Readers are often not acquainted with bibliographies and do not use them even when they are acquainted with them.

The bibliographer. --The library has never taught the use of bibliographies as it has the use of the library tools. Even so, it is apparent that the scholars who make the bibliographies use them, and there is doubt if those same scholars use the subject catalog.

The Service Department

The cataloger.--No library has yet succeeded in organizing the many thousands of subject bibliographies into a satisfactory service unit. Bibliographies are scattered all over the library, many in periodicals, many in books which are not principally bibliographies. Some are not indexed or cataloged anywhere. They can never be brought together and arranged for convenient use.

The bibliographer.--Few libraries have ever attempted to organize an efficient bibliographical service department. The modern library separates bibliography from subject cataloging and classification, subordinates it to reference work, and shelves only a few of the most general tools in the reference room. If it displayed a good collection of bibliographies as prominently as it now does the library catalog, if it provided a complete analytical subject index to that collection and to other bibliographies which could not be isolated there, and if it serviced that collection through a competent staff of bibliographers, the results might be surprising.

SUMMARY

These are the principal arguments, then, around which the controversy turns. They reflect one of the most difficult and stubborn of all problems which face modern librarianship: how to organize books in the best interests of the reader. They implicate the annual investment of millions of dollars, the occupations of thousands of librarians and scholars, and, to a large extent, the success of the library program itself. Yet astonishingly little evidence is available to support any one of those arguments. Manifestly, the problem still needs intensive study. One approach has already been undertaken by this author,[55] but many more will be required before a general solution can be found. When such a solution is found, it will doubtless be a compromise; there are jobs enough for subject catalogs, classifications, and bibliographies--all three--in the complex libraries of this day. But the relations and special uses of these devices may conceivably undergo considerable change, as the effectiveness with which particular tools satisfy the needs of different readers is more clearly understood.

References

1. Washington: Government Printing Office, 1876. Subsequent editions were issued in 1889, 1891, and 1904.
2. A Classification and Subject Index (Amherst, Mass., 1876). The fourteenth edition was printed in 1942.
3. "A Librarian's Work," Atlantic Monthly, XXXVIII (1876), 480-91.
4. "The Librarian's Work," Nation, XXIV (1877), 40-41. Dr. Hagen was an eminent entomologist of German birth and education who had come to America in 1867 at the request of Louis Agassiz to develop an entomological department in the Museum of Comparative Zoölogy at Cambridge.
5. "Dr. Hagen's Letter on Cataloguing," Library Journal, I (1877), 216-20.
6. "Libraries, American versus European," Boston Daily Advertiser, March 21, 1877; quoted in Library Journal, I (1877), 265.
7. "American Libraries," Boston Daily Advertiser, March 23, 1877; quoted in Library Journal, I (1877), 296.
8. "Libraries and Catalogues," Boston Daily Advertiser, April 10, 1877; quoted in Library Journal, I (1877), 297-98. Winsor did not become librarian of Harvard College Library until later that year.
9. B. R. Wheatley, "Hints on Library Management So Far As Relates to Circulation of Books," Library Journal, II (1877), 210-16; Eiríkr Magnússon [Discussion of Richard Garnett's paper, "On the System of Classifying Books on the Shelves Followed at the British Museum"], Library Journal, II (1878), 268.
10. See the discussion of Garnett's paper, Library Journal, II (1878), 269-70, especially the statements by E. B. Nicholson and G. Bullen.
11. "Author Catalogues in Classified Shelf Systems," Library Journal, III (1878), 371-72.
12. "The Chief Need in Libraries," Library Journal, III (1878), 49-50. See also J. T. Gerould, "An Early American Essay on Classification," Library Quarterly, VII (1937), 502-10.
13. L. E. Jones, "Cataloguing, Yearly Report," Library Journal, VII (1882), 177.
14. E. g., J. Schwartz, "A Dozen Desultory Denunciations of the Dictionary Catalogue, with a Theory of Cataloguing," Library Journal, XI (1886), 470-74.
15. J. N. Larned, "Classification, Yearly Report," Library Journal, VII (1882), 125-30.

16. W. E. Foster, "Five Men of '76," Bulletin of the American Library Association, XX (1926), 312-23.
17. "Co-operative Cataloguing," Library Journal, XI (1886), 75.
18. "Close Classification versus Bibliography," ibid., pp. 209-12.
19. Ibid., pp. 211-12.
20. Library Journal, XI (1886), 350-53.
21. Editorial, Library Journal, XI (1886), 403.
22. "Library Classification: Theory and Practice (with a Scheme of Classification)," Library Journal, XIV (1889), 22-23, 77-79, 113-16.
23. Richard Bliss, "Report on Classification," Library Journal, XIV (1889), 240-46; C. A. Nelson, "Report on Classification and Catalogs," Library Journal, XIX (1894), C72.
24. Public Libraries in America (Boston: Roberts Bros., 1894), p. 63.
25. "Uses of Subject Catalogs and Subject Lists," Library Journal, XIV (1889), 236-39; discussion, ibid., pp. 285-86.
26. "Subject Catalogues in College Libraries," Library Journal, XV (1890), 167-71.
27. "Subject Catalogs versus Bibliografies," Library Journal, XV (1890), 196.
28. Library Journal, XV (1890), 172-76.
29. "Cataloging in the Future," Library Journal, XX (1895), C24.
30. "Cataloging in the Future," Library Journal, XX (1895), C21.
31. See M. S. Cutler, "Impressions in Foreign Libraries," Library Journal, XVI (1891), C50-51.
32. London: Library Bureau, 1896. See esp. pp. 38, 57-60. Review by Cutter, Library Journal, XXI (1896), 467-68.
33. "The Proposed Subject-Index to the Library of the British Museum," Times (London), October 15, 1900.
34. See especially the Times (London) for October 27, 30, and 31 and November 3, 1900.
35. "Subject-Indexes and Bibliographies," Library World, III (1901), 155-57.
36. See N. D. C. Hodges, "Bibliographies vs. Dictionary Catalogs," Library Journal, XXVII (1902), C178-80; A. B. Kroeger, "Dictionary Catalogs vs. Bibliographies," Library Journal, XXVII (1902), C180-82; and the discussion, Library Journal, XXVII (1902), C182-86.

37. See J. D. Brown, "A Plea for Select Lists of Books on Important Subjects," Library, VII (1895), 363-66; J. D. Brown and L. S. Jast, "The Compilation of Class Lists," Library, IX (1897), 45-67 (this article was severely criticized by other English librarians); E. A. Savage, "Reading Lists," Library World, II (1900), 259-62; and W. C. B. Sayers and J. D. Stewart, "Reading Lists," Library World, VIII (1905), 147-52.
38. "Bibliography and Cataloging: Some Affinities and Contrasts," Public Libraries, X (1905), 119-22.
39. "Subject Catalogs or Bibliographies for Large Libraries?" Library Journal, XXIX (1904), 472-74.
40. E.g., W. I. Fletcher, "The Future of the Catalog," Library Journal, XXX (1905), 141-44; and Joseph Walton, "Concerning Practical Bibliography," Library Assistant, VII (1910), 7-15.
41. See C. S. Marsh (ed.), American Colleges and Universities (4th ed.; Washington: American Council on Education, 1940), pp. 59 ff., for data on the rise of graduate education in the United States.
42. See W. C. Lane, "Bibliography in America," Public Libraries, X (1905), 111-13, for the state of bibliography at that date.
43. Some Aspects of International Library Cooperation (Yardley, Pa.: F. S. Cook & Son, 1928), p. 38. This volume contains a reprint of Richardson's paper, "International Bibliography," read at the St. Louis Exposition meeting of the American Library Association, 1904.
44. See Charles Martel, "The Cataloger in His Own Defense," Library Journal, XL (1915), 33-35; [E. L. Pearson], "'The Librarian' in Reply," Library Journal, XL (1915), 35-36, 223.
45. "Conference of Eastern College Librarians," Library Journal, XLVI (1921), 1036-38; George Hibbard, "A New Way of Dealing with Government Documents," Library Journal, XLVI (1921), 490-92.
46. "The Objects of Cataloging," Library Journal, XLVI (1921), 736-37.
47. H. B. Van Hoesen (ed.), Selective Cataloging; Cataloger's Round Table, American Library Association, July 3, 1924, by T. Franklin Currier and Others, together with Unpublished and Published Papers and Extracts (New York: H. W. Wilson Co., 1928).
48. E.g., H. B. Van Hoesen and F. K. Walter, Bibliography: Practical, Enumerative, Historical (New York:

Scribner, 1928), p. 152; "News and Notes," Library Association Record (3d ser., 1933), pp. 242-43; John Anteinnson, "Dilemmas of Classification," Library Quarterly, IV (1934), 136-47; Sigmund von Frauendorfer, "Classification Problems in an International Special Library," Library Quarterly, IV (1934), 223-33; G. O. Kelley, The Classification of Books (New York: H. W. Wilson, 1937); J. J. Lund and Mortimer Taube, "A Nonexpansive Classification System: An Introduction to Period Classification," Library Quarterly, VII (1937), 373-94; Paul S. Dunkin, "Classification and the Scholar," College and Research Libraries, III (1942), 333-37, 341; and M. F. Tauber, "Reclassification and Recataloging in College and University Libraries" (unpublished doctoral dissertation, Graduate Library School, University of Chicago, 1941).

49. E.g., M. M. Kirsch, "Bibliography; An Indispensable Aid to Sociological Research," Library Journal, LV (1930), 773-74; A. C. Noé "University Library and Research," Library Quarterly, IV (1934), 300-305; and W. G. Leland, "Bibliography and Scholarship," Inter-American Bibliographical and Library Association Proceedings, II (1939), 25-33.

50. E.g., E. R. Woodson, "The Value of Bibliographies," Special Libraries, XIX (1928), 321-23; A. R. Hasse, "Bibliography: Today and Tomorrow," Special Libraries, XXI (1930), 75-80; E. C. Richardson, "The Curse of Bibliographical Cataloging," in his Some Aspects of Cooperative Cataloging (New York: H. W. Wilson Co., 1935), pt. 10, pp. 1-7; Sydney B. Mitchell, "Libraries and Scholarship," in E. M. Danton (ed.), The Library of Tomorrow (Chicago: American Library Association, 1939), pp. 68-77; T. F. Currier, "What the Bibliographer Says to the Cataloger," Catalogers' and Classifiers' Yearbook, IX (1940), 21-37; Ralph R. Shaw, "The Research Worker's Approach to Books--the Scientist," in W. M. Randall (ed.), The Acquisition and Cataloging of Books (Chicago: University of Chicago Press, 1940), pp. 299-305; Pierce Butler, "The Research Worker's Approach to Books--the Humanist," in Randall, ibid., p. 282; H. A. Kellar, Memoranda on Library Cooperation (Washington: Library of Congress, 1941), pp. 27-37; and R. E. Ellsworth, "The Administrative Implications for University Libraries of the New Cataloging Code," College and Research Libraries, III (1942), 134-38.

Subject Catalogs, ...? 27

51. E.g., Nathan Van Patten, "The Future of Cataloging," Bulletin of the American Library Association, XXV (1931), 506-12.
52. E.g., E. C. Richardson, "The Curse of Bibliographical Cataloging," in his Some Aspects of Cooperative Cataloging (New York: H. W. Wilson Co., 1935), pt. 10, pp. 1-7; see also Hasse, op. cit.
53. Paul Vanderbilt, "Philadelphia Union Catalog," in L. R. Wilson (ed.), Library Trends (Chicago: University of Chicago Press, 1936), pp. 220-22; Kellar, op. cit., pp. 35-36, 66; A. B. Berthold, "Some Aspects of the Union Catalog Situation," Special Libraries, XXXII (1941), 48-50; Ellsworth, op. cit., p. 136; and Fremont Rider, "Real Co-operative Cataloging-- the Concrete Approach," Library Quarterly, XIII (1943), 99-112.
54. See Margaret Mann, Introduction to Cataloging and the Classification of Books (2d ed., Chicago: American Library Association, 1943), p. 153. It is notable that the relations of subject catalogs to subject bibliographies are not discussed in this work.
55. The essential portion of his study, "The Organization of Library Materials for Research in English Literature," will be published in the Library Quarterly in the near future.

2. The Cost of Keeping Books

My job at this session is to say what university libraries do and why they cost so much. I am supposed also to point out some of the major financial problems of the library. To keep within thirty minutes, I shall have to generalize a good deal, and I shall have to omit all mention of library cooperation and specialization, which are the topics of the next session.

I take it also that I should help to bridge the gap of misunderstanding that often separates the library from the faculty and administration. There never was a great library that was not built by both scholars and librarians, working together--or let us say by people with both interests at heart; indeed, they are a single interest. Yet it seems to grow increasingly difficult for the faculty to diagnose the ailments of the library and for librarians to interpret the needs of the faculty. More than ever before, the closest possible rapport is needed. Librarians cannot attain goals that they do not comprehend or about which the university has failed to advise them. I hope that my remarks, although directed toward costs, will evince the great dependence of librarians upon their faculties and administrations.

The library supplies books to the faculty and students. That sounds embarrassingly simple, considering how complicated the service has become. The service has become so complicated, however, and therefore so costly, because university programs and books are complicated. Those are the elements of the library problem, and before talking about library operations as such I should like to say something about each of these elements.

Reprinted by permission from Problems and Prospects of the Research Library, ed. Edwin E. Williams. Scarecrow Press, 1955, pp. 41-55.

It needs to be said first that the library derives its very nature from the university. It has, and should have, no purpose of its own, no life apart from the institution it serves. It is what it is, does what it does, and costs what it costs primarily because the university has needed and wanted it so.

The library has, indeed, grown up with the university. It did not exist, as we know it, in the old New England college, but arose when the college became a university by assuming the functions of research, graduate study, and professional education--especially research--in addition to liberal education. Some of our problems today, like a number of other university problems, can be traced, perhaps, to the mixture of these functions in a single organization. What kind of library, for example, is appropriate for college freshmen? Certainly not a million-volume research library. And what have we done to the research library in the effort to make it comprehensible to freshmen?

It has been estimated that only a hundred thousand or so volumes should satisfy the limited and relatively stable needs of college teaching, aside from the research needs of the college faculty. Recognizing that possibility, librarians have been experimenting for a number of years with the separation of these books from the research collections, not only to provide the college with a more appropriate service but also to save the research library for the scholar. Such experimentation has seemed reasonable and good, except that, so far, the withdrawal of the college library has not led to appreciable economies, or modifications of service, in the research library. A new service has merely been added to the old.

It seems to me that any basic consideration of the library problem must begin with the functions of the university and the kinds of library service that each requires. It should include the compatibility of these functions in the library, and the economics of their fusion or separation. This is the first broad problem I would suggest for investigation.

The notable growth of the library during the last half century, however, must certainly be attributed primarily to research. Indeed, the library expresses with remarkable fidelity the ideals of scholarship that have prevailed in the university since the turn of the century. Let me mention several characteristics of that scholarship that have profoundly affected the library.

First, we have assumed that knowledge is elastic, dynamic, and ever expanding. What better monument than the library could there be to this assumption? Does anyone suppose that the library will stop growing as long as man lives and learns? Knowledge, like the human spirit, we suppose to be infinite.

Second, there is always an inconclusive quality about research. It never seems to arrive at any final state. I once heard a historian define a fact somewhat as follows: A fact is a proposition based on the best evidence critically examined and interpreted. If no fact is final, then no evidence has been finally examined and no interpretation finally rendered. That is why the scholar wants at his command the whole amorphous mass of evidence and interpretation to which he aspires to contribute. With good conscience he can and does admit no limit to the library resources that might help him.

Third, not all faculty members are natural scholars, but they make their contributions anyway. They have to, if they hope to climb the academic ladder. By requiring that teachers contribute not only to the intellectual growth of students but also to knowledge itself, we have reared a race of paper writers, whose works the world over bulk large in the research library. Literally hundreds of thousands of scientific papers are published every year. Even librarians write papers. So, when we worry about the vastness of the library, we need to remember who writes the books in the first place. Any forced selectivity of scholarly works for the library may be a richly deserved form of self-judgment.

And fourth, creative activity is unpredictable; it cannot be restricted to arbitrary or even logical definitions of scope. Knowledge simply will not stay classified, nor scholars pigeon-holed. For this reason, perhaps, the university's research program, and therefore the library program, tends to remain a vague, elusive sort of thing. The librarian is vulnerable to every imaginable kind of demand from the faculty and has no defense except lack of funds.

These are some of the aspects of the university that make the library what it is today. The mixture of undergraduate teaching and research and, in particular, the characteristics of research have confronted the library with mountainous problems which only the faculty can help to solve. These problems, like those of the scholar himself, are part of the essential pattern of higher education that has evolved since the origin of the modern university.

Books are the other element of the library problem. The quantity of written material produced in recent years is, of course, beyond all belief. Yet mere quantity, contrary to all popular notions, is not the main problem. The real problems derive from the individuality, the diversity, and the multiple uses of written material.

If books were bricks, libraries could handle billions. They could stock them and stack them and dole them out, each like every other. But books are not bricks. Every book, every article, every scribbled note is an individual, different from every other--different in authorship, title, subject, form, or purpose. The library therefore deals not merely in masses of books but in masses of individualized distinctions among books.

Diversity of form--I mean physical form--is another great complication. If only there were just books, how much simpler things would be! But library materials come in a wide variety of packages, and packages within packages, each presenting different problems and requiring special handling. Besides books, there are serial publications--journals and monographic series of all kinds and frequencies, tens of thousands of them. There are pamphlets, broadsides, newspapers, and manuscripts; archives, the care of which is another specialty; maps, charts, and pictures. There are microfilms and microprints, motion picture films, lantern slides, film strips, and phonograph records. As though that were not enough, some would also have us collect old furniture, swords, uniforms, and statues. This diversity of physical form, coupled with individuality of content and purpose, explains much of the complexity of the modern library.

The third point about books is the multiplicity of their uses. The library touches upon the work of nearly every faculty member and student in the university--from poets to conchologists, mediaevalists to physicists, freshmen to Nobel prize winners. Books, often the same books, are used in many ways for different purposes. They may be read as literature or as social documents, for information, entertainment, or inspiration. They may be associated by subjects, literary forms, languages, regions, or historical periods. They may be valued for their typography, their illustrations, or their rarity. They may report investigations, or become the subjects of investigation. The only thing that exceeds the ingenuity of man in the writing of books is his ingenuity in their use.

The university library, then, must be explained in terms of these two elements: scholarship and books--the ever expanding, inconclusive, unpredictable, paper-writing character of scholarship, and the individuality, diversity, and multiple uses of books. The complex nature of both elements is reflected throughout the library organization. Let us examine now the library as an operation--what it does to provide books for the university program.

I cannot hope to suggest the variety of activities that occur in the library--all, we suppose, of value to somebody. Few faculty members and, indeed, few librarians ever achieve familiarity with the entire operation. There are, however, four library functions that pretty well cover what libraries do. These functions correspond roughly to the four traditional library departments: acquisition, cataloguing, circulation, and reference. Acquisition is the selection and procurement of library resources, the building of the collections. Cataloguing or, more broadly, bibliographic organization, is the incorporation of these resources, once acquired, into the bibliographic system of the library. Circulation is the physical control of the collections, once acquired and incorporated into the bibliographic system--their care, location, lending, and the like. And reference is personal assistance to individual readers by the library staff.

From the point of view of costs, acquisition is the most blameworthy of all library functions, because all other costs are subsequent to it. If books were not acquired in the first place, they would not have to be catalogued, housed, loaned, and eventually mended. Every time a book is added to the library the university is committed to a series of expenditures that last the lifetime of the book--a series of which the least part is the original price of the ordinary book. Any effort to control library costs in general might well start, therefore, with an attempt to control acquisition.

How many books are enough? It may be possible to limit the number of books for undergraduate teaching, but the only apparent way to limit books for research is to run out of money. As already indicated, the faculty appetite is insatiable, because of the very nature of scholarship. We may add twenty to eighty thousand volumes a year, and never get more than a fraction of the books available. Moreover, if any librarian wilfully sought to limit acquisitions for the mere sake of economy, he would be regarded as a traitor by the faculty--a traitor to both librarianship and research.

Who selects the books? The faculty mostly, and that is as it should be. The faculty know what they need; the library is for them and their students. Yet few faculties can boast of a clear-cut acquisitional program, because of the elusive nature of their own scholarly activities. As a result, the acquisitional program is largely a composite of the individual, sometimes casual, choices of many people. It is a profile of immediate faculty interest, and that interest is frequently inconsistent and spotty. As faculty members come and go, rich collections accumulated through years of devoted effort are often suddenly forgotten. Appalling gaps are sometimes discovered in other fields. Occasionally hobbies are ridden wildly. Perhaps in the long run we could do no better, but this general lack of planning and continuity is expensive.

The library helps to provide continuity; it fills gaps, feeds suggestions to the faculty, and the like. But by and large the acquisitional program is no better than the faculty make it. It succeeds in direct proportion to purposeful, planned faculty participation. Our great collections are almost always built by devoted scholars working hand in hand with equally devoted librarians.

Do we keep all these books forever? We do, for the most part, though some of us would rather not immortalize them all. There is no doubt whatever that our libraries contain much dead wood. Some of it, such as duplicates of old textbooks, is thrown away in many cases, but it is more difficult to discard books from a research library than one might think.

There is, of course, the cost of the withdrawal procedure--the cancellation of catalogue records and the like. This is far from negligible. Also, to add a book to the collections the librarian needs the suggestion of only one faculty member--any faculty member; but to withdraw it he needs the concurrence of all faculty members who might claim any conceivable interest in it. Try as he will he is bound to overlook someone; then the fat is in the fire. There is probably no way in which a librarian can arouse faculty suspicion and mistrust more surely than by throwing away the library's books--indeed, the faculty's books--without full faculty approval, individual by individual and title by title. How to do it? I do not know, except by letting the faculty do most of the choosing, so they can blame the inevitable oversights on one another.

The librarian's share of guilt in the accumulation of dead wood is greatest in acquisition by gift and exchange. About half of all books added to some of our libraries are not selected for purchase at all. Some are solicited, some just appear. A great many should be added, but along with the good and relevant material there always arrive tons of stuff that should not. It has often been easier for the library to add almost everything than to select the best and throw the rest out. I think it can be said, however, that librarians, with faculty help, have recently tightened up considerably their selection of "free" materials. No book is ever free by the time it rests on a library shelf.

So libraries acquire books, and more and more books, and the surest way to control library costs in the long run would be to acquire fewer books. The acquisition of books is the second problem we need to study. The third is how to weed the collections of books once acquired but no longer useful.

The second function of the library is the incorporation of books, once they have been acquired, into the bibliographic system of the library. This function is far less well understood by university faculties, and even by librarians, than acquisition, and it is harder to explain. But it is absolutely fundamental to the operation of a library.

Whereas the problems of acquisition derive primarily from the nature of scholarship, those of bibliographic organization derive primarily from the nature of books--their individuality, the wide variety of their physical forms, and the multiplicity of their uses. Our catalogues and classifications, together with bibliographies, indexes, and abstract journals, try to cope with the entire spectrum of recorded knowledge as approached by a multitude of faculty and students, each pursuing his own special purposes. The bibliographic process is extraordinarily complicated. Even so,

faculty members often ask why it costs so much to catalogue
books, and librarians ask too. About all that can be honest-
ly said is that nobody yet, either scholar or librarian, has
invented a cheaper way to organize the collections.

Librarians have worked hard during the last thirty
years to economize in cataloguing--to rid the process of
extravagant, though understandable, tendencies toward legal-
ism, perfectionism, and bibliophilic snobbery. Substantial
simplifications have been achieved, and rigorous efforts have
been made to avoid the duplication in library catalogues of
information available in published indexes and bibliographies.
Yet there is a limit beyond which such economies are detri-
mental to the university. There is no point to acquiring
books if they cannot be readily found again and used, and
there is no point to the omission of important data that students will thereafter have to find for themselves, over and
over again.

The problem suggested here is how much the library
should do for the reader through its formal systems of organization, and how much the reader should do for himself.
How much cataloguing and classification is really necessary?
There is also a problem, as our libraries are now organized, of doing nearly everything with all books for all readers, instead of certain things with some books for some
readers. For example, we do not distinguish for the most
part between cataloguing for research and cataloguing for
general education. What specifically are the cataloguing
needs of the scholar; can money be saved here to buy more
books? Librarians often wonder, but they have not yet been
able to obtain clear enough data on the use of the catalogue
to risk changes that might wreck the entire service for
years. The nature and extent of cataloguing is therefore the
fourth problem I would suggest for study.

Once a book has been acquired and incorporated into
the library's bibliographic system it is ready for use. The
physical handling of the book from there on is circulation,
which is the third library function. Included here, in addition to the operation of the various loan desks, are the
maintainence of the collections; the management of reserved
book rooms, storage areas, and interlibrary loan departments; and in general the control throughout the library system of the locations of books, particularly their continual
movement from one place to another. Most of this work is
housekeeping. It is the most apparent, the most routine
part of librarianship.

There are many problems in circulation: the security of the collections, for example, their preservation, and their decentralization among many temporary service points. There is one particular problem, however, that I should like to stress: the relationship between cost and accessibility. Great numbers of infrequently used books are now commonly intershelved with frequently used books, and the percentage of infrequently used books is increasing. Storage seems to be indicated in order to clear the stack for more convenient and economical access to the active collections, or else the removal of the active collections to other, more accessible areas, such as open-shelf reading rooms. Both approaches are being tried. But certainly the insistence upon treating all books alike, intershelving them in the same high-cost stack and keeping the same hair-trigger machinery cocked to produce any one on a moment's notice, is expensive. Do we really need to produce in five minutes a book that has not been opened in the last twenty years or may never be opened again in our lifetime? A discriminating analysis of what might be called the acceptable stages of accessibility, ranging from open-shelf reading rooms to cold, dark storage at distant places, could be a great help to library economy. This is the fifth problem I would suggest for study.

The fourth function, reference, is personal assistance to individual readers. The larger and more complicated the library becomes, the more help readers need. Most reference work consists simply of helping students or faculty who cannot find what they are looking for--a book, a fact, a bibliography, a reference in the card catalogue. A lot of the work consists, however, of doing the reader's job for him. Here the range of possibilities is tremendous, all the way from answering a simple question by telephone to searching twenty-year files of several hundred journals for every reference to the topic of a new research project.

At Stanford, for example, the Biological Science Librarian knows intimately the teaching and research interests of about fifty faculty members. He and his staff examine currently every issue of more than two hundred journals, type a card for each article of interest to each person, and give it to him. For any research project, they will upon request survey the entire literature of the subject and submit a critical bibliography. The faculty in this case appear to feel that the library can do this job better, faster, and more cheaply than they could do it for themselves.

Such instances are not commonplace in university libraries, certainly not at Stanford, but they do raise an important question about library costs and values. Opinions about such services differ. Many faculty members and some librarians believe that librarians should not participate in the research process, that anybody who is dignified by the good name of scholar cannot afford to leave his bibliographic work to others. On the other hand, more and more research workers in these days have to leave some of this work to others, whether they like it or not, if they want to get anything else done. And more and more librarians are becoming scholars, or perhaps more scholars are becoming librarians. The real issue, therefore, may not be whether, but how much. And that is the sixth problem I would suggest for study. Expenditures for reference service could be greatly expanded or contracted as the university desires.

Those are the library functions--acquisition, cataloguing, circulation, and reference--by means of which books are supplied to the university. All are essential, all expensive in the present context of books and scholarship. To perform these functions the library has evolved an elaborate organization that may employ hundreds of people and divide their work into scores of departments. We may now consider the nature of that organization.

Traditionally the library organization consisted of four major departments for the centralized performance of the four library functions--acquisition, cataloguing, circulation, and reference. As the organization grew, other departments were added to handle especially troublesome forms of materials: government documents, serials, maps, and rare books, for example. Some or all of the functions relating to these materials were transferred to the form departments from the functional departments. Then, because neither the functional nor the form departments were focused on particular parts of the educational program, a multitude of subject departments were added, both inside and outside the main library--chemistry libraries, art collections, and the like. Some or all of the functions relating to some or all forms of materials on particular subjects were thus transferred to subject departments from the functional and form departments. None of the old departments, however, seemed to die; they all lingered on. By now the library is in a state of extraordinary confusion of functional, form, and subject departments, overlapping every which way.

Actually, it appears that the university library is lumbering towards the subject basis of organization, as it grows large enough to justify decentralization of functions and forms of materials. At the initial stage this trend has involved the establishment of larger subject units of organization than the departmental library--such broad divisions as humanities and social science libraries. These divisions, when staffed by competent subject specialists, have been gradually taking over acquisitional, cataloguing, and other responsibilities from the traditional departments. By now there may be enough straws in the wind to justify a review of this type of organization, and its relationship to organization by functions and forms. This is the seventh problem I would suggest for study.

One other aspect of the library organization should be mentioned briefly: the possibility of improving operational efficiency by better management and the further application of technological methods. Librarians, like many faculty members, are not always at their best as efficiency experts. Yet more than half of the entire library staff may consist of clerks, typists, and other non-professional assistants, who are engaged in procurement, accounting, paging and shelving, filing, charging out books, and the like, all jobs that are amenable to management techniques. Some librarians, at the risk of being typed by the faculty as administrators instead of scholars, have turned their attention from books to management, and significant progress in this area has been made. Certainly librarians have tried every useful gadget--from IBM to teletype--that has come to their attention. Nevertheless, the odds are pretty good that a great deal has not yet come to their attention. This is the last problem that I would suggest for study.

That is the broad picture, then, of what the library does, why it costs so much, and what problems of cost need study. Again, most of these problems arise from the nature of books and scholarship. If libraries could regiment authors, standardize forms of publication, and prescribe the uses of books, they could save a lot of money. They could save still more if universities would renounce the further advancement of knowledge, forbid the writing of more scholarly papers, and thereby end their existence. But lacking such notable reforms, we must go about our jobs the hard way.

I have suggested eight areas for possible study: (1) the functions of the university and the library needs specific to each function, (2) the acquisition of books, (3) the weeding of the collections, (4) the nature and extent of cataloguing, (5) stages of accessibility of the collections, (6) kinds and amounts of reference service, (7) types of library organization, and (8) management and the application of technological methods. All have broad financial implications, and all involve the faculty, except possibly the last. They cannot be solved by librarians alone, because they depend upon what the university wants of the library and upon how the responsibilities of the library are defined. While the library can, on its own initiative, pursue minor economies internally, the problem of costs derives fundamentally from the conception of the library in the university and therefore the conception of the university itself. No basic change in the library service can be wisely undertaken without full consideration of its effect on the university and without full faculty understanding and support.

The understanding and support not only of the faculty but also of the university administration are necessary. At present the librarian sometimes rides uncomfortably between the horns of a dilemma--the administration on the one hand urging major economy, according to the financial stringency of the times, and the faculty on the other hand demanding more and more--more books, more cataloguing, more service of all kinds--according to the expanding pattern of university scholarship. When the librarian talks to the president he feels like a faculty member, and when he talks to the faculty he feels like a president.

In the long run, the real problem is to obtain agreement about library values. I doubt that any university librarian is likely to be criticized by his faculty for acquiring too many books or providing too many services, yet even the faculty would admit, under pressure, that library costs cannot be permitted to get out of line with other university costs, or take an undue share of the funds available to the university. The presidents have a point. It is therefore essential, I believe, that, where judgments differ, the librarian get together with his faculty and administration to reconsider jointly the library program--to agree if possible on what is wanted that is really worth the cost. The library, in all its ramifications of service, is in fact capable of great expansion--or contraction. Let us not fool ourselves on that point. The nature of that expansion or contraction, however, should be defined in terms of the educational and research values that the university as a whole expects from the library.

3. The Educational Function of the University Library

This paper reviews recent trends in university libraries toward the more effective realization of their educational or teaching functions. Trends in college libraries have been recently covered in Lyle's Administration of the College Library,[1] and in Wilson's Library in College Instruction.[2] The developments identified in college libraries are also identifiable in university libraries, although differences have arisen because of the larger size of university libraries and because of their emphasis on research. By and large, the emphasis on research in university libraries has tended in the past to neglect of the instructional needs of undergraduate students.

During the last twenty years there has been a reformation in many university libraries--a reformation which does take into account the teaching as well as the research needs of the university. Intelligent and apparently successful efforts are now making possible the fuller use of the library as a tool for instruction. The idea of the library as a teaching instrument, as advanced by L. R. Wilson, B. H. Branscomb, and others, and as implemented by the creative experimentation of R. E. Ellsworth, promises to become a regenerating force of great consequence.

Several trends which are important individually in both college and university libraries, but which now tend to become merged with more general and basic trends in university libraries, will be noted first. The more general and basic trends with educational implications in university libraries will then be described more fully.

Reading is often stimulated by means of browsing rooms,[3] dormitory libraries, and other reading centers.

Reprinted by permission from Library Trends, July 1952, pp. 37-48.

For the most part, these centers are extracurricular; they are intended to stimulate voluntary reading of a general cultural and recreational nature. The successful ones attract students by means of comfortable rooms in accessible locations, pleasing appointments, an air of informality, smoking privileges, liberal circulation rules, and shelves of colorful, readable books. Although incidental to the main program of a library, the browsing room in some places has shown that a pleasant atmosphere does encourage reading. It has also suggested the educational value of wise selections of books directly accessible on open shelves.

A number of libraries use their browsing rooms for book talks, poetry readings, chamber music programs, and lecture series. Others use their browsing rooms as headquarters for organized student activities, such as literary clubs and private library competitions. These programs have shown that the library can assume a place in the cultural life of the institution and can organize students for educational pursuits.

There are readers' advisers who really help, who show that libraries can undertake counselling with good effect. Their services go beyond traditional reference service by giving unhurried, personal attention to the reading interests and problems of individual students.

Considerable attention is being paid to the instruction of students in the use of the library. For beginning students, orientation tours and lectures are widely conducted, and short courses of instruction, usually elective, are offered. [4-7] Hammond[8] has made a systematic attempt to test the effectiveness of these courses in library methods. Upper-class and graduate students may also be offered courses in advanced bibliography. While formal course work in library methods has sometimes proved disappointing because of the lack of specific curricular motivation, the effort has emphasized another educational need which the library should try to satisfy.

The desire to help students use the library more effectively has also led to the publication of handbooks on the collections, organization, services, and regulations of the library.[9] Posters and signs have been widely exploited for directing and informing students within the library building.

These are some of the methods which have been devised to increase the educational efficiency of the library.

Educational Function

But these particular methods, however useful and suggestive they may be, are too limited in their conception and application to contribute significantly to the programs of the larger and more complicated university libraries. Recently some university libraries have taken a fundamental turn which places them squarely in the center of the educational pattern of the university. The browsing rooms and readers' advisory services, the dormitory libraries and the book talks, and even the courses in library methods are but flanking operations. Now, since the establishment of Ellsworth's Colorado plan, [10] which started a remarkable series of innovations at Nebraska, Washington State, Princeton, Harvard, Iowa, and elsewhere, the university library is more completely within the scheme of things that are germane to a university education.

Open Shelves

Direct access on open shelves to all or a major part of the book collections is now accepted as a stimulant to reading, whether required or voluntary. Some of the newer buildings have been deliberately planned to coerce the reader into open stacks. The physical and administrative barriers formerly set between readers and books have been removed. Every reading room is a browsing room in which students are brought into intimate contact with teaching materials selected to enrich the instructional program. Even books for voluntary reading may be associated with curricular objectives in this setting.

There are many variations in open-shelf arrangements from simple access to a conventional book stack to flowing distributions of stacks throughout the reading areas. Access may be permitted to the entire collections or only to selections of the most important books. The new libraries at the Universities of Colorado and Nebraska display extensive selections of live materials on wall and island shelving in specialized reading rooms. The library at Princeton opens to its readers an enormous stack with carrels, study rooms, and reading tables provided throughout.

Open shelves are not only an educational stimulant in their own right; they are also a condition necessary to the success of other methods of teaching with books. Open shelves are the key to all designs for the library as a teaching instrument.

A Laboratory Situation

A large part of the teaching process is being brought into the library.[11,12] The library is no longer merely a place to read; it is a workshop in which faculty, students, and librarians work together. It becomes

> a great study center for the campus--a workshop where faculty researchers in many departments can study in convenient and stimulating quarters in close association with graduate students--a new kind of home for the College of Liberal Arts, a base that will give personality to and unify many of the now scattered activities of that College--a center where new methods of teaching and new faculty-student relationships may emerge....[13]

To create a laboratory situation, an abundance of special study facilities, in addition to reading tables, is provided in proximity to the book collections--study cubicles, faculty offices, conference rooms, seminar rooms, typing rooms, and the like. Library areas are allocated to specific instructional departments, or groups of departments, and adapted to their special needs. Tutorial and seminar classes which make frequent use of library materials are held in the library; faculty members are available in the library for consultation. As far as is possible, all the facilities needed for the scholarly use of books are conveniently concentrated in the library.

In this setting, readers' advisory and other guidance services may develop not merely as special library projects but as regular parts of the teaching program. The laboratory situation provides greater opportunity for observation of student problems, for assistance in the solution of those problems, and for general familiarity with the curriculum. The librarian and teacher work together as colleagues. Cooperation becomes integration; supplementation becomes participation.

Audio-Visual Services

The scope of the library has traditionally been extended to include a variety of visual and aural materials--maps, charts, pictures, models, phonograph records, slides, etc.-- but only recently have the educational applications of such

Educational Function

aids, especially the non-paper aids, become sufficiently important to command immediate attention. Significant current developments in the field of motion picture films, sound recordings, and slides are now leading to the organization of many audio-visual centers.

These audio-visual aids, like books, are instructional materials, and they are used together with books in the educational process. If the library is to maintain its position as the study center of the campus, it cannot afford to neglect these newer study materials. Aside from the gadgetry of audio-visual services, which often obscures the educational nature of the materials themselves, the parallel with book services is close. The essential jobs to be done are the conventional ones of acquisition, cataloging, circulation, reference, and storage, all of which may be integrated with the older library services.

Because of the elaborate apparatus, however, special facilities for the use of audio-visual materials must be provided, such as phonograph and recording booths and film and slide projection rooms. Also, because of the local production of audio-visual materials, such facilities as recording studios and photographic dark rooms are desirable. Workrooms are, of course, required for such activities as equipment maintenance and film inspection and repair.

Audio-visual services have been growing so fast in recent years that it is difficult to assess their present nature and extent. On many campuses, these services have become separated from the library and are being developed by the business office, the school of education, the extension department, or some other agency. On some campuses the services are scattered; on others they are centralized. Library-centered services have been established in a number of places, such as the University of Oregon,[14] Purdue University,[15] West Virginia University,[16] Ball State Teachers College,[17] Lycoming College,[18] and Wright Junior College.[19] Library interest in audio-visual aids has now become sufficiently general that the Association of College and Reference Libraries has appointed a Committee on Audio-Visual Work under the chairmanship of Fleming Bennett. This committee has undertaken as its first project a survey of audio-visual programs, both library and nonlibrary, in colleges and universities throughout the country.

The newer libraries, planned as teaching instruments, almost always provide in some way for audio-visual services.

The conception of the library as a laboratory presumes the concentration under good working conditions of all important kinds of instructional materials. Failure to integrate audio-visual and book resources cannot help deterring the proper development of study habits and teaching methods and most certainly will limit the contribution of the library to the educational program. It will even limit the effective use of books, since books and audio-visual materials, when used together, supplement each other in many teaching situations.

Organization by Subject

The reorientation of the library toward the educational program has now affected the organization of the service departments, especially in the larger libraries. The curriculum is divided into subject fields; the library follows suit. The traditional organization by forms of materials, such as periodicals and maps, and by types of services, such as reference and reserve, is giving way to organization by subject divisions.[20, 21] Whereas the traditional organization scatters materials and services needed by scholars working on any subject, the newer organization attempts to bring them together. Generally speaking, a subject division is an open-shelf study area, with adjacent stack, laboratory, and possibly audio-visual facilities. It is usually designed primarily for the convenience of advanced students and faculty members.

The subject-divisional organization was first applied in logical form to a university library by Ellsworth at Colorado. The Colorado plan employs three subject divisions--Humanities, Social Science, and Science--which are simply large reading rooms housing extensive selections of frequently used books, journals, bibliographies, and reference works. Some plans employ four or more divisions; variations are numerous. In the newer buildings, the subject divisions may consist of overlapping segments of continuous study and stack areas, instead of separate reading rooms in the conventional sense.

An important extension of the subject-divisional plan involves the departmental libraries in the larger universities.[22] These outlying units, instead of being separately administered by an assistant librarian as special problem children, are organized as branches of the related subject divisions of the main library. The departmental librarians

Educational Function 47

then become regular members of a divisional staff, and their libraries are placed in a definite relationship with the rest of the library system. In some instances, such as the Biological Science Division at Stanford University, a division may consist entirely of departmental and school libraries, with headquarters in the largest unit, and be located entirely outside the main library.

The educational significance of the subject-divisional plan derives from the association of library services with specific departments of the instructional program. The library divisions are given subject content and curricular motivation. Their efforts are focused on a definite clientele, with whose projects and problems the library staff can become familiar. The library's services are varied to satisfy the widely different needs of physical scientists, social scientists, and humanists. Definite parts of the library belong to them. Library staff members specialize in their divisional subjects, identify themselves with the faculties of instructional departments, and may in fact become active members of those faculties.

A General Education Division

The recent emphasis on general or liberal education, with all its many interpretations, has stimulated the development of separate under-class, or lower-divisional, and undergraduate libraries. C. L. Mowat,[23] in his "Libraries and Liberal Education," presents a review of general education programs and discusses the implications for libraries. The university library is characteristically a research library-- large, complex, and difficult to use. It is bewildering and frustrating to the underclassman without training or experience in its use. Moreover, it is superfluous for the average underclassman, whose book needs are circumscribed, and its subject departmentalization may actually be bad for the purpose of general education. By and large, the great university libraries have in the past offered less to underclassmen by way of good, appropriate service than have many of the libraries of the better liberal arts colleges.[12, 24]

The general education division is designed to give beginning students an appropriate and desirable first library experience in the university, to instruct them in the best use of the library, and to spare them the research library (and the research library them) until they undertake advanced study of a specialized nature. The division usually contains an extensive open-shelf collection of reserve books, collateral readings, periodicals, bibliographies, reference works, and a careful selection of good books for general cultural and recreational reading. While the underclassman may be freely permitted and sometimes encouraged to use other divisions of the library, the general education division is intended to satisfy most of his library needs.

The general education division may be conceived as either a lower-divisional or an undergraduate collection, although it appears that in all but the largest research libraries the lower-divisional conception may become dominant. The Lamont Library at Harvard is an undergraduate division;[25] lower-divisional libraries have been established at Colorado and Iowa.[26] When conceived as a lower-divisional library, the collection may be oriented toward some theme which is appropriate to the local doctrine of general education. The World Room at Kenyon College and the Heritage Library at the University of Iowa illustrate this possibility.[27]

The general education division is falling heir to at least two of the more conventional ways of increasing the library's educational usefulness: instruction in the use of the library and the encouragement of voluntary reading. Both are, of course, functions of the subject divisions as well, but they are especially pertinent during the underclass period when reading and study habits are being formed. Freshman orientation, formal introductory courses in library methods, and informal guidance of students working in the library all find a natural home in the general education division. They are significant parts of the general education program. So also is the formation of good reading habits, no matter whether the reading is required or voluntary. The library's effort to make a reader of every student is being focused in the general education division; and if this division is consequently used as a browsing room by advanced students and faculty, the purpose of general education is served all the better.

Since many variations of the general education division can already be found, and since the value of such a division is still controversial, the University Libraries Section of the Association of College and Reference Libraries has appointed a special committee to investigate the problem. This committee, under the chairmanship of William Dix, has

Educational Function

begun a comparative study of the under-class and undergraduate libraries which have so far been organized.

An Academic Staff

A library that participates in the academic program must develop a professional staff of real academic caliber, a staff that deserves to stand as colleagues with the faculty and that is accepted by the faculty. Faculty status or its equivalent for the qualified individuals on the staff is essential. In the subject-divisional organization, the obvious means are graduate training in a subject field in addition to library training, and direct association with the faculty by teaching a subject course or a course in bibliographic methods, by the direction of theses, or by pursuit of individual research. [21, 28]

The subject-divisional organization, implemented by open shelves, laboratory facilities, and audio-visual services, offers greater opportunity for staff development than any other general type of organization yet devised. Librarians have traditionally tended to remain too much apart from the main current of academic affairs. They have not been curious enough about what is going on and how they can help. They have not shown a convincing interest in the nature and purpose of the activities which their jobs are intended to support. The fault may be partly but not entirely their own; it is partly the traditional character of the library organization, which has not affiliated library jobs with particular fields of academic endeavor. The subject-divisional organization does define and emphasize the academic affiliations of library jobs and charges librarians with the responsibility for getting acquainted. The vacuum of library forms and techniques is broken, new channels of communication with faculty and students are opened, and the rewards for good service are more direct and tangible.

A Functional Building

Some of the methods of increasing the educational effectiveness of the library are contingent upon the creation of hospitable conditions in new or remodelled buildings. To an appreciable extent, the development of those methods has been paced by advances in building construction and design. The librarian who wishes to open his stacks to the reader, adopt laboratory situations, introduce audio-visual services, reorganize into subject divisions, or establish a general education division may be handicapped by an outmoded plant.

The change in library buildings over the last ten years has been remarkable. From the educational point of view, modular planning, dry construction, and new methods of air conditioning and lighting have produced a type of building which is sufficiently flexible to accommodate a variety of new services and to be readily modified as educational needs change. On the other hand, they succeed, with only gestures towards monumentalism, to create a comfortable, informal, friendly atmosphere conducive to a pleasant study experience.[29]

Much can be done with many older buildings, however, to adapt their form and shape to more vital educational activities. Interiors can be remodelled and additions can be built. The University of Oregon library with its recent addition offers an example of an older building modified for subject-divisional and audio-visual purposes.

A Few Questions

Taken together, these elements of the new library programs form a pattern of service which could hardly have been prophesied several decades ago. The pattern is rich in theory, fundamental in nature, and varied in practice. The new programs are still in their formative stage; all are different and every good one contains something new. It will be a long time yet before an evaluation is possible.

Toward the further development of this pattern and its ultimate evaluation, several lines of inquiry may be suggested.

First, it must be explained that in this paper the word "teaching" has been loosely used as synonymous with "educational." While it is probable that all librarians and most faculty members will agree that the library is an educational division of the university and that the librarian's work is educational in the sense that it contributes directly to the teaching program, some will not agree that the librarian "teaches" at all in the accepted sense of the word, or, if they grant that he does teach, will not agree that such teaching is a significant part of the educational program. Are his "teaching" activities as significant to the educational

Educational Function

program, for example, as his own distinctive and generally recognized contributions as a librarian? A realistic inquiry into the proper and reasonable use of the word "teaching" in this context might help to ensure that a good program is not over-promoted for the wrong reasons or under-promoted for the right ones. A survey of faculty attitudes on the contributions of the library to the instructional program might be a useful corrective at this time.

Second, it is important for librarians to look forward to the time when it will become possible to compare theory with practice. For example, what solid improvements are realized from the laboratory or workshop theory? To what extent does the theory fail to produce the expected results? How much of the educational process does actually prove in different situations to be centered in the library with good effect?

Third, what conditions should determine whether a separate general or liberal education library is desirable and whether that library, if established, should be undergraduate or lower-divisional in scope? Also, what relationships are desirable between the general education library and the research library? A study of the general education libraries now in existence at various universities, with reference to their curricular origins, would be a valuable guide to future action. The work of the Committee on Underclass and Undergraduate Libraries of the University Libraries Section of the Association of College and Reference Libraries is aimed in a general way toward finding answers to these questions.

Fourth, it is commonly charged that the subject-divisional type of organization is more costly than the traditional types. It may be or it may not; in any case the charge should be investigated, if any method can be found of isolating cost data for equivalent services. Certainly the size of the library would be an important factor in the analysis of relative costs.

Fifth, there are many aspects of the audio-visual program of which fruitful studies could be made. The most important at the moment is present services, a general survey of which the Committee on Audio-Visual Work of the Association of College and Reference Libraries has already begun. Another is the integration of audio-visual and book services in the library. What kinds of audio-visual services--acquisitions, cataloging, storage and lending of materials, production, equipment maintenance, etc. --should be performed centrally by an audio-visual department, and what kinds should be delegated to the regular library departments? Another is the exploration of library facilities and teaching methods for utilizing audio-visual aids in the library as study materials, as contrasted with their use merely as classroom aids.

And sixth, the basic problem of cataloging (discussed more fully in this issue by Mr. McAnally and Mr. Wright) will become more crucial as the trend toward subject specialization in bibliography and other services conflicts more conspicuously with the established pattern of centralization and uniformity in cataloging.[30] While the service program is undergoing important changes of an educational nature the cataloging program often remains static. How can cataloging be adapted to the specialized needs of the subject-divisional organization?

These are only a few questions, but they are enough to indicate that the recent educational trends of university libraries are reviving fundamental issues. Nevertheless, there is every reason to expect that, if present trends continue, the central position of the library in the instructional program will be strengthened, and its contributions to that program will become increasingly substantial. The library remains the only major educational division of the university which is common to all faculties, and the study of books is still the greater part of an education.

References

1. Lyle, G. R., et al.: Administration of the College Library. Ed. 2, rev. New York, H. W. Wilson, 1949, pp. 194-251.
2. Wilson, L. R.: Library in College Instruction. New York, H. W. Wilson, 1951, pp. 292-308.
3. Vahey, Mary Ricarda, Sister: 1948 Survey of Browsing Rooms. Catholic Library World, 20:242-246, May, 1949.
4. Brown, Helen M.: Librarian as Teacher in the College Library. College and Research Libraries, 10:119-123+, April 1949.
5. Hughes, A.: Instruction in Use of Library in Alabama Colleges. Alabama Librarian, 2:7-8, Jan. 1951.
6. Sellers, Rose Z.: What Shall We Do for Our Fresh-

Educational Function

men? Wilson Library Bulletin, 24:360-365, Jan. 1950.
7. McCann, Eleanor: Custom Made; Student Instruction Tailored to Our Needs. Wilson Library Bulletin, 24:367-369, Jan. 1950.
8. Hammond, Norma M.: Influence of Academic Experience on Proficiency in Use of the Library. Unpublished M.S. Thesis, Columbia University School of Library Service, 1949.
9. Hinten, Mary L.: Evaluation of College and University Library Handbooks for Students. Unpublished M.S. Thesis, Columbia University School of Library Service, 1950.
10. Ellsworth, R. E.: Colorado University's Divisional Reading Room Plan: Description and Evaluation. College and Research Libraries, 2:103-109, March 1941.
11. Iowa University. University Library Planning Committee: Library as a Teaching Instrument. Iowa City, State University of Iowa, 1945, pp. 4-6.
12. Burchard, J. E., et al., eds.: Planning the University Library Building. Princeton, Princeton University Press, 1949, pp. 9-11.
13. Hancher, V. M.: Statement in Iowa University, op. cit., p. 3.
14. Swank, R. C.: University of Oregon's Audio-Visual Service. College and Research Libraries, 9:299-307+, Oct. 1948.
15. Moriarty, J. H.: Campus Center. Library Journal, 76:1183-1185, Aug. 1951.
16. West Virginia University. Library: Annual Report for the Year Ending June 30, 1948. (Mimeographed) Morgantown, W. Va., The Library, 1948, pp. 8-10.
17. Grady, M. B.: Nonbook Materials in a Teachers College Library. College and Research Libraries, 9:311-315, Oct. 1948.
18. Whitten, J. N.: Audio-Visual Services at Lycoming College. College and Research Libraries, 9:308-310, Oct. 1948.
19. Peskind, I. J.: Organization of an Audio-Visual Unit in a Junior College Library. College and Research Libraries, 12:62-66, Jan. 1951.
20. Burchard, op. cit., pp. 27-28.
21. Iowa University, op. cit., pp. 11-12.
22. McAnally, A. M.: Coordinating the Departmental Library System. Library Quarterly, 21:113-119, April 1951.

23. Mowat, C. L.: Libraries and Liberal Education. College and Research Libraries, 8:388-395, Oct. 1947.
24. Metcalf, K. D.: To What Extent Must We Segregate? College and Research Libraries, 8:399-401, Oct. 1947.
25. Metcalf, K. D.: Lamont Library. Function. Harvard Library Bulletin, 3:12-30, Winter 1949.
26. Ellsworth, R. E.: To What Extent Can We Integrate? College and Research Libraries, 8:401-404, Oct. 1947.
27. Iowa University, op. cit., pp. 9-10.
28. Ellsworth, R. E.: Training of Divisional Reading Room Librarians. College and Research Libraries, 6:4-7+, Dec. 1944.
29. Ellsworth, R. E.: Educational Implications of New Ideas in Library Construction. College and Research Libraries, 7:326-329, Oct. 1946.
30. Swank, R. C.: Subject Cataloging in the Subject-Departmentalized Library, in Shera, J. H., and Egan, Margaret E., eds.: Bibliographic Organization; Papers Presented Before the Fifteenth Annual Conference of the Graduate Library School, July 24-29, 1950. Chicago, University of Chicago Press, 1951, pp. 187-199.

4. Sight and Sound in the World of Books

My topic, to open this audio-visual workshop, is sight and sound in the world of books, the role of audio-visual materials in libraries. What I have to say, unfortunately, would be better spent on some other audience, because most of you are already convinced that audio-visual materials belong in libraries. The librarians who are not convinced--may the Lord make fewer of them--do not attend audio-visual workshops. But it is imperative that we keep on talking, even though only to ourselves, in the hope that, one by one, the uninitiated will eventually hear us.

If any doubters are within hearing distance now, let it be understood at the very beginning that we do not wish to detract one iota from the greatness of the printed book, or of the illuminated manuscript before it. We are first of all librarians, and to all our profession books are basic. We had no quarrel with Lawrence Clark Powell when he said at the ALA conference a year ago: "For half a millenium the book has been accumulating a power which it alone has today. A good book bears at once the bloom of youth and the patina of age.... I know that my bookloving art librarian at UCLA is also thrilled by the sight of a slide collection, and a battery of televisions would raise Skip Graham's blood pressure ... but for me books are basic...."

Reprinted by permission from Library Journal, September 15, 1953, pp. 1459-64, published by R. R. Bowker Co. (a Xerox company). Copyright © 1953 by Xerox Corporation.

The soundest audio-visual enthusiasts I know are also booklovers--those who cherish books for the good they do to people and who transfer their enthusiasm to anything else that does a similar good to people. Goodness is no vested interest. There is no additional glory for either books or audio-visual materials in the depreciation of the other. I have no patience with the fanaticism of either bibliophilic or audio-visual sectarians, who can see no good in the works of the other and who seek salvation alone.

It is difficult to discuss audio-visual materials sensibly, because of the stigma attached to the word. It is a controversial word, and the very sound of it raises the hackles of many good people, who, I firmly believe, have no real objections to the proper use of the materials. Somehow, the word summons a whole host of prejudices, misconceptions, and malignancies, which effectively block all further understanding.

Before we consider the role of audio-visual materials in libraries, let us clear away a few of those prejudices and misconceptions--a few of the more popular fallacies.

Popular Fallacies

The first is easy: the tendency among people predisposed against films, radio, or whatever it may be, to compare the best in books with the worst in audio-visual materials. You have heard people say, after seeing a questionable TV program or cartoon, "See what I mean? I'd rather settle down with a good book any day." Such people forget that a large part of the books printed today are at least as questionable as the worst in films or TV. Perhaps they have never even seen a good educational film. You can't argue with such people. They have to be shown.

When Lester Beck, back at the University of Oregon, decided to sell me on the role of films in the university library, he did not argue with me. He invited me to dinner and casually screened a few top-notch films for after-dinner entertainment. I began to ask questions. Were there other films as good as these, and where could I see them? The next time I went to an ALA conference I sought out the Audio-Visual Committee and attended its meetings. I've been attending them ever since.

But to this day, there is still no place around my home town, where I can see the good new educational films. Most librarians have never seen any; that is half the trouble. Within the limits of their present knowledge, the only thing they can compare with a good book is the commercial movie, TV, or radio. If comparisons must be made, and I doubt that they need be, let us compare the best of both--story with story, social study with social study, travelogue with travelogue. And if both are found good, who cares which is the better?

A second fallacy is the tendency to blame the poor quality of many audio-visual materials on the nature of the media themselves. This misconception usually takes the form of disparaging remarks about cellophane, or vinylite, or electronic tubes, or loud speakers. How could anything born of the false gods of technology be expected to be any good? Paper, printers ink, and even library paste, on the other hand, are wonderful. As a matter of fact, the printing press and paper-making are as much the products of technology as the color film. Quality comes from the sensitive and artistic use of the medium chosen. If the educational films with which we are familiar do not measure up to our standards, let us put the blame where it belongs--on their creators--and try to interest better artists in the creation of better films.

A third fallacy is that books are richer in spiritual and intellectual values than the audio-visual media. Books demand thought and sensitive awareness of the reader; they are capable of penetrating our innermost experiences. The audio-visual media, on the other hand, are immediate, sensuous, and superficial; the audience is passive and uncritical. Again, let me say, <u>some</u> books and <u>some</u> audio-visual materials! Many trivial books are read passively and uncritically, and at least a few films, radio programs, and recordings--enough to demonstrate their potentialities--have stirred audiences at high intellectual and spiritual planes. The fact that films can be used so provocatively at forums and other meetings where audience participation is desired, should satisfy any further doubt on this point.

The fourth fallacy is that audio-visual materials are strictly mass media while the book is an intimate and individual medium. The film, the radio, the recording, and the slide are conceived as productions inflicted upon large groups of people who are swayed in unison by whatever message the

producer wishes to put across. This may be true, but the
masses are composed of individuals who can accept or reject
as they please. The experience is still personal. Also, I
am not certain that a much different effect is achieved by
the mass distribution of popular magazines or pulps, the
contents of which are determined by the publisher.

More important to us, however, are the educational
uses of audio-visual materials by individuals or small groups
in the library, the classroom, or the community organization. This is one of our most important responsibilities to
education and this is not mass communication. The slide,
the recording, and the film, even the radio and TV program
as recorded for future use, can and should be made as accessible for individual study as the printed word. At the
same time, we should of course take advantage of every opportunity to reach the masses with good audio-visual productions, as well as with good books.

The fifth fallacy is that audio-visual materials are
embattled against books--that the world of books is antithetic
to the audio-visual world, and that a struggle to the death
is in the making. "People don't read any more; they go to
the movies or watch TV." Pretty soon there won't be any
readers, and then there won't be any books. The superficial, the trivial, the quickie types of entertainment, which
demand nothing and offer nothing, have so far won the day.
The library world, the publishers, the booksellers, and all
true book-lovers everywhere must join forces to save the
book, and thereby humanity.

"Capsule Culture"

There is enough truth in that position to keep one awake
nights; yet the problem is not so simple as fighting a battle
of books against audio-visual materials. The two are not
antithetic, though the best in books and the worst in audio-
visual materials symbolize two conflicting aspects of our culture today. The same conflict is symbolized, though less
dramatically, by the best in audio-visual materials and the
worst in books. What they symbolize is our common struggle against the human compulsion in this age to be educated
and entertained on the run. This quickie, capsule culture
is manifest not only in the popularity of the mass audio-
visual media but also in the periodical digest, the picture
magazine, the book condensation, and the compendium of the

world's knowledge. It appears in the conversations of the cocktail hour, the bustle of commuter suburbanism, and the razzle-dazzle of our summer resorts. It may even be manifest, just a teeny bit, in that especially alluring capsule, the Great Books. It is ourselves who are embattled, not just books, and one of the sorriest, least noticed, but most valiant allies we have is the small, educational film producer who knows that films can be better and who is dedicated to making them better. Another is the film society which encourages the development of the film as an artistic medium. If you think book-lovers are in a bad way, you should take a look at those heroic people. They are fighting the same battle, but without half a millenium of experience behind them.

It may be true that people who go to movies and watch TV read fewer books, but I am not yet ready to believe that the people who watch poor movies or poor TV read fewer good books. It seems more likely that the immediate competition is between poor books and poor movies, both of which appeal to undiscriminating minds, and that the thoughtful and discriminating reader will be equally choosey about his audio-visual fare. Again, the enthusiasm generated by either a good book or a good film is readily transferred to the other--more than that, the one encourages the other and gathers strength from it. In the last analysis, this is not a battle of the media for men's minds; it is a battle of men's minds, fought with every kind of medium.

The last fallacy is the tendency to ascribe a kind of unity to the audio-visual field, to regard it as a single type. The phrase itself, audio-visual materials, is unfortunate because of the mechanistic imagery which it evokes. The phrase is equally unfortunate because it lumps together in our minds a large number of widely different media, such as: motion picture films, records, slides, television, maps, pictures, filmstrips, and radio. Actually, this conglomeration is not a type at all; it is simply everything but the printed word.

Some so-called audio-visual media, those capable of being printed on paper, have always been associated with the printed word in the book. It is hard to say, for example, whether illustrations and maps fit more comfortably with books or with slides and filmstrips. It is also foolish to argue such a question. On the basis of content and educational purpose they belong in both places.

A Unified Approach

This leads me to the most important point I want to make. Instead of emphasizing the mechanical separateness of the various media--instead of imagining conflicts between them--we should, I think, as librarians, concern ourselves with the content and educational purposes of all of them. If we think in terms of content and purpose, we will unhesitatingly relate books with films, slides, or recordings whenever they supplement each other, any place in the library. We will consciously use them together. Let me illustrate.

Many of us read poetry. In print poetry is literature, certainly one of the highest forms of literature. But poetry is not just literature; it is also, as one of my colleagues defines it, "memorable words." The best poetry needs to be heard as well as read in order to grasp fully its emotional quality and technique.

Not long ago I read several of the longer poems of Robinson Jeffers. As soon as I began to feel the movement of the lines, I slowed down and read aloud. Then I wondered how Jeffers would read them--what kind of voice he has, where his accents would fall. They are strange poems; their meaning is not at all clear to me. I wanted to know more about Jeffers--his personality, his way of life. I wanted to walk over his countryside and watch for myself the storms beating on Point Sur. Of course, I could not. But second best would be to find in the poetry room of the library not only the printed text of Jeffers' poems but also recordings of his own readings of these poems. I would like to read, to listen, then to read again. I would like also to find there pictures, slides, or even motion picture films of Jeffers and his countryside, in addition to the more conventional biographical data.

The point is that all these media, when taken together, contribute to a richer understanding and appreciation of the poet and his work. A great many recordings of the living poets are already available. Harvard, especially, has acquired an outstanding collection.

If poetry is not just literature, neither is the story or the play. A good story needs to be told as well as read. We still read stories aloud to children; it would be a good thing if we read aloud more as adults. Again, the recording can help us, and so can such well conceived motion picture films as Quartet, The Ox-Bow Incident, and Of Mice and Men. The Stanford Library had a happy experience recently when, for one of its Intermezzo programs, it displayed and publicized the book, The Ox-Bow Incident, and then showed the film, with the author there to talk informally about both works.

The play, even more than the story, needs the aural and visual record, because it is written to be performed, and the performance is heard and seen by the audience. Years ago, after attending a performance of Robeson's Othello, I bought the phonograph recordings that Columbia put on the market. No reading of the text alone can now recall to me so vividly the Moor as Robeson's words. Better still would be a sound film of the production--such a film as Henry V. If this is not so, then why should a play ever be produced? If it is the play itself that we would teach, not just the text as literature, then our drama collections should be supplemented as fully as possible with films, recordings, slides, and pictures, and the wherewithal to use them--not off somewhere in an audio-visual center, but in the room with the books.

In the closely related field of speech, the aural record is a great aid to the book for studies of interpretative reading, oratory, and dialects. I note that at Stanford the recorded speeches of Franklin D. Roosevelt, for example, are used by speech classes. Similarly, in the study of foreign languages, if the objective includes conversation as well as reading, the value of the recording is apparent. In all these cases, the uses of the book and of the audio-visual media are intimately related, because the content and purpose are essentially the same.

Visual records in the field of art and aural records in the field of music are so obviously important that it is difficult to understand why it is still necessary to argue the point with librarians. The subjects by their very nature are visual and aural. Fortunately, in both these fields, librarians have moved much farther toward the integration of audio-visual materials with the book collections than in the fields of literature and drama. Many music libraries have excellent record collections, and many of our art libraries have excellent slide and picture collections. May we soon do as well in some of the less obvious fields.

The Social Sciences

One of the less obvious fields is social science. Here more has been done with the film than with other audio-visual media, if radio and TV are excluded. The sensitive and thoughtful documentary film can vividly portray how people look, feel, and act. This sense of immediate reality is especially valuable in supplementing written analyses when the subject is totally unfamiliar to us. I think of Julien Bryan's film studies of the people of China, Japan, Yugoslavia, Russia, Britain, and other countries--intimate studies of personality and family life. A few outstanding anthropological documentaries have also been made. We Americans, for all our books, are deplorably un-informed about other peoples in the world. We should read a lot more about them, and see as many films as we can in addition. That educational TV can also help was demonstrated this year by Stanford's popular TV series on People, Places, and Politics over San Francisco's station KPIX.

I think also of the increasing number of film studies of family and community problems, of abnormal psychology, of industries, and of institutions. I do not say that these films are better than books, but I do say that they are good. I would like to see the social science departments of our libraries crowded with such films as well as with books--the film Brotherhood of Man, for instance, in the same department with the pamphlet Races of Mankind.

History is still less obvious, I suppose because we can't see the forest for the trees. No group of scholars that I know is less interested in audio-visual documents than the historians. The real reason may be that, unlike diaries and newspapers, our audio-visual records of social and political events, of customs, peoples, and institutions, are not yet old enough to have been discovered for historical purposes. Recently early photography has attracted serious historical interest, but the full richness and variety of the documentation of this age has not yet risen to the surface of the academic consciousness. I have no doubt that the written record will remain of the greatest significance, but it need no longer stand alone.

Even in the fields of philosophy and religion, in spite of the contention that pictures and voices cannot penetrate the recesses of the mind and spirit--a contention which I think is wrong--films and recordings are useful. Several weeks ago the Stanford Library in co-operation with the University Church presented the French film, God Needs Men, at an Intermezzo program. The reaction surprised and pleased us all. For days afterwards students called at the Vestry Library to comment, or seek comment, about this film. There is no doubt whatever that the film raised in a most provocative manner a number of basic spiritual and ecclesiastical questions, and raised them in living terms. A passive, uncritical audience would have been impossible. Such a film, I am certain, would stimulate thoughtful reading. It belongs with good religious books.

Examples could be multiplied in a number of fields. In each case, where audio-visual materials have common cause with books, they belong together--in our libraries, in our schools, in our homes. There is no battle between them; neither detracts from the other. They are allies in the common struggle against the shoddy, the commonplace, or superficial, whether in books, films, magazines, or TV.

I have said that audio-visual materials are not a single, separate type of medium, but a wide variety of media serving all kinds of purposes. These media, as I think I have demonstrated, are more closely related functionally to books that serve the same purposes than to each other. Thus a recording of Robert Frost reciting his own verses is more akin to the printed text of those verses than to a motion picture film on the rearing of children. There is a lesson in this for us, who think of ourselves as audio-visual specialists, prepare courses for audio-visual instruction, and attend audio-visual workshops. We are not a separate profession, and we ought not isolate ourselves or our work.

We have come to think, for example, in terms of audio-visual centers, either inside or outside the library organization. These are centers which handle all kinds of audio-visual materials in an atmosphere dissociated for the most part from books. I have promoted audio-visual centers as vigorously as anybody, but in the last few years my ideas about them have been modified somewhat. I now feel that they should be primarily administrative units to maintain and expedite the use of the equipment and to operate photographic and other laboratory services, but that the collections and the facilities for their immediate use should be associated as closely as possible with the related book collections. We should not permit an isolated audio-visual library to arise within the library or anywhere else, unless unavoidable circumstances, such as the nature of a library building, dictate a separate arrangement.

This is a very important point that needs careful analysis in each local situation. I am now sure that I have retarded audio-visual development at Stanford by insisting upon a center, whereas individual projects in their regular library context, such as drama films in a drama library and poetry records in a poetry library, can be sold quite readily. We are working at Stanford on reference services by our regular reference staff, on film rentals, and on the development of individual audio-visual collections wherever they fill a recognized need. When the technical problems become too difficult to be managed in this way, there will be time enough to set up a central service.

If there is any unity in the audio-visual field, it derives from the gadgetry, the mechanical appurtenances, necessary to the use of most audio-visual materials. I think we should minimize this aspect of the work as much as possible, keep it out of sight. The less conscious our readers are of the apparatus, the better. We give our readers not wax, not phonographs, but the spoken word--the poem, the story, the drama told aloud. We give them not film, not projectors and beaded screens, but the vision of life recreated for their pleasure and understanding. These are the things that books are made of too, and therein lies real unity. When sight and sound are fully accepted in the world of books, when the unity of content is fully recognized, we will have better libraries, better readers, and better people.

5. Too Much and Too Little; Observations on
the Current Status of University Library Resources

The current status of library resources is an elusive topic that I have skirted warily in this effort to represent the position of the university. It was futile, for example, to try within the scope of this paper to evaluate the resources themselves. Evaluate for what? If asked whether a great university library had enough resources, I would answer no, from one point of view. If asked whether it had too many, I would answer yes, from another. And I would be right both times. The library is too small and yet too large. In trying to cope with this paradox we continue feverishly with one hand to extend the collections, while with the other we probe nervously for ways to constrain them, to create optimum selections of manageable size. In one breath we cry for quantity, in the next for quality. It is this paradox that I want to explore--this manifestation of the contradictory and confused conceptions which guide the university library in the acquisition and disposition of resources.

The status of the university library in the academic world is changing; its current position is difficult to estimate. The rising intellectual tide of the century has engulfed one position after another. The role of the scholar has been revolutionized; his life and habits have been transformed since the day he worked alone in his private study. The methods and organization of research have been altered profoundly. There is no reason to suppose that the status of the library is any more final than that of research or of the scholar himself.

Our confusion arises from the difficulty of assessing our position in what begins to resemble another intellectual

---

Reprinted by permission of the American Library Association from Library Resources & Technical Services, Winter 1959, pp. 20-31.

revolution, perhaps as great as the one that created the modern university. This new revolution, like the earlier one, is a function of growth. The advancement of knowledge once required that teachers become productive scholars, that they join with independent researchers to form schools, and that these schools unite to form the university, which became the organized center of both teaching and research. The new structure enabled the scholar, through specialization, interdependence, and the pooling of resources, to deal with quantities and complexities of knowledge that he could no longer encompass alone. For over fifty years this structure was adequate. Since the end of World War II, however, it has become increasingly evident that even the university can no longer encompass the task alone. It is still the center of learning, but the full responsibility for the advancement and transmission of knowledge is again being widely shared. Undergraduate teaching is regaining separate status, both within and without the university. Independent research agencies, to which the university is often a mere sub-contractor, have been sponsored on a very large scale in government, industry, and elsewhere. Even the university's role in the advancement of knowledge is now becoming specialized, its contribution dependent in large measure upon those of other agencies. The organization of research and the pooling of intellectual resources have begun to assume national, even international, proportions.

In this context, we have a right to be confused about the status of the university library in the acquisition of resources, and I expect that our faculty colleagues have an even better right. As long as the university could embrace substantially all knowledge and organize its contributions independently, the acquisitional policy of the library was fairly clear. For many decades the librarian busily acquired everything of present or potential use to the university program. From time to time new fields of acquisition were recognized and exploited--newspapers, diaries, government documents, house organs--as intensified scholarly methods and the advancing boundaries of knowledge demanded. But eventually recorded knowledge grew faster than the library. Even at a geometric rate of growth, the library ceased to gain upon the expanding literatures of fact, opinion, and interpretation that it had helped to germinate. While growing faster than ever, it could no longer hold to the traditional goal of completeness and self-sufficiency with any hope of success.

Discussions of acquisitional policy then tended to emphasize selectivity, quality, and the focus on local, specialized needs. In the evaluation of prospective acquisitions, distinctions were drawn between needs that are improbable or unlikely and those that are likely or certain. Perhaps everything isn't worth acquiring after all. Perhaps money is being wasted in the building of monstrous, inefficient machines. A discriminating policy that is based on the known needs of important scholarship might actually be more productive as well as more economical.

In our darker moods we have tended to emphasize the phrase "important scholarship." A great many books deserve our attention, perhaps most of them; some have changed the world. But how many are just grist in the academic mill! About this time we take Barzun's Teacher in America[1] down from the shelf and reread a number of tasty bits about the academic nonsense that has caused much of our trouble. We meditate then about all the information that was never worth discovering, the ideas that never needed expressing, and the books that never should have been written. If only the academic world itself were more discriminating, if only it could practice some measure of verbal economy, the problem of the library might be solved.

There is some sense in this. Somewhere in the blind rush of discovery there is need of evaluation and synthesis. It is just as important now to see life whole as it was a century ago; it is only more difficult. The academic man might well forego the discovery of some new facts in order to digest the ones he already has and turn them to human use. Knowledge is infinite, and the everlasting pursuit of it will do no good unless we can still sift the more meaningful from the less and perceive the essence.

Thus the goal of the carefully selected, well rounded library is still valid--the library that the mind and spirit can embrace. Indeed, it is needed now more than ever before. The range and magnitude of resources in the modern library are beyond the capacity of any one man to comprehend. The library has become an enormous conglomeration, the greater and still increasing part of which is rarely used by anybody. The improbable and the unlikely have engulfed the likely and the certain.

This thinking, especially when supported by financial necessity, commends a policy of ruthless choice, not only in

the acquisition of additional books but also in the weeding out
of those already acquired. It commends discrimination, proportion, and balance in the molding of a library that can be
used with the greatest possible effect and efficiency. It argues for a library that is well within the means of every
major university and that satisfies a current, significant local need. Moreover, it is consistent with the recent reemphasis on undergraduate education, particularly general education, in the university curriculum. The university itself
has begun to realize that the essence of learning has been
dissipated in the proliferation of knowledge, that summary
and evaluation are still basic to the education of man.

Yet the proliferation of knowledge continues. The
exploration of the unknown leads by definition to paths that
are neither likely nor certain. Nothing is more improbable
than great discoveries not yet made; and who can evaluate
in advance the seemingly off-beat investigations from which
they sometimes come? And books are the record, in many
fields of raw material, of discovery. It is a platitude that
any scrap of poor paper indented with pale print might sometime reveal something of value to somebody. Probably not;
but should the librarian judge? Dare he ruthlessly choose?
Can he commit to oblivion any appreciable part of the record
without violence to his calling? Can he assume the mantle
of prophecy by declaring that these are useful but those are
useless bits of knowledge?

There is sense in this too, such compelling sense as
to justify the amassing of even our largest collections, however costly, inefficient, and incomprehensible. Even though
it is clear that the universe of knowledge, like that of research, can no longer be circumscribed by the university,
the librarian is still impelled to try. Thus the goal of completeness, the fullest possible coverage of all existing resources, is also still a valid objective.

The necessity of selection on the one hand and of
coverage on the other is enough to induce schizophrenia in
the best of us. Both objectives are valid, and although in
these times they catch us coming and going there is no real
conflict of principle between them. Discovery has always
been followed by the consolidation of new positions; the expansion of knowledge should result in new syntheses and
evaluations. Again, at this juncture the confusion seems to
derive from a new period of transition in the structure of
the intellectual world, a period in which these two objectives

Too Much and Too Little

only appear to be in conflict. I have no doubt that we will still have coverage in the future and we will also have selection, but not necessarily in the same old places.

Such transitions have occurred before, and possibly with every bit as much confusion. The whole history of the coverage and selection of library resources is embellished with conflicts over where and how they should be kept. Even their present disposition is still not gracefully accepted by all members of the faculty. It might be reassuring, if not enlightening, to re-examine the past and present from this point of view.

I expect that every true scholar would still hang the library if only he could get all of his books back into his private study. This impulse is so obdurate that, seventy-five years after he lost this battle, he still adheres to the principle that a symbolic number of library books should never be returned to the library shelves. I take a tolerant view of this. For centuries the scholar depended upon his private library and worked as hard as any of us, perhaps under even greater financial stress, to achieve what we now call coverage. He was the center of learning, and his scholarship depended in very large part upon the adequacy of his personal book collection.

But he had in due course to give up the struggle. However reluctantly, he had to narrow his field and pool his library effort with that of his colleagues. Even so, he did not give up his private library; and he still has it, although its functions have changed. He relinquished the goal of coverage to agencies of broader base but retained two things: the everyday tools of his specialty and the broader selection of best books that enriched his personal life.

Whether this agency of broader base was first a school, an institute, or the university itself, my history does not tell me; but we know that eventually it was the university. We know also that the library of the college that antedated the university was small and relatively unimportant. But once the scholar transferred his loyalty from his private to his university library he labored zealously to strengthen the latter. The library of the university came alive. The university was now the center of learning, and the community of scholars depended upon a common library resource.[2] This was a significant transition. Indeed, to some extent it is still going on as the private research libraries, begun

fifty or more years ago, of some of the elder members of
our faculties are finally bequeathed to the university.

So the university library, as a device to deal with the
expansion of recorded knowledge, had a recent beginning.
The scholarly traditions upon which it was based were old,
but the method was new, as were the place and the scholar's relationship to it. It was a response to necessity, a
product of growth. Possibly nobody really wanted it, but
few could deny it.

When the confusion of loyalties that attended this
transition had been resolved, the university library had a
clear field. With the help of the faculty it now assumed the
full responsibility for amassing the printed record, and it
was equal to the task for a number of decades. It was not,
I suppose, until the 1930's--again my history is wanting--
when the new structure began to creak. I think it was about
that time when the generations of free-wheeling, acquisitive
librarians began to succumb to the present breed (myself included) of penny-pestered, size-conscious, schizophrenic administrators. It took the depression, coupled with the distinguished success of our predecessors in building collections, to bring on our present dilemma.

For one thing, some faculties, particularly in the sciences and professional schools, never had fully transferred
their loyalties to the university library as such. Not being
so oppressed by an over-abundance of resources as other
faculties, or merely preferring to keep their books closer
to themselves, or perhaps still distrusting this new superlibrary scheme, they had continued to maintain school and
department libraries for a selection of their essential books.
Nobody seems to have worried about this as long as the goal
was simply to acquire more books. But when the pressure
for economy, for the reduction of duplication, and for greater efficiency of management set in, some administrators
undertook to complete the transition to a centralized university library. They did not always succeed, and perhaps fortunately so, because now that the general library is twice as
large as it was then, it doesn't seem very efficient either,
and the newest trend is back toward decentralization. In any
case, these department libraries still hold a position somewhere between the main university library and the working
part of the scholar's private library. They represent, in
one degree or another, the valid need of keeping at home a
substantial though limited part of the books in a special field

and of falling back on a larger, general reservoir for marginal materials and for the storage of infrequently used books when space at home is exhausted.

Another early symptom of distress was the browsing room. If the department library is regarded as analogous to the working part of the scholar's private library, augmented and one step removed, the browsing room may be likened to the other part. Granted that, where browsing libraries are concerned, the gentleman was sometimes confused with the scholar, the general idea was to set apart from the indistinguishable masses of research materials a comprehensible selection of best books. The main collections had grown so large as to become ineffective in the stimulation of thoughtful, discriminating reading. They now failed to inspire a sense of values, to enrich the understanding, or to sharpen the critical and interpretative faculties. In effect, the browsing room was a new synthesis in the disposition of library books.

It did not, however, succeed very well. The idea was sound; it responded to a perennial need that is still keenly felt. But the method was inadequate. Basically, the room had no curricular counterpart; it was extra-curricular. It looked and felt like a bit of fluff on the academic tide. Not until the tide itself was turned did the idea begin to take realistic form. In response to the same need there followed in due course a revival of general education as against the proliferation of special studies. The curriculum too had grown so large as to fragment the whole man. The idea of the browsing room was then embodied with greater substance in the undergraduate library.

The undergraduate library, whatever the specific form it may take, is a selective counterpart of the library of record. It is quality as against quantity, the summation as against the accumulation of raw data. The very contemplation of it improves our mental health, in that it promises new fulfillment of a major responsibility that had necessarily been sacrificed to other responsibilities. This sacrifice, of course, had never been required of the college librarian. Indeed, the undergraduate library is a college library, re-created within the university.

The undergraduate library, however, offers no appreciable relief from the growth of the research collections. It is a palliative but not a cure. The quantitative problems of coverage still harass every large university, as the collections overflow the stacks into attics and basements elsewhere. Thus storage becomes another symptom of distress. The formalization of book storage has the willing approval of probably no faculty in the country. Again, no one really wants it. Yet some universities have found it necessary to erect specialized storage buildings to supplement the main stack. These buildings do offer relief, but still no long term cure. They can cut the cost of retaining existing little-used collections, and they can cushion the eventual transfer of collections to more distant places; but in twenty, forty, or eighty years they will have overshadowed the main libraries of many universities. The ogre of exponential growth will have merely been shunted to the backyards of our campuses.

All these organization devices--the scholar's private library, the school and department libraries, the main university library, the undergraduate library, and the storage library--all have served on the one hand to extend the overall coverage of book resources or on the other to separate selected collections from the whole. The extension of coverage has entailed the progressive pooling of less frequently used resources in larger organizational units, a process that has been accompanied by further specialization and selectivity in the earlier, smaller units. The newer larger units have been superimposed upon but have not superseded the earlier ones. As the responsibility for the coverage of less frequently used materials has been transferred to larger units, the earlier ones have been focussed more sharply upon frequent local needs, such as the working tools of special fields and the general selections of best books. Each stage in this progression has resulted to some degree in confusion and the conflict of loyalties, because an ever increasing proportion of the total resources comes to rest in more distant places under agencies farther removed from the individual scholar.

The next transition to agencies beyond the university--a transition that has, of course, already begun--may be expected to be particularly difficult. Although it is apparent that the university can no longer cope individually with all its own library needs, the subordination of university interests and the development of extra-university loyalties will take time, patience, and probably the cudgel of necessity. The definition and acceptance of a modified role for the university library will be required. The acquisitional policy of the individual library will need to be reoriented to a larger frame of reference.

The general nature of this reorientation seems reasonably clear even now. As the individual scholar once relinquished his responsibility for library coverage to the department and main libraries of the university, the university library must now relinquish some of its responsibility, first for a few troublesome classes of materials, then for increasingly large parts of the universe of resources. This does not mean that the university library will become smaller; on the contrary, I would expect it to continue to grow larger. It simply means that the library will acquire locally a smaller proportion of the total, that it will become more selective within a universe that is growing faster than itself. It will tend to focus more closely on local institutional needs and to respond more readily to teaching and research in progress, while the more abstract and conjectural function of completeness is gradually reassigned to extra-university agencies. The dominant goal of the individual university library will shift, like that of other organizational units before it, from coverage to selectivity.

The idea is clear enough, but the method of its implementation is not. Two problems must be faced: first, clarification of the bases of local selection and, second, establishment of extra-university agencies to extend the coverage of materials that cannot be acquired locally. We may now examine briefly each of these problems, which are in effect a re-statement of the two horns of our dilemma--the valid need of both completeness and selectivity.

If the individual university library must become more selective, which books should be kept at home and which resigned to the next more remote stages of accessibility? It is one thing to select books for an undergraduate library; it is another to choose among resources for research. The answer seems to lie somewhere in the analysis of resources and of their uses and in the determination of their best distribution through various stages of accessibility, from department libraries and browsing rooms on up. This analysis, moreover, is not so simple as the identification of more or less frequently used titles. It consists of the identification of categories of materials and the definition of their relevance to scholarly needs, past, present, and future. Herman Fussler has noted that "there may be, in many fields, real and predictable differences among little-used books."[3] When millions of titles are to be sorted, only a knowledge of these categorical differences will enable us to dispose them to the greatest advantage.

The selection of categories for the university library will depend first, as always, upon the objectives of the institution--the levels of teaching and research and the definition of central and marginal fields. Second, it will depend--and this is where we are most weak--upon the analysis of resources in those fields. The nature, extent, and uses of library resources vary widely from field to field. And third, it will depend upon such variables as cost, rarity, bulk, and durability. However desirable some resources might be, their acquisition by the individual library might never be practical. It is the second factor that needs our most urgent attention.

The analysis of resources by fields involves first the varying roles that books, journals, and other materials play in the service of scholarship. In some fields, particularly the physical sciences (except history of science), their role is reportorial--that is, they report, as well as summarize, teach, and popularize, the results of past research. In the historical disciplines, some materials are reportorial (the secondary sources) and others documentary (the primary sources). Reports of early investigations, including those in the physical sciences, may of course shift their role to the documentary in the history of the discipline. Then, in other fields, such as literature and the graphic arts, library resources play a third role in addition to the reportorial and the documentary. This might be called the substantive, in that books in their own right are themselves the subjects of study--the novel, the poem, the illustration. And these may also shift their role to the documentary when used as historical evidence. Indeed, every book, regardless of its nature or initial purpose, eventually becomes part of the retrospective documentation of its time.

These functions are useful to the analysis of resources by date and place of publication, physical form, authorship, or other characteristics. Date, for example, has different meanings in the reportorial and documentary functions. In the reportorial it suggests the timeliness of the information reported; in the documentary it indicates the period documented. In the substantive function, as in literature, authorship has a special, personalized significance which is largely lacking in the reportorial, where the objectivity of the data is more important. The journal, as a form of publication, plays a particularly significant reportorial role in the sciences.

Too Much and Too Little

Some data are already available from citation and other studies of use, such as those by Fussler,[4] Stevens,[5] McAnally,[6] and Gosnell.[7] These data in general suggest--and again I give credit to Fussler,[8] who has thought deeply about these problems--that in some disciplines, particularly the experimental sciences, a relatively small selection of recent books and journals, well within the reach of most major universities, will satisfy a very high proportion of current research needs. Conversely, the satisfaction of the last few percentage points of need will require extremely large collections, the great bulk of which will be used very infrequently, if at all. In the historical disciplines, however, this line is fuzzy, because use is more evenly spread throughout a larger proportion of the total literature, so large a proportion, in fact, that no university can hope to satisfy at home a very high percentage even of current need.

The great problem seems to reside in the documentary function, where obsolescence is low or absent, use is infrequent, and research is highly specialized. This is the problem of the library of permanent record, which strives to preserve at least one copy of virtually every piece of library material. Where retrospective coverage is the goal, selection is hardly possible. But selection for current local use is feasible from resources that serve the reportorial function, where obsolescence is higher and use is more heavily concentrated. This appears to be true in the historical as well as the experimental disciplines. And selection is surely possible from resources that serve the substantive function-- that is, for example, from literary works.

I should expect that such analyses and interpretations, if sufficiently detailed and refined, would help to clarify the bases for increasing the selectivity of the university library, provided a suitable superstructure were created to cover the resources that were not selected. Here, then, is the second problem: the establishment of extra-university (or inter-university) agencies for the pooling of resources that are beyond the means of the individual libraries. A number of such agencies are, of course, already in existence, and my comments here will be limited to a few personal observations about their long-term adequacy.

These agencies, taken separately or together, should comprise a common reservoir that might be fed from at least four sources. First, it might absorb the withdrawals of less useful materials from individual libraries that practice "de-acquisition." Second, it might acquire directly the current production of some kinds of peripheral materials. Third, it might acquire directly many retrospective materials that have not yet found their way into the individual libraries. Included here might be such blocks of materials as the Wing or Evans titles when reproduced in micro-form. And fourth, it should be assigned other resources which for reasons of cost, bulk, durability, or the like cannot readily be handled by the individual library. Beyond these obvious sources, there are probably unfashionable fields in every period of scholarship, the resources for which, if they could be identified, could be appropriately pooled. In general, these extra- or inter-university agencies should be capable of stocking almost everything that ought to be preserved and kept available to all but which need not, or cannot, be stocked locally.

Traditionally the functions of this reservoir have been assumed by a few individual libraries, such as the Library of Congress, the New York Public Library, Harvard, and Yale, the combined resources of which have long supplemented those of other research libraries. Undoubtedly these libraries will continue in the future to perform those functions, but in lesser degree. Not even they can hold against the rising flood of print, nor should they be expected to bear alone what is truly a national or even an international responsibility. The Library of Congress, being under the federal aegis, might be an exception. Its national role could conceivably be very much extended.

To spread this responsibility for national coverage more equitably, the research libraries of the country are now engaged in programs of specialization by subject fields, notably the Farmington Plan. This type of super-structure appears to be useful as a supplement to the existing structure but inadequate as a long-term solution to the problem of exponential growth. By this method the university library, which is becoming more generally selective, would become less selective in the field of its specialty. Eventually, if pursued long enough, this imbalance would seriously distort the university collection, as the relatively unselected quantities of books in one field loom ever larger beside the regular collection. Also, the national distribution of resources would in time bear less and less relationship to the distribution of need. Increasing proportions of the resources needed by one university would be scattered among the others, without benefit of any direct method of centralized access. There is the further likelihood that the program of some universities might change in such degree as to render their own specialties of little use to themselves. Then, we may note a suggestion by Rolland Stevens that the separation of "fringe" from "core" materials often does not follow subject lines.9 However useful a systematic plan of subject specialization may be for limited purposes, the solution of the long-term problem will, I expect, have to rest on other methods.

Another type of superstructure that might help to do the job is exemplified by the Midwest Inter-Library Center. This embryonic library's library of record has, I understand, already experimented with all the sources of acquisition noted above. It does acquire for the region some kinds of current peripheral materials, such as government documents and foreign newspapers. It does store fringe materials withdrawn from the participating libraries--college catalogs, textbooks, and the like. It does acquire blocks of retrospective materials that are not widely available--the Evans microtexts, for example--and files that are usually costly or bulky. It is, moreover, capable of great expansion as an organizational device. It can supplement without distorting the individual library, and it does not scatter fringe materials by subjects. Its clear long-term goal could well be the full coverage of marginal resources for libraries that are resigned to a future policy of greater selectivity. It is a new general book stack, one step further removed from the department library and the scholar's private library.

The MILC is, however, regional. If it were the true prototype, then similar centers should be anticipated in other regions. Yet similar conditions do not appear to exist in other regions, nor is it clear that they ever will. The resources of the Far West, for example, are strung out in a line 1500 miles long. The quest of research materials, moreover, is typically national, or even international, in scope, not regional. Even the MILC recognizes this fact in its support of the national union catalog, as against a regional catalog, and in its administration of the foreign newspaper microfilm project, which includes libraries throughout the country. We may also note that the collections at MILC, like those at the New England Deposit Library, are so little used that they might well be sufficient for the whole country, possibly for the whole world. This suggests that such a center, at least while it is still small, could perhaps be

more amply financed and more fully exploited if organized
on a national base. Yet if a national inter-library center
were to exist, why should it not be the Library of Congress,
with federal subsidy? I do not know. It does seem clear,
though, that the functions adopted by the MILC are precisely
those that would in the long run enable the university library
to rationalize its local acquisitional policy on a more selective basis and yet insure the coverage that is required especially by the historical disciplines.

    A serious problem of such a center, as exemplified
by the MILC, still seems, however, to be the reluctance of
some librarians, or their faculty constituents, to transfer
the necessary degree of responsibility and loyalty to the
center. [10] While acknowledging intellectually the paradox of
their situation, they nevertheless still do not, or cannot,
modify their local acquisitional policy to fit the broader context. Perhaps the pressures upon them are not yet severe
enough; perhaps the illusion still persists that everything
needed can still be had at home. If so, time will take care
of that. The transition has barely begun. Even if nothing
of importance is transferred from the existing collections to
any center, the centers will grow from new acquisitions; they
will increase by absorbing larger proportions of the materials
that the individual libraries cannot acquire in the future.
The transition might eventually be achieved through inunda-
tion by resources not yet created. Remember, we are looking toward not only the next twenty years of growth but also
the next forty, eighty, one hundred sixty, and so on. In
American librarianship, the past is short; the future, we
hope, will be very much longer.

    Even now, I should think that an inter-library center
would offer a practical alternative to the local selection or
discard of doubtful materials. As long as the university
stands alone, each librarian makes unilateral decisions about
books that are presented for possible acquisition. There are
exceptions, of course, but mostly each librarian independently preserves or commits to oblivion whatever books come to
hand. The center, however, offers the alternative of rejecting a book locally and still preserving it by committing it to
the center, with a reasonable degree of accessibility to the
rejecting library. This degree of accessibility now promises
to be greatly increased by xerographic reproduction of texts
from microfilm. If one copy of a book is available at a
suitable library center, any university in the country will be
able in the future to get a reproduction at reasonable cost at

any time the need actually arises. Acquisition for the improbable or unlikely need can in the future be deferred until that need becomes likely or certain, if ever. The negative choice becomes practical at the local level when the positive choice may follow later without penalty. Indeed, "deferred acquisition" may actually be the key to greater, acceptable selectivity at the local level. But such selectivity depends upon the evolution of a comprehensive collection elsewhere. Contraction at one point relies upon expansion at another.

The progressive specialization and interdependence of fields, and the pooling of resources, lead inevitably to broader bases of organization--unless, of course, some technological development changes our perspective of the disposition of resources. The full realization of the inter-library center will undoubtedly depend upon the invention of devices that are more effective than the camera in reproducing materials and faster than the mails in transmitting them from place to place. The possibilities of electronic reproduction and transmission suggest that distance, as a deterrent to inter-library centers, might some time be largely removed. I shall not elaborate upon this possibility, except to point out that our faculties would still probably hang the library--and I mean our present university library--if by some miracle of technology the full coverage of their fields could again be restored to their private studies--if, having come full circle, we could cut through all these organizational strata, these stages of accessibility, and the scholar could again retire to the convenience of his own armchair. Let us not count too much upon the loyalty of our faculties even to the university library, let alone to an inter-library center. All these loyalties are born first of necessity and then perpetuated by habit; there is nothing natural about any of them.

Meanwhile, the status of resources in the university library is still too much and too little--too much for understanding, too little for research. The librarian is still torn between constraint in the molding of a library that responds effectively to local institutional needs and the impulsion to stock everything for any possible investigation. The problems of library service, like those of research itself, have outgrown the university as an independent organizational base. To be selective at home, as I believe we must, and yet to insure the full coverage required by research, as I believe we also must, requires the pooling of some resources at an extra-university level. The issue is not selectivity versus coverage; it is selectivity plus coverage.

Paper presented at the program meeting of the Resources and Technical Services Division of ALA, San Francisco, July 16, 1958.

References

1. Barzun, Jacques. Teacher in America. Boston, Little, Brown, 1945.
2. Bestor, A. E. "Transformation of American Scholarship." Library Quarterly, 23:164-79, 1953.
3. Fussler, H. H. "The Research Library in Transition." University of Tennessee Library Lectures, no. 8:22. December 1957.
4. _____. "Characteristics of the Research Literature Used by Chemists and Physicists in the United States." Library Quarterly, 19:19-35, 119-43. 1949.
5. Stevens, R. E. "The Use of Library Materials in Doctoral Research." Library Quarterly, 23:33-41. 1953.
6. McAnally, A. M. Characteristics of Materials Used in Research in United States History. Unpublished Ph. D. dissertation, University of Chicago, 1951.
7. Gosnell, C. F. "Obsolescence of Books in College Libraries." College and Research Libraries, 5:115-25. 1944.
8. "The Research Library in Transition." op. cit., 35-36.
9. Op. cit., 41.
10. Esterquest, R. T. "Aspects of Library Cooperation." College and Research Libraries, 19:203-08, 263. 1958.

6. The Help We Give

Directing the International Relations Office is a remarkable experience, one that I wish could be widely shared. Actually, the director directs nothing. He is a kind of cultural relationist who travels abroad to study library conditions and needs and to promote programs of library assistance, especially in library education. His geographical area is Latin America, the Middle East, Africa, and Asia. During his three years with IRO, Jack Dalton covered a large part of the world. As his successor, I have barely begun. So far I have traveled only through Latin America and around the Pacific basin. Yet I have seen enough already to unsettle many old thoughts and to stimulate some new ones. The experience is not only remarkable; it is also disturbing.

It is disturbing in fundamental ways. In the valleys of the Andes, among the rice terraces of Taiwan, and on the streets of Djakarta I have burst into sweat as I asked myself again and again what my mission really is. What is the help we give? Who really wants it and why? How can it be useful and inoffensively given?

The help we give, or should give, is not easily defined. I might at one time have thought that I knew the answer. By now I think that I have only begun to know the question. When we go abroad, what do we offer? Dollars? Yes, in many instances we do--dollars that are sometimes appreciated, sometimes not. Technical assistance? Again, yes--assistance that can be useful if wisely applied, but that is not always received with as much enthusiasm as we feel in the giving.

Reprinted by permission of the American Library Association from the ALA Bulletin, September 1960, pp. 657-62; copyright © 1960 by the American Library Association.

More pointedly, do we offer a superior technology to underdeveloped peoples? Do we offer to raise backward peoples to our level? Do we offer to make other peoples as good as we?

There is nothing wrong with financial and technical aid. It is needed, and anyone who has the resources should give it. The crux seems to be the human values that are given along with it--or taken away. No help that deprives a man of his self-respect is wanted. No superior creatures are welcome. No foreign systems are desired that negate a man's own cultural traditions. The help we give must first of all serve a man's own purpose--his purpose as well as ours.

I suppose there are goals, or values, that are common to all mankind. I do not know. Perhaps we could all agree on the pursuit of happiness. We might agree for the most part that we all seek to establish institutions of individual freedom and social order, and that the library is one of those institutions. But there are differences, particularly between the East and the West--differences if not in goals then at least in the methods of achieving the goals. There are historical, social, and ethical differences, even differences in modes of thought. And these differences are frequently very difficult to perceive. Yet perceive we must if the help we give is not to hinder.

I cannot analyze these differences in any fundamental way. But let me try to illustrate by calling attention to a few conditions that affect libraries--conditions that differ between the United States and many other countries and that have resulted in different forms of library development.

Availability of Books

First, the availability of books. We are accustomed and our libraries are geared to a plenitude. If we lose them we replace them. They can be easily reproduced in one form or another as often as necessary. We therefore display them on open shelves, lend them even to school boys, and take pride in how many wear out. We can afford to regard some of them as expendable.

But this idea that books are expendable is quite new in the world. It does not, perhaps it cannot, obtain in any

country where each copy of every book--not necessarily even
a good book--is still a treasure, where all books are rare
and irreplaceable. In those places all books are protected
exactly as we protect our own treasures. They are locked
behind glass, shielded from careless hands by chicken wire,
or secluded in dark stacks. The librarian bears a special
custodial responsibility; he is often made personally liable
for every loss. Of course the books are carefully guarded.
Their use is a privilege, a very special privilege, reserved
for those who earn it--the mature scholar, the distinguished
public servant.

The point is that many of our modern concepts of library service are really predicated upon the condition that books and more books, and books to replace books, are cheaply and universally plentiful. Open shelves, popular circulation, readers' advisory services, the encouragement of independent reading, even standards of book selection and programs of interlibrary cooperation--all are predicated upon that condition. What shakes me is the ease with which we assume that we are advanced and others are retarded because the facts of life that we face are different from those that they face. Believe me, they face their facts just as realistically and intelligently as we do ours.

Even the availability of paper is a condition of that of books. We take paper for granted, enough to keep any number of secretaries busy just filing it. But paper is not abundant in some parts of the world. No paper, no books; no books, no free popular libraries. Then imagine the local reaction to an American library expert who enters those parts with the preconception that any enlightened librarian would at once open his shelves, send the books home with any and all readers, and encourage them to come back for more. Where paper is scarce the books might even be regarded as more valuable than the readers.

Methods of Scholarship

Second, methods of scholarship. We have the idea that university scholarship is best served by a central or main library, and some of us are quick to recommend one wherever it does not already exist. Yet there are scores of central university libraries from Mexico to Kyoto that cannot discover why they exist. Some are vestigial; they have lost their historic meaning. Others are imitative; they have not yet found their meaning. We know that, given certain conditions, they do have a meaning. But what are those conditions?

Those conditions lie in the nature of the university itself, its organization and curriculum, as well as its teaching and research methods. The United States university emphasizes general education and the interrelationships among specialized fields of knowledge. During about half his undergraduate career the student moves back and forth among the several disciplines in order to gain a broad understanding of the world and to choose his specialty wisely. Even during the other half he may be required to strengthen his knowledge of related specialties. There is a role for a central library in this curriculum.

But in many universities of the world each department, or faculty, is an airtight compartment. A student chooses his discipline when he enrolls in the university, and all the courses he ever takes are offered by the faculty of that discipline. Each faculty, moreover, has its own library, sometimes a very good library, and there is no curricular reason why a student should ever use another library. What role, then, for a central university library? None but to store books that nobody needs and to supervise a study hall. It is folly in this context to suppose that building a central library would solve anyone's problems.

Suppose we got the idea that, regardless of university organization or curriculum, a central library of our type would at least advance research. It conceivably might, but another significant condition of research is a full-time faculty devoted to research. The fact is that in South America, for example, most faculty members are part-time teachers who earn much of their living as practicing lawyers, doctors, engineers, or businessmen, or as part-time teachers in other universities. They have neither time nor incentive for research. So why the library? Who would use it?

There is a central library function, however, aside from the physical centralization of the books themselves, that is being developed in South American universities and promises to be useful. This function is the coordination of a decentralized, faculty library system by means of centralized bibliographic and documentation services--literature searching through a strong collection of bibliographies and indexes and abstract journals, the compilation of union cata-

The Help We Give   85

logs, the centralization of acquisitional and cataloging processes, and the provision of interlibrary loan and photoduplication services. These are library functions that can and do exist apart from the faculty libraries themselves and that few of the faculty libraries could ever provide for themselves. But we North Americans are used to dividing the library between technical and readers' services, or between main and departmental libraries, not between book collections and library functions. Here the documentalists have the edge on us. Understanding the South American university and the kinds of library services that would fit its needs requires a wrench of our imagination.

Classification of Knowledge

Third, the classification of knowledge. Suppose, for example, we decided that the reclassification of a library in Argentina from a fixed-location to the Dewey System would advance library service. Why? Because students will be encouraged to browse in the library stack? Because Dewey discovered the natural order of the universe? Nonsense. Until books are abundant the students cannot be allowed to browse in the stack. And Dewey did not discover the natural order of any universe, except that of New England in 1870.

The amazing thing to me is the extent to which the Dewey classification has already been adopted throughout the world. Apparently for two reasons. First, its decimal notation, which is indeed universal in its appeal and utility. Second, its stability and reliability, which commend it to people everywhere, regardless of the order of whose knowledge. But Dewey was never conceived as an international classification. It is oriented to the West--indeed, the nineteenth century, Protestant, New England West. The intellectual and political violence that it does to a Taiwan Buddhist of this generation could not conceivably have been anticipated by its author.

The world-wide acceptance of Dewey for practical as against intellectual reasons raises doubts about the intellectual importance of shelf classification in any country. But what about classification for bibliographic purposes? The librarian in the United States is hardly aware of this problem, because he uses a dictionary catalog. To him classification means shelf classification. This might be one of the reasons why he is so indifferent to the University Decimal Classification. The UDC, I find, is commonly used in South America in classified catalogs, while the books are shelved in fixed locations. I wonder if any of us would seriously argue that Dewey should replace UDC in classified catalogs.

Really, I wonder how many of us would seriously argue that in a foreign scholarly library the classified catalog should be replaced by a dictionary catalog. In this instance I am not sure that United States librarians made the right decision on the basis of their own conditions.

It seems to me that United States librarians should be particularly cautious about the classification systems they recommend. For one thing, we know that our own systems leave much to be desired. For another, we know that the organization of information can be accomplished by several combinations of shelf arrangements, card or sheaf catalogs, and bibliographical supplements, the usefulness of which depends on a variety of conditions, such as stack access, methods of study, mechanical equipment, and cooperative indexing or cataloging services. And then there is the order of knowledge itself. What knowledge ordered for whom? The content of the book collections, the arrangement of disciplines, and the very categories of thought differ widely between the East and the West.

Library Education

Fourth, the education of librarians. In the United States there has evolved a graduate professional program based on a four-year, undergraduate, liberal arts degree. This pattern fits neatly our university curriculum and our ideas about the qualifications for librarianship. But the difficulties of applying this pattern in other countries are legion. In Indonesia, for example, the undergraduate program is three years, not four, and the master's program is two, not one. The purpose and content of the undergraduate program, moreover, are different. In some countries a graduate school that is not based upon an undergraduate program in the same subject is unthinkable. For such reasons as these there are no graduate library schools in Latin America or Asia; all the existing schools are undergraduate. Is our system better? Yes, for us. But for Asia and Latin America, no, or at least not until basic changes in the structure of higher education have occurred.

The Help We Give

Meanwhile, foreign librarians who want our type of graduate library degrees must come to the United States to get them, and they must face the chance that their own undergraduate backgrounds may be so different from ours that they will encounter grave difficulty. And they must also face the chance that when they go back home their peculiar United States degrees may be neither understood nor appreciated.

Librarians' Status

Fifth, the status of librarians. In our country a career librarian can climb, in his own right as librarian, through the academic ranks of the university to achieve the status of professor and dean. The public librarian can become an intellectual leader in his community, a person of influence and prestige. Not so in many other countries. A Japanese University librarian, for example, can rarely become the director of his library, even if he has earned a graduate library degree. This post is reserved for a senior professor, who is usually elected by the faculty for a term of several years, and who continues his teaching and research. This practice does not deprecate the library. The president of the university is also elected by the faculty for a similar period. The election of either does honor to both the individual and the office. Librarianship as such simply does not rate the honor.

As long as this condition exists--and this is a condition that does not imply backwardness in either the professors or the librarians--the elevation of a career librarian to the directorship of the library could be disastrous to both the individual and the office. In his own land, and by means that are appropriate to that land, the librarian must earn the status that merits the honor. He cannot import his prestige from the United States, nor can we export it to him.

Administrative Procedure

Sixth, administrative procedure. This is a broad rubric under which I would like briefly to suggest several differences that affect the operation of libraries. Take an organization chart, for example. The fact that an Asian library might adopt a chart that looks like one of ours does not mean that the organization will work like one of ours. The way people work together, the way they get things done can be very different. Calling a committee together or creating an administrative council to talk out a problem and establish a consensus might not work at all, because nobody could act ethically in that kind of situation. There might even be class restrictions upon who can meet and talk together. The processes of winning support, of assigning or withdrawing responsibility, or of reaching decisions may follow ground rules that the American does not comprehend at all.

At the community level the public library in some countries is regarded as strictly a government responsibility. The people have nothing to do with it. There are no citizens' committees or boards that assume a public responsibility, if necessary in opposition to the government, for the improvement of library service. The idea that the people themselves might contribute in their own interest to better educational facilities does not exist. Library books belong to the library, the library belongs to the state. Neither belongs to the people. Under this condition the procedure for stimulating library development bears little resemblance to that in a Middle Western American city.

Literacy

And last, literacy. In the United States public libraries thrive among a people whose rate of literacy is high. Among peoples whose rate is low, who wants or needs or could use a public library? Do we suppose that the creation of public libraries would teach people to read? Perhaps in some degree. But generally speaking, there must first be schools and books for the schools. In some places, Fiji for example, I have seen schools that did not even have suitable primary readers. Under these conditions it would be folly to criticize the libraries that do exist because they serve the educated elite and are not organized for popular use. The popular library cannot evolve faster than popular education. It should evolve, however, just as fast. Just as soon as there are people who can read, or schools where people are being taught to read, the library becomes a necessary part of the movement toward literacy.

These are all examples of conditions that affect library development--the availability of books, the methods of scholarship, the classification of knowledge, the education and the status of librarians, administrative procedures, and literacy--conditions that vary widely between the United States and many other countries. Because of these and other conditions, libraries are different in other countries. They develop along different lines and function in different ways. If the help we give is not to offend or embarrass our colleagues in those countries, if it is to do more good than harm, these differences must be sought out and appreciated.

Lest there be any smugness left in us, let us recall the recency with which librarianship in the United States has advanced beyond that in the so-called underdeveloped countries. How long since the Williamson report on library education? How long since the Graduate Library School was opened at the University of Chicago? How long since career librarians achieved the directorship of some of our major university libraries? How long since college librarians achieved academic status, and how many have not yet achieved it? How long since many of our libraries adopted personnel classifications that differentiate professional from nonprofessional work? How long since public library service was extended to large rural areas? How long since our own bookstacks were opened? Most of us can probably remember when these changes were taking place, and some of these changes are still taking place. And what is still the popular image of the librarian in this country? We are not so much farther advanced in either substance or time as we like to think.

On the other hand, there are hundreds of important libraries throughout Latin America, Asia, and other areas-- libraries about which we know depressingly little. Some are centuries old. Many preserve resources of outstanding cultural and historical significance. They served a mature and useful purpose before all but a very few of our libraries were born. They look and act differently from our libraries. Different people use them. But they are attuned to the purposes, the methods, and the means of the societies they serve. My visits to such institutions as the Academia Sinica at Taipei, the Museum at Djakarta, the Children's Library at São Paulo, and the Municipal Library at Lima were memorable experiences.

If we knew more about these libraries and the conditions of their development, if we were better acquainted with the societies in which they exist, we would be less inclined to assume the superiority of our own methods and judgment. Isolated by geography and particularly by language, we often fail even to search for the values that do obtain. We analyze organizational procedures, count volumes and staff, measure square feet, and estimate the circulation of books per capita, then draw conclusions that might be neither relevant nor useful. The least we can do is pay attention to why other people act and think as they do. If we did we could all be the wiser. The Orient is full of the richness of human creativity, cumulative through time that began before the Occident was discovered.

I do not belittle our own culture. I want only to put it in its proper relationship to other cultures. In many ways we have a great deal to offer that is needed elsewhere in the world. But in other ways we have a great deal to learn. Above all we still need the humility, the understanding, and the flexibility of spirit to be one people among many. We are all developing nations in one way or another. We still need the wisdom of history and the perspective of a world that did not begin in 1776 and is not likely to end in New England or California.

What, then, is the help we give? What is the role of the cultural relationist? The wisest answer I have yet heard was offered by René d'Harnoncourt of the Museum of Modern Art when he spoke last fall at the Denver Conference of the U.S. National Commission for Unesco. He said in effect--I can only paraphrase--that the modest role of the cultural relationist is merely to see to it that the cultural products of one country that are useful to another are made available. Like a plumber, he keeps the pipes open. A country benefits only when individuals recognize the utility and feel the need of an available product. This conception is wise because it assumes a relationship of mutual respect and assistance. It implies no superior or inferior cultures, no advanced or retarded peoples. It advocates the imposition of no method or system by one people upon another. Instead, it awaits the readiness of each people to discover, modify, and adopt for itself whatever cultural products of another people it needs and can use.

My job in the International Relations Office is to keep the library channels open.

This paper was read May 26, 1960, at the annual dinner meeting of the District of Columbia Library Association.

7. Librarians and Librarianship

The dedication, competence, and enthusiasm of Soviet librarians impressed the American delegation very favorably. The quality of people who enter the profession, the nature of their training, their status in the intellectual community, and their methods of improving librarianship itself are all striking and stimulating. A strong sense of professional rapport was quickly and easily established between American and Soviet librarians in every city and village visited.

Education of Librarians

A person may enter the field of Soviet librarianship at several levels and through different doors. The chief training agencies are (1) the library institutes, (2) the universities, (3) the technical high schools, and (4) the in-service training programs. 1

The four major library institutes--Moscow, Leningrad, Kharkov, and a recently created East Siberian Institute in Ulan Ude--offer four-and-one-half to five-year curricula to high school graduates who are training for the higher professional positions. A fifth Middle Asia Library Institute is now being organized at Tashkent. These institutes are separate educational agencies under the republic Ministries of Culture. The curricula are uniform, except for local variations of language and culture, and are self-contained. The Leningrad State Library Institute, visited by the delegation, will be described in general terms below.

Equal in status with the programs of the institutes are the training programs of a number of universities in

---

Reprinted by permission of the American Library Association from Soviet Libraries and Librarianship, by Melville J. Ruggles and Raynard C. Swank, pp. 104-118. Copyright © 1962 by the American Library Association.

Lithuania, Latvia, Estonia, Belorussia, Georgia, Azerbaidzhan, Kazakhstan, Uzbekistan, and Armenia. In some instances the faculties of librarianship are parts of the pedagogical institutes of the universities. The entrance requirements, the curricula, and the standards of these university programs are similar to those of the separate library institutes.

Many scholars with university degrees in fields other than librarianship are welcomed to the profession after a period of either formal or in-service library training in a manner similar to the normal pattern of postgraduate training in the United States. A diploma course for university graduates is offered, for example, by the Leningrad State Library Institute.

A lower level of library training for smaller mass and children's libraries is provided by many technical high schools or tekhnikums. There are now fifty-five such schools in the Soviet Union, with twenty-three in the Ukraine alone. Many thousands of students are graduated each year.

Numerous in-service training programs are also available to working librarians. Until 1960 a special Refresher Courses Institute was responsible for part-time seminars. This institute has now been dissolved, and its functions have been assigned to the regular library institutes. Three- to twelve-month courses with examinations are supplied by correspondence. Locally sponsored seminars, workshops, conferences, and refresher courses are continually going on everywhere. Many are organized by the library methodological centers for the smaller libraries within their jurisdiction; others appear to be staff projects of a more or less spontaneous nature. In Tashkent, for example, special "circles" are held to enable young librarians without higher education to improve their knowledge of libraries and librarianship.

The Leningrad State Library Institute, since it was the only one visited by the delegation, will be described here as an example of the higher professional library schools of the Soviet Union. The delegation was told that the standards and curricula of all the library institutes and university training programs were essentially the same. This particular Institute was established in 1918 and is now administered by the Ministry of Culture of the RSFSR. Its full title includes the name of Lenin's wife, Krupskaia, who is revered as the founder of Soviet librarianship.

There were 4,070 students enrolled during the spring of 1961. Of these, 3,300 were enrolled in the library division, the rest in the division of cultural work. Six hundred and sixty students were to be graduated in 1961. There is apparently no difficulty in recruiting good students; many librarians are needed in all types of libraries, and librarianship is regarded as a desirable career. High school graduates (about age seventeen) are selected on the basis of a competitive entrance examination in general literature (both Russian and foreign, but chiefly Russian), the history of the USSR, and one foreign language (usually English, French, or German). An essay must also be written in the Russian language. (This is the same examination that is taken by all applicants for higher education in any field.) About 50 per cent of the successful applicants at the Institute are men. None is foreign, although the delegation was told that some foreign students (their nationalities were not specified) attend the Moscow Institute.[2]

About 85 per cent of the students attend the Institute on state scholarships that cover tuition, textbooks, room and board, and even clothing. A token fee of one (new) ruble and fifty kopeks is collected monthly to instill a sense of responsibility in the students. The 15 per cent who do not get scholarships are either well-to-do or notably less competent than the recipients of awards. A few of the weakest students are expelled.

The curriculum is divided into (1) general courses in the social sciences, humanities, physical sciences, and foreign languages and (2) special courses in library science. The general courses occupy 60-65 per cent of the entire curriculum. The special courses cover the historical and technical aspects of librarianship and include specialized programs for children's and technical librarians. An elective course is offered in the history of the arts (theater, cinema, and the like), and all students are required to take courses in the fundamentals of Marxist and Leninist ethics and aesthetics and in the principles of scientific atheism.

This curriculum is applied uniformly to students in the day, the evening, and the correspondence departments. Of the 660 graduates in 1961, 180 (27 per cent) attended the day department, 50 (8 per cent) the evening department, and 430 (65 per cent) the correspondence department.

Students may take courses in the day department if they have had two years of work experience in any field;

most of these students have actually had library experience. Students with no work experience are required to take daytime library jobs and attend only evening classes the first year. From the second year on all may attend the day classes. After three and one-half years, the graduates leave the Institute to work a full year in a library, then return at the end of the year to take the Institute examinations.

Then follow the state examinations, which are administered by a special committee of the Ministry of Culture. These examinations cover the history of the Communist Party, literature (varied by field of specialization), librarianship, and bibliography. The successful candidates, having received their diplomas, are obligated to return to the libraries to which they had been assigned during the previous year for an additional period of work before moving on to other positions.

The program of the evening department covers five years. All students work in Leningrad libraries and take sixteen hours of classes per week. Each year they are given thirty days of leave, at full pay, from their jobs to prepare for the Institute examinations. An additional thirty days of paid leave is granted when students prepare for the state examinations.

About 98 per cent of all correspondence students are also working librarians, many in the more remote republics. Entrance examinations and the general course examination may be taken in the student's home town, but the student must go to the Institute or one of its branches for his examinations in the special library courses. Paid leave and transportation are provided by the state. The three branches where the student may take all the state examinations are at Khabarovsk (in the extreme eastern part of Siberia, near the Pacific), Kirov (over 500 miles east of Moscow, near the western approaches to the Ural Mountains), and Kaliningrad (formerly Königsberg of East Prussia on the Baltic). Correspondence students must go to Leningrad for the same state examinations the day students take.

A three-year postgraduate course is offered to persons who already have the higher degree in librarianship. The purpose of this program, which is similar to the doctoral program in American library schools, is training for research and for the highest administrative positions. After the submission of a major thesis, the degree of Candidate of Pedagogical Sciences is granted. The Institute also maintains a department of research which investigates library problems, develops new methods, and recommends the adoption of improved furnishings and equipment, such as lights, compact stacks, and microfilm projectors.

The American delegation could not assess the quality of the teaching or the content of the curriculum, but the product seemed to be satisfactory as judged by the spirit and ability of the graduates. By comparison with American library schools, the Soviet institutes are conspicuously strong in field work and practical experience. A full year of field work is required of the day students. The specialized library courses appear to take about the same amount of time (35-40 per cent of three and one-half years) as the master's program in the United States.

On the other hand, the Soviet library institutes require much less general educational background (60-65 per cent of three and one-half years) than do American schools, which require graduation from a four-year college or university, with a university degree in some field other than librarianship, for admission to the one-year specialized library curriculum. Indeed, the delegation questioned whether the graduates of the Soviet institutes are given sufficient opportunity to become as broadly educated as American librarians. The only Soviet library recruits who might possibly enjoy wider scope are the university graduates in fields other than librarianship who later transfer to library work, that is, who enter librarianship after receiving an undergraduate university degree. It is hoped readers will not assume that these observations are made in ignorance of the differences between United States and Soviet educational systems in general. The delegation is aware that the Soviet student receives a liberal arts program of study throughout the first decade of matriculation--comparable to the gymnasium level of Western Europe--and then begins specialization. Nonetheless, it seems to the delegation that on balance the graduate of a Soviet library institute is more narrowly specialized-- and less broadly educated--than his counterpart in the United States.

One other aspect of the Soviet library institutes raised questions in the minds of the American delegates--the lack of university affiliation. It has been the experience of American librarians that general cultural courses as offered by the faculty of a special, nonuniversity institute are often less adequate than the same courses offered by the regular departments of a university. Standards may be lower, and the materials may be slanted too sharply toward professional interests; the product may be second-rate from an academic point of view. For this reason all but a few American library schools have long since been affiliated with strong universities, and the students are required to compete with other university students in the fields of their specialization. A prospective librarian, for example, who is majoring in chemistry in the university before entering library school must hold his own in competition with prospective, professional chemists. There is no special curriculum in the United States in chemistry for librarians.

Status of Librarians

The delegation inquired on many occasions into the status of librarians in the Soviet Union. Is librarianship regarded as a desirable career? Is it attractive in comparison with other careers? Are librarians well paid? Generally speaking, the answer seems to be that Soviet librarians enjoy a respected position in Soviet society, and that salaries and status are on a par with those of other professional groups requiring comparable training. It is a relatively stable profession with considerable opportunity for personal advancement and for significant social service, according to Soviet standards in this field. There are many jobs waiting; working conditions are good; the future of any student who can gain admission to library school and complete the state examination is relatively secure.

Uniform salary schedules are recommended by the Ministry of Culture, in consultation with the State Committee on Labor and Salaries, and are approved by the Council of Ministers. Three criteria are used: amount of education, type of library, and climatic zone.

The basic criterion is amount of education--a criterion which applies equally to teachers, research workers, and other professional groups, as well as to librarians. A librarian with a higher academic degree draws the same pay as a scientist with a comparable degree, and a scientist working as a specialist in a research library is paid the same as if he were working in a laboratory. The salary of a mass or school librarian who has graduated from a technical high school is equal to that of an elementary school teacher who has been trained at the same level. The mass or scholarly librarian who has graduated from a library institute draws the same salary as a university graduate. A person who has a university degree in a field other than librarianship and has later qualified as a librarian earns 10 per cent more than the graduate of the library institute. A librarian with the degree of Candidate (similar to the American doctorate) is paid on a par with university professors and other scholars who are also Candidates.

Dr. Nicholas DeWitt found that--as of the mid-1950's --"librarians" (rank unspecified) were in a wage category which he designated "below level" (61-80 rubles per month), sharing this position with preschool teachers, elementary grade schoolteachers, semiprofessional medical personnel, and the like. In his "above average" wage category (121-170 rubles per month), Dr. DeWitt found "senior librarians" on a level with secondary school directors, editors and translators, junior research workers, chief physicians and directors of medical establishments, ordinary engineers, designers, and economists. In the "high" salary category (171-400 rubles per month) library directors share the company of professors and associate professors in higher education, directors and deputy directors of higher educational and research establishments, senior research workers, and the like. In the "very high" (401-700 rubles per month) and "extremely high" (700 rubles and over per month) categories librarians do not appear.[3]

These uniform salary schedules are varied, however, by type of institution. All research institutions, including libraries, are classified on the basis of the significance of their work in relation to the economic and cultural needs of the country. The Council of Ministers, on recommendation of the State Committee on Labor and Salaries, has established four categories of institutions. Research libraries, such as the Lenin Library, are in Category II--next to the top. Only the highest-priority research institutes belong in Category I. The only library that is said to be in Category I is the All-Union Library of Foreign Literature, which is administered directly by the USSR Ministry of Culture. Most, or perhaps all, of the smaller mass libraries, and many of the larger libraries in the outlying republics, appear to belong in Category III.

It was understood by the delegation that the highest salary schedules are applied to institutions in Category I, the lowest to those in Category IV. People with a given academic status are therefore paid more or less depending upon the significance of the institution in which they work. It was noted in the Ukraine, however, that the Ministry of Culture was considering the elimination of type of institution as a criterion for the determination of salaries, presumably because the present system discriminated against the mass and school libraries, which urgently need more highly trained staff.

The delegation collected no information about the third criterion determining rates of salary: climatic zone. It assumes that it relates to "hardship posts," such as in the Arctic regions.

In brief, the delegation concluded that, except in the smaller libraries, the status of Soviet librarians is good indeed. Libraries are highly rated among other kinds of educational and research institutions, and librarians get the same pay as other graduates or scholars with comparable academic qualifications.

The relatively low qualifications required of librarians for the smaller mass, children's, and school libraries seemed to the delegation to pose a serious problem in the Soviet library system. The graduates of the library institutes and the universities take positions in the republic, state, oblast, academy, university, and other large libraries which require their competence. Very few of them now direct raion (comparable to the United States county) and rural libraries, which in the judgment of the delegation also require their competence. The vast majority of the rural and raion librarians are graduates only of the technical high schools, which are designed to serve this market. The line has been drawn by size of library, instead of by the professional nature of the work required.

Conversely, a surprisingly high proportion of the staff of larger libraries are fully trained as professional librarians. Very few graduates of the technical high schools are employed in large libraries. To the American delegates, who are accustomed to dividing library work not so much by size of library as by its professional or nonprofessional nature, this fact also raised a question. It appeared to the delegation that the larger Soviet libraries were using fully professional people to do many kinds of routine library work, such as attending loan desks, that are assigned to nonprofessional assistants in American libraries.

Librarians and Librarianship

The American pattern is to use fully professional librarians in key positions in both large and small libraries--the professional nature of the work being regarded as essentially the same--and to support the professional staff, especially in large libraries, with many clerical or subprofessional assistants. The ratio of subprofessional or clerical to professional staff is often as high as two to one. To the American observers, the Soviet pattern of concentrating almost all of the best people in the larger libraries, where they are often expected to do subprofessional or clerical as well as professional work, is wasteful of professional talent; while the concentration of the less well-trained people in the smaller libraries, where they must try to do professional as well as subprofessional and clerical work, is a disservice to the masses of readers.

Efforts are now being made, however, the delegation was told, to recruit larger numbers of library institute graduates for service in the rural and raion libraries. In the Ukraine especially was this need expressed to the delegation; and, as noted above, the possibility of discontinuing type of library as a determinant of salary and status is being considered. The further possibility of using larger numbers of technical high school graduates for the more routine, subprofessional work of the larger libraries might, it seemed to the delegation, also be usefully considered.

Some data were collected by the delegation on the size and composition of the staffs of individual libraries. Three examples might serve as illustrative.

The staff of the Lenin Library consists of 2,150 people, exclusive of cloakroom attendants, janitors, and employees of the printing department. (The comparable Library of Congress statistic is approximately 2,600.) Of these 2,150 people, 1,750 are librarians and 400 are technical staff, such as engineers and shopworkers. Assistant librarians who have only technical high school training are included in both groups. About three fourths of the 1,750 librarians are university or institute graduates. Many are subject specialists with one year of in-service library training.

The main library of Kiev State University employs 70 people, excluding cloakroom attendants and janitors. About half are graduates of library institutes, 5 hold their positions on the basis of experience, 3 or 4 are graduates of technical high schools, and the rest are university graduates in fields other than librarianship. There are 3 clerical positions in the cataloging and acquisition departments. Loan desk attendants are required to be library institute graduates. Branch librarians are not included in this total.

The special library of Shoe Factory No. 4 at Kiev has 4 full-time staff members. Two are library institute graduates, 1 is a technical high school graduate, and 1 is a graduate of the Institute of Light Industry. The library supplies both technical and general literature to 5,000 factory workers, including 300 engineers.

It was impossible for the delegates to evaluate Soviet library staffs in terms of size. Many libraries, especially the smaller mass, children's, and school libraries, seemed understaffed. A few of the larger libraries seemed overstaffed in relation to the nature and extent of their services. Possibly lack of mechanization is partly responsible. No generalizations are feasible, except that a great and growing army of librarians is widely spread throughout the country. The delegation was told that there are 100,000 librarians in the Ukraine alone, 30,000 of whom work in mass and other libraries within the network of the Ministry of Culture. Such statistics include, of course, nearly all regular library employees and are not directly comparable to American statistics. One can only admire the energy and determination with which this large reservoir of qualified personnel is being created.

Its creation is a responsibility primarily of the Ministry of Culture, which supervises the library institutes, establishes standards and qualifications, and recommends salary scales. When the Lenin Library, for example, requires new or additional staff members, the Director applies to the Ministry of Culture, which supplies names of available people from which he may choose. Other applicants, such as persons moving from place to place, may offer their services. A personnel department attends to problems arising from routine turnover, marriages, and the like. Successful applicants are assigned to the Library by the Ministry.

Centralized Guidance and Assistance

One of the greatest differences between American and Soviet librarianship is the way in which the profession is advanced. In large degree, Americans rely upon individual initiative and enterprise in the discovery of new methods and upon voluntary acceptance of those methods which prove to be most useful. Responsibility is essentially local. The Soviets plan their improvements centrally and at a high level of political authority; officials at the top identify a problem, find what they believe to be the best solution, then apply that solution more or less uniformly throughout the country. The responsibility is essentially centralized in the Ministry of Culture. Having determined policy and procedure on a countrywide basis, the Ministry passes down this competence through an elaborate network of methodological centers to the least and most remote hamlets in the country.

There are, therefore, no library associations in the Soviet Union--associations, that is, in the American sense of voluntary, nongovernmental organizations of individuals who seek to improve themselves and their profession. No distinction is drawn between official and nonofficial activities. When the Soviet delegation visited the United States, the delegates seemed to be searching for some kind of official status of the American Library Association--some covert way (there being none overt) in which it establishes and enforces national library policy, or at least carries out policies determined by whatever higher interests it serves. The Soviet guests were simply trying to understand the American system in terms applicable in the Soviet Union. American librarians will commit the same error if they try to interpret the Soviet system in terms applicable in the United States. The lack of library associations in the Soviet Union means only that librarianship, like all other activities, is an integral part of national planning, and that the improvement of librarianship is therefore pursued primarily through official channels. Individual interests are subordinated to group interests, and group interests are, by definition, official.

As already indicated, responsibility for the improvement of Soviet librarianship throughout the entire USSR is now centralized in the Main Library Inspection Office of the Ministry of Culture of the USSR, which coordinates the activities of the library networks of all the ministries. The general methodological center for the country is the Lenin Library. The Foreign Literature Library bears a special responsibility for methods of handling foreign literature. Moscow University Library is the national center for the network of the Ministry of Higher Education. Within each network subordinate centers are dispersed at various geographic or administrative levels throughout the land. For state and mass libraries, for example, the Ministry of Culture has designated certain libraries as methodological centers in each republic, district, oblast, and raion; the centers in the raions provide technical assistance to the village and rural libraries within their jurisdictions.

The nature of these centers was first revealed to the American delegation at the Lenin Library. The Scientific and Methodological Department of this Library, as described by one member of the delegation, is like the American Library Association, the Special Libraries Association, the Library Services Branch of the U. S. Office of Education, the H. W. Wilson Company, and the Council on Library Resources all rolled into one. Its purpose is to conduct research, to compile bibliographies on various subjects, and to provide methodological assistance to the libraries of the USSR. Assistance includes consultation with librarians on such problems as cataloging and classification, the publication of textbooks and manuals on library science, and the organization of conferences and seminars for the exchange of information.

The Department has eight sections: (1) Service for Readers and Selective Bibliography, which compiles book lists for the guidance of readers and for use by libraries as aids to book selection; (2) Book Stocks and Catalogs, which is concerned with problems relating to the acquisition and organization of library collections; (3) Organization and Planning for Librarianship, which includes standards and techniques of library services and the training of librarians; (4) Local Bibliography, which publishes guides for district libraries on the handling of local history collections and materials on topics of current popular interest; (5) Service to Children, which covers all aspects of work with children, including selective bibliography; (6) History of Librarianship and Bibliography; (7) Information on Librarianship and Bibliography Abroad; and (8) the Special Library, which is a library science library of some 40,000 volumes. The Department employs a staff of about fifty people, including lawyers, historians, and physicists.

Another staff of fifty people is employed by the Department of Bibliography and Librarianship of the Saltykov-Shchedrin Library, which shares responsibility for guidance in methodology with the Lenin Library for the northeastern areas of the RSFSR. Like its equivalent in the Lenin Library, this Department prepares publications on librarianship, compiles bibliographies, and gives methodological assistance to various libraries, especially mass libraries. Its specialists go into the field to inspect libraries and to advise working librarians on all such problems as technical services, the stimulation of library use, and how to help children with their reading. Conferences are organized for the exchange of information and experience.

The methodological center for the Ukraine is the Ukrainian State Republic Library, that for Uzbekistan the national library for the Uzbek Republic. These republic centers follow in large degree the principles and policies derived from the Lenin Library, to which major issues are referred, but they also assume initiative in developing local practices that are appropriate to their own regional climates, languages, and customs. The Ukrainian State Republic Library, for example, issues bibliographies in editions up to 20,000 to help librarians deal with literature concerning local problems of agricultural production.

Below the republic centers are the district, oblast, and raion centers. The Moscow City Library serves other libraries in the Moscow district with bibliographical aids to Chinese, Indian, and American literature. There is an active Methodological Department in the Kalinin Oblast Library. The Borispol Raion Library has a methods person who inspects and advises twenty-six village libraries. Monthly seminars of two days each are held for the village librarians, and each library is visited two or three times every three months. Theoretical conferences are held annually. Workshops are arranged for young, untrained librarians. The center assures that the work of all libraries is well carried out and gives advice on cataloging, shelving, book selection, recruiting, and the like.

The methodological centers for children's libraries are sometimes parts of more general centers, at other times separate centers in special children's libraries. The Lenin Library, the Saltykov-Shchedrin Library, and the Ukrainian State Republic Library, for example, have children's sections in their general methodological departments. In the Kalinin Oblast Library, on the other hand, the responsibility for assistance to sixty children's libraries is vested in the Pushkin Children's Library, which is a branch of the Kalinin Oblast Library. The Pushkin Children's Library even distributes the books and catalog cards to the libraries within its jurisdiction. It issues instructions on the proper management of children's libraries and, like other centers, inspects the libraries and holds meetings of the librarians.

The Kiev Oblast Library for Children serves the school as well as the separate children's libraries of the area. Its Methodological and Bibliography Department performs all the usual functions of inspection and instruction and compiles many bibliographies, including an extensive annual index to articles on children's books and education. As a reference center on children's books, it gives out information by telephone and letter as well as in person. A separate children's library at Borispol oversees the twenty-five school libraries in that raion.

The Soviet library profession is thus officially organized in such a way that instruction and guidance toward the improvement of library work are handed down step by step from such national centers as the Lenin Library or the Moscow University Library to the grass roots of the entire country. New ideas are diffused, standards are raised, techniques are taught, and, above all, bibliographies are disseminated in large numbers to guide libraries and readers everywhere in the best ways of achieving the economic and cultural goals of the Soviet society. Within the framework of that society, this system of professional organization is well developed and probably very effective. By contrast, the American system of voluntary, unofficial associations and other private agencies seems loose and casual.

The American system of professional library organization, however, has certain advantages over the tightly knit, closely controlled Soviet system. In particular, it encourages a maximum of varied, individual experimentation. In viewing Soviet libraries, the American delegation was struck by what it regarded as an excessive uniformity of practice, despite local adaptations, that was inconsistent with the wide range of cultural patterns of the several Soviet republics. The same exhibits, the same designs of exhibit cases, the same sets of statistics, the same division of reader privileges, even the same lack of such items as mechanical equipment, tended toward monotony.

While standardization of many practices (e.g., statistics) is a desirable goal of libraries everywhere, the delegation felt that the Soviet system tended to standardize undesirable practices as well as desirable. The emphasis was not so much on individual initiative in the development of new and more effective techniques (e.g., exhibits) as on group conformity in the most effective application of predetermined techniques. For this reason Soviet libraries in general seemed to the delegation less inventive, less varied in their methods of achieving their goals, and indeed less interesting than the libraries of most Western countries. Nevertheless, their power to carry out a national program, once a method has been designated and to the extent that a single method is adequate, is highly impressive. Librarianship in the Soviet Union is an extremely well-organized profession.

International Relations

The American delegation had little opportunity to inquire into the international activities of Soviet librarianship. Some foreign students, it was learned, do attend the Moscow Library Institute; how many and from what countries was not learned. There was no mention of Soviet librarians working as consultants in the uncommitted countries of Africa, Asia, or Latin America. Many foreign librarians, especially from the satellite countries, do visit the Soviet Union; relatively few Soviet librarians appear to visit countries outside the Soviet bloc. There have been notable exceptions, particularly in connection with various international meetings of librarians and bibliographers. The Soviet Union has been represented at several such meetings and has contributed importantly to their success.

Soviet librarianship, as such, does not seem to be involved in any direct way with the distribution of Soviet books for propaganda purposes in other countries of the world. The international relations of Soviet librarianship are largely restricted to the acquisition and dissemination of foreign library literature and the development of contacts with international professional organizations, such as the International Federation of Library Associations.

The Lenin Library, as noted above, has a section on Information on Librarianship and Bibliography Abroad in its Scientific and Methodological Department. About 40 per cent of its special library science collection is foreign. The Foreign Literature Library, which bears central responsibility for international library relations, has a Foreign Library Literature Section and an International Relations Section. The Foreign Library Literature Section collects, indexes, and annotates foreign library periodicals and compiles bibliographies of those periodicals. It has four professional staff members. The International Relations Section, with five professional staff members, compiles manuals on the International Federation of Library Associations, the International Federation of Documentation, and the International Standards Organization. It issues a selective Russian edition of the Unesco Bulletin for Libraries and other Unesco publications, works with numerous foreign library delegations, and exchanges information with international library organizations.

The Director of the Foreign Literature Library, Mrs. Margarita I. Rudomino, is Chairman of the Committee on Librarianship and Bibliography of the Soviet National Commission for Unesco. She is also Chairman of the Committee on International Relations of the Council on Library Problems of the Ministry of Culture of the USSR. In general, the Foreign Literature Library appears to be the central agency that represents Soviet librarianship in international affairs and international librarianship in Soviet affairs.

References

1. A survey of library training in the USSR by the Director of the Foreign Literature Library appeared in a recent issue of Libri: Margarita Rudomino, "Library Training in the USSR," Libri, 12, No. 1:1-7 (1962).
2. In the academic year 1961-62, the first United States librarian--so far as the delegation knows--was a student at a Soviet library institute. Robert Karlowich of the University of Illinois was one of thirty-seven United States graduate students chosen as exchange students under the U.S.-Soviet Cultural Exchange Agreement for that year. His field was library science, and he was enrolled at the Leningrad State Library Institute.
3. Nicholas DeWitt, Education and Professional Employment in the USSR (Washington, D.C.: National Science Foundation, 1961), p. 543.

8. Six Items for Export:

International Values in American Librarianship

Librarianship has always evinced an international character, and the international relations of American librarianship are strong and traditional. The international exchange of library resources helps greatly to disseminate information among the peoples of the world. American librarians have long been conscious, moreover, of their international responsibilities and have sought to cooperate with their foreign colleagues in every practicable way--the exchange of library staff, the education of foreign librarians in American library schools, the establishment of native library schools in other countries, the provision of technical assistance to overseas libraries, and the strengthening of their book collections. Several scores of American librarians are now working abroad each year in Japan, Korea, the Philippines, Indonesia, Thailand, Burma, Pakistan, India, Nepal, and in as many other countries of the Middle East, Africa, and Latin America. The foreign librarians who travel or study in the United States are counted in the several hundreds each year. The professional library associations, such as the American Library Association, Special Libraries Association, and the Medical Library Association, sponsor many of these activities with foundation or government aid. The Department of State, the Agency for International Development, the United States Information Agency, and the Pan American Union are all significantly involved, together with a number of international agencies, including Unesco, the International Federation of Library Associations, and the International Federation of Documentation.

American librarianship thus advances international librarianship along a wide and varied front. All kinds of li-

---

Reprinted by permission from Library Journal, 88 (Feb. 15, 1963), pp. 711-17, published by R. R. Bowker Co. (a Xerox company). Copyright © 1963 by Xerox Corporation.

braries are affected--national, academic, public and juvenile, and those in such special fields as medicine, agriculture, and industry. The full history and description of these programs, and their evaluation, will someday make an absorbing study. I think especially of the personal contributions of many such individuals as Arthur Bostwick, Harry Lydenberg, Verner Clapp, Marietta Daniels, Keyes Metcalf, and Robert Gitler, who have distinguished themselves in service overseas. But this is not my story.

My purpose here is to identify the characteristics of American librarianship that justify all these efforts, particularly in the newly developing nations of the world. When we work abroad, when foreign librarians study here, what do we offer that is worth the trouble? What is our cultural product that merits emulation?

There are six characteristics of American librarianship that I perceive as valuable for export: first, the conception of the library as an organization of books; second, the evolution of a library profession; third, the attitude of service; fourth, the function of the library as an educational institution; fifth, its role in the advancement of intellectual freedom; and last, the conception of organized information as a public resource and responsibility.

Before talking about these characteristics, I hasten to emphasize that none is exclusively American. The roots of American librarianship emerge from other times and are shared with our colleagues in many countries. We did not invent the library catalog, or bibliography, or adult education. But we have enriched these and other traits of modern librarianship and have shaped a corpus of librarianship that is characteristically American.

I hasten to emphasize further that American librarians are not the only ones who do good in the world. For us ever to overlook the contributions of British librarianship in Africa, or French librarianship in Latin America, or Australian librarianship in Indonesia would be inexcusably parochial. We share a strong Western heritage in international library affairs, and we are beginning to understand that there also exists an Eastern heritage from which Western librarianship may benefit richly.

Organization of Books

First is the conception of the library as an organization of books. Historically and universally the library has been defined as a collection of books, but only within the last century, and particularly in the United States and Great Britain, has the idea grown that the library should become a collection of books organized for efficient use--an organism designed to interpret and exploit its intellectual resources. This is a dynamic new dimension of librarianship that is still but vaguely understood by some American scholars. Overseas in many places it has hardly been recognized, as is clearly evident from even a cursory view of the dusty disorder of hundreds of libraries around the world. The books may be arranged in some order on the shelves, but often not for convenient use. The catalogs may exist only for inventory purposes. There may be no coordination, administrative or bibliographic, among the several collections of a single institution. The idea that the library is not only an agency for the collection and preservation of books but also an agent of their intellectual organization may still not have crossed the threshold of the imagination.

The organization of the American library embraces many techniques that are the stock and trade of the professional librarian--bibliographies, classification schemes, union catalogs, serial records, and so on. It embraces the departmentalization of library functions and the coordination of library services, including the entire field of interlibrary cooperation. It extends to the architecture of library buildings. These are the obvious, how-to-do-it characteristics of American librarianship.

Many of these techniques are exportable, though rarely without major adaptation to local customs, materials, and human resources. The Dewey classification has, for example, been modified in a multitude of ways for use in a surprising number of foreign countries. We should encourage these adaptations; there is no reason to resist them. The techniques have no value in themselves. The value derives only from the conception of an organization that works well for the particular communities to be served.

Among the technical advances of American librarianship are also the mechanical devices that improve the efficiency of the library organization--book trucks, typewriters, multiple carbon forms, accounting machines, office copying equipment, electric erasers, microfilm cameras and readers, conveyors and lifts, and so on. These gadgets are much desired by librarians in newly developing countries-- sometimes wisely, often not. Like new buildings, they may be sought as the symbols of modern librarianship and may be proudly displayed whether or not they are useful, or even work. Among the exportable values of American librarianship, these products of mechanical ingenuity are the least important; they may actually detract attention from the more important values. The library is not a building, and its organization not a machine.

The significance of the library as an organization of books arises first from the exponential growth of recorded knowledge and second from the variety of uses to which this knowledge is put. There are multi-millions of individual books, each different from every other, that serve the manifold purposes of multi-millions of individual readers. The organized library is really a vast extension of the individual reader's capacity to collect and sort out the books he needs. In these times it is no exaggeration, I believe, to suggest that the modern library is a late, high refinement of a civilization that is built on the accumulation of printed words. The intellectual organization of this accumulation promises to become one of the most critical, consequential, and incredibly complex problems that mankind faces today.

American librarianship has begun to understand its new mission in the large, and there is foresight in this understanding for other peoples of the world. Even the simplest, smallest, most unpretentious popular library in the African bush should still be conceived as an organized way of increasing the utility of books.

Evolution of a Profession

Second is the evolution of a library profession--a young and often uncertain profession, but a real one. The organization of books into useful libraries depends heavily upon the knowledge and skill of the people who make librarianship their career. In Great Britain, the United States, the Soviet Union, and elsewhere, the profession has clearly paced the growth of the modern library. In Burma, by contrast, there is no such profession. There is no public library legislation and no classification for librarians in the government service. Librarians are clerks, whether educated or not. In the universities, only the chief librarian enjoys a modicum of prestige, which is usually borrowed from other scholarly pursuits. The low status of librarianship, and therefore of the library organization, is a major deterrent to both formal and informal education. Yet in other countries, such as India, the Philippines, and Japan, the profession is seen to be emerging gradually, as it did in Great Britain and the United States, as the social and intellectual values of the library are recognized.

The exportable values of the American library profession are typical of all professions--a body of unique, technical knowledge, a specialized literature, a system of professional organizations or associations, a social mission, and a sense of ethics. Lacking any of these, the progress of librarianship in any country is certain to be limited. In the effort to stimulate indigenous professional movements overseas, the American library profession, working primarily through its professional associations, has concentrated on education for librarianship--that is, on the education of foreign librarians who can in turn stimulate their native professional movements. With American help, new library schools have been established in Israel, Japan, Turkey, Colombia, Uruguay, China, and elsewhere, and existing schools have been strengthened in such other countries as the Philippines and India. Many hundreds of foreign librarians have been educated in the United States, and many among them now teach in foreign library schools or serve in other posts of professional leadership.

As leadership emerges in foreign professional movements, more attention will be drawn to other aspects of librarianship, especially professional literature and associations. Adaptations and translations of American and European library literature are sorely needed in Asia, the Middle East, and Latin America, together with new texts, codes, and manuals written specially for local use. The library associations in most of the developing countries still need to be strengthened. The recent effort to organize an Asian Federation of Library Associations has been handicapped by the inability of many of the member associations to represent their national professions adequately or to finance the travel of their delegates to international meetings. The American librarian abroad needs not only to organize libraries and to educate librarians but also to nurture in every possible way the growth of indigenous professional organizations. The struggle for status, for the opportunity to do a professional job, indeed, for recognition that there exists a professional job to be done, may be several generations behind the same, continuing struggle in the United States.

Service Attitude

Third is the attitude of service. This characteristic of American librarianship could well have been included with other attributes of the profession, but I am listing it separately because of the particular significance that American librarians have attached to it during their service abroad. The attitude is no different from that of physicians, ministers, and members of other professions who are dedicated to their social missions. It is simply the attitude of helpfulness, the motive of being useful to other people. This is what takes us overseas in the first place, and whether at home or abroad, service is a cardinal principle of American librarianship.

Nothing impresses the American librarian abroad more immediately and forcefully, and often unexpectedly, than the unhelpful attitude of some foreign librarians. Whether the reason be the lack of professional development or the granting of library jobs as sinecures, the librarians of some countries are often not devoted to helping readers. Their official positions may denote prestige for themselves, and they may use this prestige against the welfare of less important people. They may abet a social elite by kowtowing to their superiors and brow-beating their inferiors. Excessive red tape, frustrating regulations, and other ceremonial impedimenta may be evoked as symbols of power and status.

Our own virtue in this department of human behavior is not unquestionable. But by and large we have come to believe that public institutions are utilitarian devices to further the general welfare. A government official is a public servant. An administrator creates conditions that are favorable to the worker. The business man feels a responsibility toward his customers. The librarian serves people who need books--the people for whose welfare the library exists.

American librarians, in their dedication to service, have adopted many practices that stimulate the use of books. Liberal lending regulations, long hours of service, recommended reading lists, film forums, book clubs, lecture series, book reviews on radio and TV, and "new book shelves" are all good examples. Most significant is reference service, in which librarians personally help readers to explore the resources of the library. This personal, outgoing relationship of librarian to reader is still unknown in much of the library world.

Educational Function

Fourth is the function of the library as an educational institution. It is probable that the libraries of no country other than the United States, except the Soviet Union, have been so clearly conceived as playing a positive role in the lifelong education of all the people. Books and reading are central to learning, and the stimulation of learning is the affirmative job of the library, whether ancillary to a school, college, or other institution of formal education, or separately constituted for informal education.

This is common knowledge of course. Yet the foreign librarian, and occasionally his American counterpart, may become so preoccupied with the accepted forms of librarianship that he overlooks the educational reason for them. No length of open book shelves, for example, will be useful unless the people are first taught, and then persuaded, that the books are really displayed for their benefit, and that they are really allowed to read them. This idea may be entirely new to them. There may be social distinctions that preclude for whole classes of people any presumption of learning--the women of lower-caste India, for example. The value is not in the open shelves; it is in the process of education that open-shelf libraries are designed to encourage.

There are many superb libraries throughout the developing world that do serve a significant educational purpose; the Makerere College Library in Uganda and the Children's Library at São Paulo, Brazil, are examples. But for every one that does there are scores that do not. I do not now refer to the many fine archival and other rare book depositories that are properly restricted; these constitute a special custodial problem. I do refer to the numerous public, school, and college libraries that are also still restricted--college libraries in South America that are closed to students, subscription libraries in Africa (even some that are now ostensibly multi-racial) that are unavailable for all practical purposes to black Africans, and national libraries in Asia that, while open to readers, have never dreamed of leading a national popular library movement. These libraries do not yet exert, or conceive that they might properly exert, a deliberate, aggressive influence toward the enlightenment of all the people.

The exportable value of American librarianship is really, then, that libraries can and should take the initiative in the education of the people. The establishment of children's reading rooms, the promotion of adult educational programs, the extension of book services to rural areas-- these are all manifestations of an educational idea that American librarianship can convey to our neighbors overseas. We can demonstrate how a collection of books, selected for specific educational purposes, and so organized that people are encouraged to read them, can strengthen a whole community. We can show how a regional network of libraries can reach large, underprivileged populations. Books for fun and relaxation, books for inspiration, books for social ideas, books for science and technology, and books for the everyday business of living are all needed in the universal quest of learning.

Intellectual Freedom

Fifth is the role of the library in the advancement of intellectual freedom. Like other basic values of American librarianship, the freedom of inquiry and expression derives not only from library services; the library is only one among many institutions that embrace this principle. But the library is elemental in that books, as contrasted with the mass media, are the private forum of the mind. Whatever else may happen, there can be no final abridgement of intellectual freedom as long as individuals, privately and voluntarily, can choose their own reading from libraries that honor the Library Bill of Rights.

The very existence of the Library Bill of Rights testifies, of course, to our continuing struggle to advance its principles not only overseas but also in our own back yards. The Committee on Intellectual Freedom is one of the busiest groups in the American Library Association. Instances of library censorship, covert as well as overt, are legion; and aside from the outright, local censorship of library collections there are instances of impressive violation, or misun-

Six Items for Export

derstanding of intellectual freedom in high places. Let me cite two examples.

First is the proposed U.S. Postal Revision Act of 1962, H.R. 7927, which, had it passed, would have restricted the mailing at regular postal rates of "Communist political propaganda financed or sponsored directly or indirectly by any Communist controlled government." This language was so loose, so broad, and so difficult of administration that it could have obstructed severely the flow of information about Communist peoples even to our research libraries. Ignorance is dangerous, no matter who pays, or does not pay, the postage.

Second is the general practice of the United States Information Agency of restricting the 177 USIS libraries overseas to books written by American authors and published in the United States. This practice has recently been modified to permit USIS librarians to buy books in local languages on the local market. Other exceptions can be found. But in general, the world over, only American books about the United States, and only American books about the rest of the world, including the host country, are displayed for local reading. This is not censorship in the usual sense that people are prevented from reading anything else; people can go across the street to the British Council Library or the USSR Library for other reading if they wish. But the practice does misrepresent the freedoms that we cherish for ourselves, and it advertises our lack of interest in those freedoms for other people.

The idea, presumably, is to sell America, but what is really sold would be unrecognizable in the United States. The book stock of the USIS library disavows, for example, our entire indebtedness to the Classic and Renaissance worlds and our heritage in the English, Scandinavian, Polish, Russian, German, Japanese, Mexican, and a score of other cultures. Can you imagine an "American" library without Aristotle, Tolstoy, Shakespeare, Cervantes, or Rousseau? And what African, however deeply he may appreciate the excellent services of his USIS library, could be persuaded on the basis of this example that we really believe in the freedom to read, that we do not censor the cultural products of other nations, and that our purpose at home as well as abroad is other than to propagandize our exclusive political interests?

We have a long way to go before intellectual freedom is finally achieved at home and we are not yet secure enough in our own wisdom to offer other people the freedom of choice that we value for ourselves. Meanwhile, we misrepresent what we preach in the very method of preaching. But many American librarians overseas are free agents who can, if they will, help to export one of the basic values of American life. They can recruit our foreign colleagues for a crusade that has already lasted several centuries in the Western world and in which the library, if worse should ever come to worst, is certain to be the last stronghold.

Public Responsibility

Sixth, and last, is the conception of organized information as a public resource and responsibility. We are accustomed to thinking of natural resources, such as oil, water, forests, and other material wealth that are crucial to the public welfare. We may also think of educational, industrial, and other cultural resources and we often characterize book collections as resources. The acceptance of public responsibility for supplying book collections to all the people is by now traditional in many countries.

This traditional acceptance of the public library is, however, only the beginning. We noted earlier that libraries, in the modern sense, are more than collections of books; they are complex organizations of books for use. Similarly, organized information is more than a collection of facts. We are now beginning to understand that the totality of recorded knowledge, collected, controlled, and analyzed intellectually for use, is itself a public resource that is vital even to the welfare of nations. The problem is no longer just the availability of some good books; it is the universal command of all important books.

This conception is now sharpest in the fields of science and technology, where organized knowledge is increasingly crucial to the strength of nations. The National Science Foundation, the Atomic Energy Commission, the National Institutes of Health, and the Armed Services are all deeply concerned, together with industry and universities everywhere. The USSR is tackling the problem through its Institute of Scientific Information. In the developing countries, such as Egypt, India, Pakistan, and Indonesia, a number of national documentation centers have been started in

Six Items for Export

support of new research programs. But the idea is by no means limited to the sciences; it applies equally to history, geography, anthropology, the fine arts, and other humanities and social sciences.

One of the most important things that librarians can do abroad is to teach the idea that information is not just the private concern of an educated elite but also a significant public concern, and further that the organization of information through libraries, bibliographies, and documentation centers has become so great a problem as to require public attention. The orderly, continuing control of recorded knowledge is both a present utility and the foundation of future knowledge. In all modern, technological societies, organized libraries have become a critical national resource.

These, then, are the international values that I perceive in American librarianship; these are the qualities that enrich our international library relations. Libraries are books organized for effective use, and a strong library profession is necessary to their organization. A distinctive trait of this profession is the devotion to service, the attitude of helpfulness to all readers. Indeed, libraries teach; they are educational institutions, and they may secure to all readers their individual freedom of inquiry. As agencies for the organization of knowledge, they comprise in modern society a cultural resource that is vital to the welfare of nations. These are ideas that foreign librarians may learn from American librarianship and that may exert an influence for good in the affairs of the world.

These values define, of course, our own domestic library goals; they are not for export only. Indeed, we offer nothing that has been finally achieved at home. We have made progress, but it should be candidly made clear both at home and abroad that a long road is still ahead for librarians everywhere before any of these goals is reached; in fact, there may be no such thing as reaching them. No organization of books is ever perfect, education is never complete, and there will always be people who seek to coerce the minds of others. We offer only to share with others our experience thus far, to help them when we can, and to enlist their help in the continuing pursuit of values that we believe are good for everybody.

This paper was given at the Cornell Library Conference and Dedication, October 1962.

9. Documentation and Information Science in the Core Library School Curriculum

A year ago in a paper "The Graduate Library School Curriculum"[1] I suggested that, in incorporating the newer content of documentation and information science into the library school curriculum, we need to go all the way back into the core courses to take a new look at them in the light of important changes in librarianship to which the curriculum must be adjusted.

> First is the expansion of librarianship, with respect ... to the range of functions within it and of interests without. By functions within I mean new or alternative or more intensive kinds of services--selective dissemination of information to readers, the delivery of photocopies to offices and laboratories, literature searching, and other activities of which many are embraced by the rubric "documentation." By interests without I mean other fields of information service, such as information centers (as Weinberg defined them), data banks (in social and political fields), management information systems (in business), and command and control systems (in the military)....
>
> Second, in this process of expansion, librarianship is again reaching out to other disciplines for new knowledge and methodologies. In the nineteen thirties we found new strength in the social sci-

---

Reprinted by permission from Special Libraries, Vol. 58 (no. 1): 40-45 (Jan. 1967). Copyright © 1967 by Special Libraries Association.

ences--sociology, education, communications, and statistics. Today, in the quest of advanced technologies, we are searching out mathematics, electronics, business and industrial management, linguistics, philosophy, and psychology.

Third is the emergence of additional, exacting specializations in librarianship, especially in the area of information science, including operations research, systems analysis, and mechanization.

And fourth is the development of librarianship itself as a more rigorous discipline. The growing complexity of the profession requires the discovery and application of more precise methodologies for the study of library affairs....

The new content represented by these changes is impressive--the extension of librarianship into new fields of information handling, the intensification of library services, the infusion of new knowledge and techniques from other disciplines, with emerging new specializations, and the evolution of a more exact library science. But let us never forget that the traditional content of librarianship is also impressive. The long experience and tested values of librarianship are still our most reliable and sophisticated resource for the solution of information-handling problems in most contexts, whatever additional help may now be needed. An imaginative curriculum revision will build upon this resource, explicate its values, and extend its application to information problems far from the four walls of the library.

Blending Old and New

There are three ways of relating the newer content of documentation and information science to the older content of librarianship. First is the addition of specialized courses to the existing curriculum, as many schools are now doing. This is useful and expedient but achieves no basic integration. The old curriculum remains substantially untouched. Second is the offering of separate new curricula in information science that are parallel or alternative to the old curriculum, as a few library schools and the separate schools of information science are now doing. This approach not only fails of integration but actually emphasizes the apparent dichotomy between the new and the old. The third way, to which I subscribe, is the blending of the new content into a basically revised version of the old curriculum--or, if the converse pleases more, the blending of the old content into a basically new curriculum.

I prefer the integrated approach because I do not believe that information science is a field separate from librarianship. It is rather a fresh insight into the nature of librarianship--an insight derived from broader concepts, more exact methodologies, and more varied applications. Its content cuts across the entire spectrum of librarianship and even penetrates the core curriculum. Like documentation, it is an extension of librarianship. The processes of collection building, organization, and utilization are, for example, common to all library and information systems.

Let us look back at the nature of librarianship and try to identify the broad areas of content that are common to all information-handling systems and to which documentation and information science are applicable. The conceptualization that works best for me divides the content into three main areas.

First are books and readers, including all forms of recorded knowledge and all manner of people who use it, both inside and outside the library or information agency. Second is the intellectual organization of recorded knowledge, including bibliography, cataloging, classification, and indexing of all kinds, regardless of origin or place of application. And third is the library itself, and other kinds of information centers, as institutions for the operation of book and information services. These three--recorded knowledge and its users, its intellectual organization, and the service agencies --are, I believe, comprehensive of both librarianship and information science.

Of Books and Readers

The world of books and readers is conceived here broadly as the content, the substance, the meanings with which we are basically concerned. It is also the environmental aspect of libraries as institutions--the sources of policy and criteria for evaluation. Books to cover the whole panoply of forms in which information is recorded, including journals, technical reports, newspapers, manuscripts, films, and magnetic tape. Reading to stand for the full range of uses to which books are put, the scholarly needs they serve, their selection and dissemination. The emphasis in this area is on the content of the collection (or file) and on its scholarly origins and interpretation.

It might be argued that books and readers are two fields instead of one. I prefer to think of them as one, because I find it impossible to consider such functions as book selection and literature searching without simultaneous reference to both. The two merge in the concept of reading, or, more broadly, in the retrieval and dissemination of ideas and information from recorded sources. It is the interaction of writers and books and readers that is central to our purpose, regardless of how diverse our specializations may be.

This area relates also to the beginning and the end of the information cycle, to both the input and the output of a library or information system. The principles of book selection and literature searching are essentially the same for the acquisition librarian, the reference librarian, the information specialist, or the reader.

Specializations in this area, without reference to specific courses, may be broadly outlined as follows. First the history of books and printing and the field of rare books. Second are selection of books and the evaluation of collections, whether for acquisition or use. Third are reading interests and user studies, which branch out into the theory of learning, the sociology and psychology of communication, and the nature and methods of scholarship. Fourth is reference, which branches out into the various fields of subject literature specialization; specializations by forms of materials, such as government documents, technical reports, and audio-visual materials; and specializations by reader levels, such as children's and popular adult literature. The term reference is used here not simply to denote a familiarity with dictionaries, handbooks, encyclopedias, indexes, and the like, but more broadly the knowledge and exploitation of book collections and information files, including the tools of their organization, the strategies of seeking out the desired resources, and the methods of their dissemination.

To this entire area of librarianship there is an introductory or core content that I wish could be shared by students in all specializations, for the purposes of perspective, of understanding the relationships between one's own specialization and those of others, and of communication among the

Information Science in the Core Curriculum   123

specializations. This would be an introduction to the major
forms and movements of publication that fill up libraries
and information centers, including their origins in the history of scholarship and the scholarly uses to which they are
put. It would not be just the history of the printed book or
the rise of the technical report, though it would include
something about each. It would treat of the beginnings and
present status of the scientific journal, the uses of microforms and audio-visual aids, the purposes of government
documents, and the acceptance of newspapers as historical
evidence. It would touch upon current changes in the concept of publication, as texts begin to be reproduced in single
copies upon demand from microforms, just as the concept
was changed in the fifteenth century from the production of
single to multiple copies by the new technologies of printing.
The survey though necessarily superficial in many respects,
would try to make certain that librarians, documentalists,
and information scientists alike share a broad view of the
full range of library resources and the manifold reasons for
their existence. While a course such as this might be impractical, and certainly difficult to teach, it does represent
an approach that ought at least be explored.

Of Organization

The second broad area is the intellectual organization of recorded knowledge--the bibliographical schemes within which
the content and meanings of books are arranged and described
for retrieval. These are the intellectual road maps of the
world of books and reading. Included are all varieties of
classifications, vocabularies, catalogs, bibliographies, and
indexes, whether applied in manual or mechanized systems.
Indeed, the theories and principles of bibliography, as the
broadest term available for this area, are separable from
the technologies of particular libraries or information centers. Also, the design and preparation of bibliographical
schemes, which are the main concerns of this area, are
separable from the methods of utilizing those schemes at the
point of reference and retrieval.

The specializations in this area include notably the
field of enumerative bibliography, and especially subject bibliography, as well as library cataloging and classification,
the many special indexing schemes, such as coordinate, citation, and key-word-in-context, and the systematic study of
problems common to all types of file organization, such as

the derivation and control of subject headings, or descriptors, and the measurement of relevance. Here especially do the disciplines of logic, mathematics, and linguistics come into play.

For a core program in this area I would suggest a comparative introduction to the many species of bibliographical schemes. This would define the elements that are common to all schemes and explore the variations in the treatment of those elements for different bodies of recorded knowledge, different groups of readers, and different uses. Some of these elements are 1) the scope or coverage of a catalog, index, or file--what it really contains; 2) the scheme of intellectual organization, which may be broken down into a) the principles and concepts of classification used, b) the derivation and control of the terms applied to the concepts, c) the order or arrangement of the terms, as in alphabetical, hierarchical, coordinate, and random schemes, and d) the notations or codes that facilitate filing and searching; 3) the rules of entry, that is, the choice of books or information that are represented under particular concepts or terms, as in specific, analytic, or generic entries, and including depth of indexing; 4) the fullness of description, that is, what is told about a book or an item of information when it is entered under a term, and this includes abstracting, and finally 5) the physical attributes of the scheme, its form, the ease of scanning, the method of cumulation, and so on. These are all variables that must be measured or controlled in the evaluation of any bibliographical scheme, however ancient or ultra-modern.

It should be noted that each of these elements, except the last, comprises a continuum from broad to narrow, general to specific, complete to selective, or complex to simple, and that every bibliographical scheme represents a point on each continuum--a scope and completeness of coverage, a detail of vocabulary, a specificity of entry, and a fullness of description. The core program would introduce students to the nature of these elements and their continuums, compare their applications in selected bibliographies, catalogs, and indexes of widely different kinds and purposes, and analyze the reasons for the differences observed. In this way the elements of bibliographical organization should come clear to all students, whether they specialize later in library cataloging or automatic indexing, and a common theoretical basis for the comparison and evaluation of all schemes would be laid.

Of Institutions

In the third area are the institutions that operate information services--the libraries, information centers, data banks, or whatever other forms they might take. This is the engineering and administration of library and information systems, including both manual and mechanized technologies and the integration of human and machine capabilities. It is the institutional manifestation of books and their intellectual organization for service to particular communities or types of readers.

Specializations in this area begin with the history of libraries and other information handling agencies. There follows the general administration and management of these agencies, including 1) organization, staffing, and control, 2) line operations, such as order work, reference service, and circulation, and 3) staff functions, both internal and external, such as systems analysis and mechanization, and product research and public relations. Finally specializations by types of communities served--academic, public, state and national, school, business, industrial, governmental, and many others. These treat of the books and other resources and the kinds of bibliographical organization, as well as the institutional forms, policies, procedures, and services, that are peculiar to their own specific communities of readers.

The best core program in this area would probably be an introduction to the various types of libraries and information centers--their history, the characteristics of the communities served, their social or scholarly goals, the kinds and levels of the services they perform, and the peculiarities of their administration, management, and operation. This might sound like the traditional, and often berated, "introduction to librarianship" that takes up the several types of libraries one by one, competitively, and conveys no meaningful relationships among them, but I have something different in mind. On the one hand, the program would cover information centers, data banks, and the like, as well as conventional libraries. But more importantly, it would follow a topical outline in drawing comparisons among the several types of institutions. There would be less emphasis on the types of libraries as such as on the diversity of scholarly and social environments, the wide range of reading interests and needs, and the different extensions and intensions of service that explain the institutional forms that libraries take. With this background, a student could move on into general administrative or technological specializations and to specializations by type of library with an early appreciation of the environmental variables upon which the design of all information systems should rest.

These three core programs, then, suggest a basic curricular structure that might bring the older content of librarianship and the newer content of documentation and information science into a rational and mutually constructive relationship. In the area of books and readers, or of information and its users, there could be a survey of the major forms and movements of publication, their origins in the history of scholarship, and the principal uses to which they are put. In the area of the intellectual organization of recorded knowledge, there would be a comparative study of catalogs, bibliographies, and indexes, both conventional and unconventional, with respect to common variables, such as scope, vocabulary, entry, and description, and with emphasis upon the treatment of those variables for different purposes. And in the area of libraries and information centers as institutions, there would be a topical comparison of institutions by their origins, the types of communities served, the kinds and levels of service required, and other environmental factors that determine the design of information systems.

I have suggested also some of the specializations in each of these three areas, and there are both conventional and unconventional specializations in each. The subject literature specialists, for example, would concentrate in the first area, along with reference and acquisition librarians and researchers in the scholar's use of books and information. Library catalogers would concentrate in the second area, along with bibliographers and coordinate indexers, and researchers in file organization and the measurement of file operating effectiveness. The managers and operators of libraries and information centers would concentrate in the third area, along with personnel directors and data processors, and researchers in the design of information systems. The specialists by type of library--the academic, the public, the industrial, the school, and so on--would look back over all three areas as they relate to the design of institutions for service to particular communities of readers.

Some Implications

There are three implications of this approach that would have to be reckoned with in a detailed curriculum revision.

First is the likelihood that, after the core programs had been taken, students who were specializing in fields other than the practice of conventional librarianship could probably not be required to take as much library cataloging and reference as some schools now require. Beyond a certain point, these traditional courses would have to be viewed as elective specializations that are parallel to other elective specializations, such as indexing and literature searching in science and technology. To all specializations, including conventional librarianship, the new core programs would provide general introductions.

Second is the certainty that no such curriculum as is here envisaged, with extensions backward into still more generalized introductory courses and forward into still more intensive specializations, could be completed in one year of graduate study. At least a full quarter of newly organized content would precede the beginning of the present curriculum, and the subsequent programs in at least the new specializations would have to be expanded. My guess is that we would have to plan for two full years of graduate study for the basic professional degree.

And third is the probability that undergraduate, or even graduate, subject prerequisites would soon have to be specified for some specializations, particularly those that emphasize subject literature fields or use unfamiliar techniques from other disciplines.

Librarianship could become a deeper and broader discipline if its basic studies were first detached from institutional applications and then adapted to the widest range of service situations and technologies.

This paper was presented at the Second Forum on Education for Special Librarianship at the SLA Minneapolis Convention, June 3, 1966.

Reference

1. Sarah R. Reed, ed. Problems of Library School Administration: Report of an Institute, April 14-15, 1965, Washington, D. C. U.S. Office of Education, 1965, p. 20-27.

10. Interlibrary Cooperation, Interlibrary Communications, and Information Networks--Explanation and Definition

The purpose of this paper is to state the principal issues and parameters of concern at this conference on interlibrary communications and information networks. As I conceive my task, I should map the entire field of our concerns and describe in general terms its topography. I should not analyze specific problem areas, offer solutions, or recommend plans for action. These are the tasks of the papers that will follow.

Definitions

I will begin with definitions of information and communications networks. In my review of the literature--the literature specific to this definition is very recent and sparse--I found the most help in the publications of Carl Overhage, Joe Becker, and Launor Carter.

Overhage identified five different contexts in which the term "networks" is used.[1] The first is "science literature," as in networks of citation-linked papers. The second is "organization structures," as in the ERIC clearinghouses. The third is "cooperative arrangements," as in interlibrary loans. The fourth is "communications systems," as in press wire services. And the fifth is "computer-communications systems," as in the NASA Recon system. He went on, then, to explain that, while networks of scientific literature, of organizational structures, and of libraries are all important, none specifically characterizes the com-

---

Reprinted by permission from Interlibrary Communications and Information Networks, ed. Joseph Becker; Proceedings of a Conference. American Library Association, 1971, pp. 18-26.

munications links to be used. The primary topic of his annual review of "information networks" was networks of communications and of computer-communications systems, which do specify the use of electric signal transmission. For the purpose of his paper, therefore, he adopted the following definition: "... when these [communications] channels are used for the transfer of certain categories of information they are customarily said to constitute an information network. In this usage ... the essential feature of an information network is the utilization of a set of communications channels through which the information is transferred by electric signals."[2]

 Becker and Olsen also noted the varieties of contexts in which the term "network" is used, then divided the definitions first by class of equipment, as in telephone, teletype, facsimile, and computer networks; second by form of data, as in digital, audio, video and film networks; and third by functions, as in financial, library, education, and management networks. He continued: "Information networks include some combination of the above three elements, which when coupled with a communications system, provide the desired pattern of information exchange."[3] The main concepts of an automated information network--and he pointed out that none yet existed--would be:

    1. Formal Organization. Many units sharing a common information purpose recognize the value of group affiliation and enter into a compact.
    2. Communications. The network includes circuits that can rapidly interconnect dispersed points.
    3. Bidirectional Operation. Information may move in either direction, and provision is made for each network participant to send as well as receive.
    4. A Directory and Switching Capability. A directory look-up system enables a participant to identify the unit most able to satisfy a particular request. A switching center then routes messages to this unit over the optimum communications path.[4]

 Becker and Olsen then noted that the word network is also widely applied to "the banding together of existing information systems into some type of communications cooperative, e.g., referral centers, information analysis centers, industrial departments, airline tickets offices, and police precincts, in order to satisfy a functional goal."[5]

Carter took a somewhat different line, in that he introduced the data base and remote users into his definition.

An information network, or a library network, I think, has the following characteristics. First we have two or more nodes, or centers of intercommunication and of data bases. One node or center, by itself, is not a network.... The nodes are interconnected and are able to use each other's data bases, and that is very important. Each node has a unique data base or capability--in terms of a bibliographical apparatus, in terms of unique holdings, in terms of the power of the computer center--and each one is able to call upon the others for assistance. You have nodes, then, which are interconnected by communications, and that is my second point. Third, each node in this system has remote users--the users are quite separated from the nodal center. Nodes in, say, Olympia, Bellingham, Hoquiam, Vancouver, Spokane, etc., could all be switched more or less automatically to a node in, say, Seattle or some other place. Those, then, are the three characteristics I think of a network as having: It has nodes, with a unique data base at each node; it is of course electronically switchable and has high-speed communications; and it has remote users. [6]

For the purpose of balance, let me add a definition that I used in 1967 with reference not to any particular class of communications equipment or type of data but to what Becker and Olsen called the banding together of existing information systems, in this case libraries and information centers.

The network concept includes the development of cooperative systems of libraries on geographical, subject, or other lines, each with some kind of center that not only coordinates the internal activities of the system but also serves as the system's outlet to, and inlet from, the centers of other systems. The concept is also hierarchical in that the centers of smaller systems are channels to centers of larger networks at state, national, and even international levels. A familiar analogy is the telephone service, in which local systems were first coordinated and then hooked up into national and international networks. [7]

Overhage, Becker and Olsen, and Carter, while acknowledging the importance of networks of existing library and information systems, as in my definition above, all defined information networks in the modern sense as utilizing communications by electronic signal transmission. This is appropriate, I think, as an ideal. I do not think, however, that we should limit our discussions to networks that specify particular types of communications channels, for two reasons. First, many of the evolving networks of existing library and information systems tend toward that ideal. In mixed ways, and in varying degrees, they do use electric signal communications through telephones, teletype, and sometimes computer applications, and they are doing so increasingly. Second, overemphasis on the communications technology sometimes obscures other essential components of information services that are not dependent, strictly speaking, upon any particular technology. For example, Becker and Olsen included "a directory look-up system" in their definition. This to me is an understatement of the central problem of the intellectual organization of documents and data, a problem that grows more and more crucial as information systems are elaborated into networks. Carter included the "data base" in his definition, and this is an abstraction of the tremendous problems of the selection, acquisition, and purging of the information resources to which access is the very reason for networks. Carter also included "remote users," which leads us again into the maze of user studies--the audiences to which network services should be addressed and the needs to be met. The technology changes and grows more powerful, but these problems remain essentially unchanged. The more widely our networks spread, the greater should be our concern about these indispensable components of all library and other information services.

I like to think of library and other information services as extensions of the home, the office, or the personal library. There a man collects his books, journals, and data files, according to his own wishes. When he has enough that he can't readily find what he wants, he begins to organize his collections--to arrange them systematically on the shelves and in file drawers and to make catalogs and indexes. The breadth and variety of the data bases that are accessible to him are then extended stage by stage through local libraries, information centers, and other communications channels to regional systems and national networks until ideally he should have the world's knowledge at his finger tips. The extensions of his data base are accompanied by corresponding extensions of his powers of analysis through increasingly more comprehensive and sensitive schemes for the intellectual organization of that knowledge. The methods by which he can get his hands on the desired materials--that is, gain physical access--are similarly extended. To accomplish these extensions, larger organizational units of service are created, and new technologies are brought to bear upon the data bases, the schemes of intellectual access, and the methods of physical access. At every stage along the way there is a shifting balance between what the user does for himself and what the system does for him. There are trade-offs between values gained and values lost, as well as between cost and effectiveness. But the perfect information network would be the one that took us full circle to the personal library again--that would make the world's knowledge an extension of his private collection, that would give him intellectual access to the whole of it at home, and that would put copies of anything he wants on his own desk.

In this perspective, the modern information network would be new and different primarily in its technological power to extend tremendously a set of elemental functions that started at home, that are running the gamut of library and information systems and networks, and that ought sometime to end at home. So let me define an information network, for present purposes, as having these characteristics:

1. Information resources. Collections of documents or data in whatever medium. The data bases. The input.
2. Readers or users, usually remote from the main sources of information.
3. Schemes for the intellectual organization of documents or data, as directories for use by readers or users.
4. Methods for the delivery of resources to readers or users. The output.
5. Formal organization of cooperating or contracting information agencies, representing different data bases and/or groups of users.
6. Bidirectional communications networks, preferably through high-speed, long-distance electrical signal transmission with switching capabilities and computer hook-ups.

These are the broad areas of concern at this conference, and I will organize the rest of this paper around them.

The Information Resource

I tried once before to say in the most general terms what this commodity, the information resource, is as it relates to the library and information needs of society.[8] What is it that we collect, store, organize and disseminate? We may think of it as books, journals, or other texts; as audio or visual documents; or as smaller units of information or data that can be separately manipulated, as by a computer. All of these forms of records comprise parts of the information resource; but it is helpful, I think, to perceive that recorded resources are still only a part of a society's general cultural resource, which consists of an accumulation of concepts, habits, skills, arts, instruments, institutions, etc., that are handed down and built upon by each generation. I suspect that much of the learning of mankind has been forgotten, and has had to be relearned many times, if it was worth knowing in the first place. What is worth remembering comes down to us through many channels--our parents, teachers, and friends; our churches and other social institutions; our manners and customs; our folk tales and arts; and our radio and television channels. In advanced societies, a substantial part of the culture also comes down to us in recorded forms of one kind or another, and this is the part that concerns information networks.

I put the matter this way in order to emphasize the crucial role that recorded knowledge plays in advanced societies. Let us hypothesize that the more advanced the society, or the greater the totality of learning, the greater is the dependence upon the record for access to that learning. A person, or all the persons in a society, can carry only so much of it in mind; for the rest they must call upon the record. And the proportion of the total that can be recalled only from the record is ever increasing. Let us hypothesize further that no society can advance beyond a certain point without effective access to its collective memory of record; or, conversely, that an advanced society that loses control of the record will regress. In this perspective, modern information networks could be seen as a late high refinement of societies that depend increasingly upon recorded information for their further advancement.

This basic concern about the social significance of information in recorded form should not, however, be misconstrued as requiring the preservation of the totality of recorded information. A great deal of learning, whether recorded or not, has deservedly been forgotten throughout history, and the act of recording does not of itself make a piece of learning more deserving of preservation. There is a concern, then, about the problem of completeness. The goal of complete coverage of foreign materials of scholarly interest is found in the Farmington Plan and the Shared Cataloging Program under Title IIC of the Higher Education Act.[9] A report of the Committee on Scientific and Technical Information (COSATI) urged that it be "... the Federal Government's responsibility to insure that there exists within the United States at least one accessible copy of each significant publication of world-wide scientific and technical literature.[10] These are reasonably qualified goals, far short of the totality of recorded information. Carter seriously questioned the need of anyone, including scholars, to know the holdings of every library in the country and suggested that information networks be confined to selected research libraries. A nationally integrated computer network might not be required at all, except in certain discipline oriented fields.[11]

The further problem of preserving the totality of unrefined data, as against published documents, in recorded form was dramatically illustrated by James Fava in his account of the massive amounts of raw data accumulated by the space programs.[12] On the one hand, as in archival administration, large packages of related data might have to be calendared as a whole; and, on the other hand, a line might have to be drawn somewhere between the potentially infinite floods of raw data and the generalizable products of that data, after compacting, editing, correcting, merging, and interpretation--that is, between the raw data and the eventually published document. Total access to uninterpreted data appears to be a vastly greater chimera than that to unevaluated publications. But still, within narrowly specialized communities of scholars, continuing access to raw data for the purpose of reanalysis and reinterpretation could be essential until better data are produced.

There is the further concern that the information resource, as we should be viewing it, includes documents, or records, in all media.[13] Printed documents, yes, but also audio records, as in discs and tapes; video records, as in films, slides, and tapes; and digital records, as in cores, tapes, and discs. The recording media are being increasingly varied by technological extensions of the written word, the picture, and the sound. We need to insure that information networks of the future are flexible enough to embrace all forms of record that are useful to society.

Here are three major concerns, then, about the information resource:

1. The general nature and significance of the recorded information resource to society.
2. The completeness with which the information resource can be usefully acquired and stored for future access through information networks.
3. The varieties of recording media that are utilized as information resources by information networks.

Users

In the broad area of the users of information network services, we are concerned primarily with the increasing numbers of users and the growing varieties of their needs, the rights of people to equal access to information services (including realistic access at local points of service), the categories of people to be served, and the general problem of user studies.

I have already noted the growing dependence of advanced societies upon their collective memories of record. Individuals, too, can carry only a limited proportion of the world's knowledge in mind even in narrow specializations. The larger the number of people and the greater their dependence upon the record, the greater the burden upon information services. Data on the number of users of science and technology data and documents were recently published by SDC.[14] Similar data should be developed about users in other fields. There is real concern about the ability of future information networks to cope with the demands that will be made upon them. Certainly the present information systems are already in trouble.

Further demands upon information networks could, however, be influenced as much by the democratization of information services as by increasing numbers of special categories of users. In some societies--perhaps most at one time or another--access to libraries has been a privilege reserved for an educated élite, those who have earned or inherited the privilege, who bear the social responsibilities, and who hold the power. More recently, access to information has been claimed as the right of everyman for purposes of universal enlightenment, regardless of his social class, ability, or responsibility. In Western concepts of democracy, power resides not with a privileged élite but with an educated and informed populace. One could go a step further and postulate that in advanced, technological societies, information becomes not just a privilege or a right but a necessity for essential social and national purposes. A sense of national urgency now pervades many library and information programs not only in the United States but also in certain developing countries, where the goal may not be so much to foster individual rights as to train the manpower required for the achievement of national goals, such as health, economic welfare, and security under threat of war. But whether because of individual rights or national imperatives, information should be as widely available as possible to all the people.

One of the goals of library and information networks should therefore be more realistic and effective access to information resources, wherever they may be, for every citizen.[15] Weinstock set a similar goal for special libraries: "Every library should provide every patron with any published information required."[16] As in the acquisition of the total information resource, the ultimate goal can probably never be reached. Not all parts of the total resource could probably ever be made immediately accessible to everyone, but there is a continuum along which each man's opportunity can be measured.

The principle of equality of access to information everywhere raises some real problems. People are accustomed to thinking of local library and information centers as more or less self-sufficient resources to satisfy local needs, and many centers reflect those needs with remarkable sensitivity. But we are still stuck with the notion that the need varies with numbers of people, or with the size and wealth of communities. Smaller, poorer communities are presumed to need less. Larger, richer communities are presumed to need more. There are certainly valid differences among community needs on the basis of subject interests and emphases, but the principle of "books per capita" should be persuasively investigated. The college freshman, the engineer, the school teacher, the doctor, and the business man in rural, north-mountain California have no less need, as individuals, of the total resource than do their counterparts in the San Francisco-Bay Area. The basis of need is not political, geographic, demographic, or economic; it is personal; and the need finds expression not simply as a relationship between a community and its locally supported library but as one between the individual, wherever he may be, and the total information resource, wherever it may be.

For people everywhere, moreover, realistic and effective access should mean their ability to discover, at any local point of contact with the information network, what books and information are available from the network, and then to get prompt delivery, also at the point of contact. Here again the ideal may never be fully achievable, but progress could be made along this continuum by means of computer and communications applications to the dissemination of bibliographical information on the one hand and to document delivery on the other.

The existing inequities of realistic access to information throughout the country are staggering;[17] and they merit our most serious study. They involve, of course, a wide range of categories of users. Our concern is not only with scientists, engineers, and professionals in other critical fields but also with the lay public, including the underprivileged. We are concerned with non-users of information as well as with users. We are concerned with education,[18] business, and recreation as well as research.

For all these categories of users, a further concern is the paucity of data about their information problems and needs. A careful analysis of user studies in the fields of science and technology by SDC revealed a number of useful recent studies but also pointed out the limitations of most of them.[19] Almost all the studies used questionnaires and interviews with scientists to ask what they think or say they need at some point of time. One wonders if other methodologies could be developed to assess the needs of scholars, such as, say, an analysis of a field of scholarship itself; its goals, the types of research done, the kinds of data used and the methodologies of their use, the sources of data, and so on, all of which points are germane to the general structure of an information system. More studies are also needed of other categories of users, such as suburban communities, the public schools, rural neighborhoods, small business organizations, and the ghettos. Such studies should supply criteria for the design and the evaluation of information networks.

Cooperation, Communications, and Networks 139

The major concerns, then, in the area of users (following the three for resources) include:

4. The growth in numbers of users and in the varieties of their information needs.
5. Equality of access by individual users to information resources everywhere, including realistic and effective service at local points of contact with the information network. The inequalities of existing access.
6. The categories of users and the range of purposes that information networks should serve.
7. User studies of the various kinds of readers to be served, as criteria for the design and evaluation of information networks.

Intellectual Access

The next broad area of concern is intellectual access to documents and data or, in conventional library terminology, bibliographical organization. I will not give much space to this area because of its great complexity; but it is, I believe, the really unique, gut problem of any library or information service. The communications and computer technologies for information network development are already at hand, but the logical means of organizing the information resource for discriminating access are not. The intellectual problems far outweigh the technological.

One way to express this problem is to postulate a direct relationship between the size of the data base and the selectivity required in its intellectual organization through catalogs, indexes, bibliographies, or other schemes. The larger and more varied the information resource to which access is desired, and the greater the numbers and heterogeneity of users who need access, the more refined, sensitive, flexible, and discriminating must be the schemes of intellectual organization. These schemes are like sieves that sort huge quantities of grossly related things into sequentially smaller quantities of more closely related things, until what is pertinent to a special need is sifted out. The Library of Congress classification and dictionary catalog are already tremendously complex sets of sieves, but the schemes that would be needed to sift out for everyone everywhere the few materials wanted from a nationally integrated network of the total information resource are still almost unthinkable.

This problem, it appears, would be exaggerated by mechanized retrieval systems unless highly reactive, or interactive, schemes become practicable. Our traditional manual schemes permit a user to enter and reenter the system at different points, to narrow or broaden his search strategies, to browse, and to select as many or as few references as he wants. A similar capability must be built into mechanized systems, and, indeed, impressive progress has already been made. But there are still big bottlenecks in the logic of the structure of very large files and in the programs for reorganizing stored information in response to the differing and changing needs of users.[20]

The reactive process, moreover, must occur where the user is--again, at his local contact with the information network--either by means of manually searched catalogs produced by machine for distribution to local service points or by means of direct interrogation of computer files.

There is a plethora of problems behind these broad concerns: the concepts and terms around which documents and data are organized, and the derivation of those concepts and terms; their arrangement for speedy access; the rules by which documents are entered under them or by which they are assigned to documents; and so on and on. Automatic associative indexing and question-answering systems are possibilities, but still in the future for large scale applications. Major new insights into the logical problems of information organization will be required before the network capabilities of electric signal transmission can be fully exploited.

Our concerns here (added to those previously mentioned) are primarily:

8. The further refinement of existing schemes, or the creation of new and more sensitive ones, for intellectual access to the hugely augmented information resources to become accessible through information networks.
9. In particular, the development of reactive, flexible, mechanized retrieval systems that simulate the user's interchange with manual systems.

Physical Access

By physical access I mean the getting of copies, in whatever form, of the documents or data selected through the process of intellectual access. Our concern is that the information network be able to supply copies, within reasonable periods of time, for users who want them. I suspect that, on the whole, this is a much less critical concern than intellectual access. Many users might want only the bibliographical references, or abstracts, and others might be in no great hurry for the full texts. But the modern information network should have as one of its goals the prompt location of desired documents or data anywhere in the country and the delivery of some of them, or parts of them, by such means as long distance facsimile transmission, computer print out, or CRT display, as well as by conventional interlibrary loan. The potentially huge volume of traffic along these delivery lines might necessitate rigorous priorities.

In future fully automated networks, physical access might form a single continuum with intellectual access. A reactive system of intellectual access might be able to display not only conventional bibliographical references but also annotations, abstracts, and selected segments of the text (as microfilms are scanned); then, desired parts of the work, or the whole of it, could be printed out. The potential spectrum of representation of a document extends from brief citation to full text. For a good long while, however, the practicable methods of physical access appear likely to remain separate from those of intellectual access and to employ different kinds of equipment.

Our main concern is:

10. The prompt location of desired documents or data anywhere in the country and the delivery of copies, within appropriate periods of time, to users at local outlets of the network.

Formal Organization

The preceding areas were mainly related to objective concerns--the why, the who, and the what of information networks. I now turn to the operating agencies that comprise service systems and networks and the organizational structures that bind them together. This is a large, practical area that, together with technological concerns, will probably dominate the discussions at this conference.

To Becker and Olsen a formal network organization occurs when "many units sharing a common information purpose recognize the value of group affiliation and enter into a compact."[21] I would add that such organizations are often conceived also as having hierarchical levels of cooperating units and affiliations. From any local service point, the search for documents and data might rise, if need be, through several layers of cooperating information systems--local, regional, national, or even international--each system at each level having its own communications center or node. The network idea, in a sense, is the full modern extension of a drive that began many decades ago to organize larger units of public library service, a drive that has resulted in county, regional, and, to a certain extent, state-wide public library systems. Characteristically, such organizations consist of centers or nodes of local service that are then affiliated under second-level centers or nodes with higher switching capabilities, and so on. Theoretically, at least, the ultimate national network should have some sort of super-node at the apex of the hierarchy.

One major concern, then, is the conformation of such hierarchical organizations. What, for example, would be the optimum size of systems at each level of the network? What would be the best balance between resources that are locally available from any particular node and those that must be sought through nodes at higher levels? What levels of local sufficiency would be most cost-effective, given varying levels of back-up capability? For network purposes, how should a region be defined? What would be the functions of a regional center or node? Under what circumstances should requests for service by-pass regional or other intermediate nodes and proceed directly to coordinate or higher nodes? At what levels of centralization should certain technical processes occur, such as accounting, circulation control, and the production of union lists? There has been a great deal of pragmatic experience with these and similar concerns, but the general conformation of network organizations has, to my knowledge, received very little systematic study.

More attention has been paid to the kinds of information agencies that should be banded together. Separate cooperative systems may be formed by type of library or information center, such as public, academic, or special libraries; by form or medium of record, such as technical reports, motion picture films, or journals; or by discipline, such as medical, agricultural, or chemical information services. Title III of the Library Services and Construction Act promotes cooperation among all types of libraries. Carter has argued that national networks might be developed most usefully along subject lines.[22] I have argued for mixed networks of geographical systems, embracing public, school, and small college libraries, with separate subject systems of special libraries, and with our great university and research libraries backing up all on a broad contractual basis.[23] The geographical boundaries of public and subject systems might differ greatly. Many patterns are possible, and perhaps no consistent pattern is needed, as long as the nodes of each system are in communication with each other, so that public systems may be served also by subject systems, subject systems by media systems, and so on. The real-life mosaic of special interest systems that will comprise the information network of the future could be very complex indeed.

Another problem is the nature of the compacts that bind governmental units, public and private institutions, and business and industrial organizations together for the common purpose of sharing information. What legal bases have been or could be used for financial and service agreements? What is offered, what is received, and by what accounting?

More fundamental is the problem of overall responsibility for and control of information networks, particularly at the national level. Some sort of central coordination, either by a federal agency or by a national commission, seems needed.[24] The federal and state governments have a basic responsibility for the equalization of information service opportunities and a financial interest in the performance and promise of information networks.[25] Yet the contributions and interests of the private sector must be respected and protected. No satisfactory formula has yet been evolved for the allocation of these responsibilities, but some observers believe still that modern information networks of national scope are not likely to be built until the federal government has been persuaded to finance them.[26]

Planning at the national level is certainly essential. In the last two decades, wave after wave of national document-handling plans have been advanced by various agencies. Fifteen of the best known plans were reviewed by SDC.[27] Most of them concentrated on the organizational aspects of the national information problem, few dealt with the acquisition of resources, the needs of users were generally overlooked, relatively little attention was paid to technical problems, and still less attention, perhaps, was devoted to existing operating library systems.

The experience of existing library and information systems should not, I think, be neglected in the design of national networks. The SDC analyzed a selection of federal and nonfederal libraries; information analysis centers; publication, announcement, and distribution groups; document generators/users; and administration, policy, and support groups in the fields of science and technology.[28] This analysis is impressive, and similar studies of information agencies in other fields would be most helpful. So also would be equally thorough studies of the evolving patterns of cooperative systems and networks. Some surveys have been made,[29] and these are revealing, even though they are often more discursive than systematic.

The national planners would often impose entirely new networks from above, on the assumption that the tortuously evolving efforts from below have failed. The revolutionary tends to by-pass due process. The evolutionary prefers to build upon existing institutions, which are, for better or worse, the only operational ones we know. Perhaps both approaches are needed--planning from above and building from below--, each with full appreciation of the other.

In support of the evolutionary approach certain points can be made. This is the real-life world of information service, the best yet. A national document system that tried to ignore it might wash down the drain because of the absence of grass-roots delivery facilities. The understructure of local facilities, educated and experienced staff, and even informed readers is indispensable. The proof of any network is the goods actually delivered to people who understand what they can ask for from staff who know how to get it through well developed organizations at the local level.

In support of national planning, certain other points can be made. Existing institutions are bound by tradition and motivated by self-defense. They eschew new ideas and technologies that disturb their sense of security and success. They fail to face the future. The only way to get on with the business is to create de novo new systems based on broader concepts that exploit more advanced technologies.

There is some truth, I suggest, in both positions, but not the whole truth in either. Within the realistic economic and social constraints of operating library and information services, new ideas and technologies have, in fact, been readily espoused. But the more revolutionary ideas and technologies that are not yet achievable within those constraints have been understandably resisted. Revolutionary approaches might be possible, but only, and then not likely, by the intervention of such a deus ex machina as the federal government.

So, our areas of concern under the rubric of formal organization include:

11. The conformation of network structures. The optimum size of systems at each level. The balance between local and back-up resources. Centralized processing, and so on.
12. The kinds of information agencies to be formed into systems. Geographical, type of library, media, and subject systems. The linking of mixed systems into networks.
13. The compacts that bind information agencies together into systems. Financial and service agreements.
14. Responsibility for and control of information networks. Contributions of the governmental and private sectors. The federal government and national network development.
15. Planning for national networks. The need of new national structures.
16. Evolution of existing cooperative systems and networks. The importance of building upon operational experience.

The New Technologies

Earlier in this paper I noted that the modern information network would be new and different primarily in its technological power to extend tremendously a set of elemental functions that started in the personal, home library. These extensions of power should enable us to amass larger data bases without filling miles and miles of book shelves, to search them more deeply without thumbing millions of catalog cards, and to obtain copies of documents without travelling across the country or sending for them by mail. Telecommunications and computers, in particular, are magnificent tools that should help us in our trade, as the hammer helps the carpenter.

There are many kinds of new technological developments in such fields as document miniaturization and reprography, printing, and audio and visual techniques, all of which are of general interest to us. But for network development our primary concerns are telecommunications and computers. These are the particular tools that encourage us to plan toward national information networks that might in fact bring true the century-old dream of interlibrary cooperation. It is the potential power of their application to information services that has justified this conference.

Becker gave us a brief description of modern telecommunications devices, classified by type of signal (audio, digital, and video) and by signal carriers (telephone lines, radio broadcasting, coaxial cable, microwave, and communications satellites).30 For the technological layman, like myself, he also reviewed in simple terms the history and significance of the computer interface with communications. He described the growing capacities of telephone lines; the advent of wide-band facilities that will easily accommodate the language of the TV camera, the facsimile scanner, the teletype machine, and the computer; the role of switching stations; and the nature and potentialities of satellites. He then illustrated the use of communications for remote access to computer-manipulated data bases, including audio as well as digital messages.31 The wedding of on-line computers with communications networks and remote user terminals is the key to expanding information services through network development.

It would be presumptuous of me to undertake any discussion of these technological developments. The latest developments were covered by Overhage in the 1969 Annual Review.32 Taking my cues partly from him, I will outline briefly the following major areas of our concern:

There is first the general need for the further development of communications and computing capabilities as they relate specifically to large scale document and data handling systems. I refer particularly to storage capacities, reactive retrieval systems, and high-speed, high-data-rate, low-cost communications channels.

Second is the need for further applications to operating information systems at various levels, from relatively simple teletype and facsimile transmission through computer-communications configurations. Such experiments should certainly include mixed systems that might be based, for example, partly on computers, partly on microforms of one kind

Cooperation, Communications, and Networks

or another, and partly on conventional texts. A "pure" computer-communications network might never be technically or economically feasible in the field of information services. The most fruitful immediate computer applications appear to be in the area of intellectual access to, or bibliographical organization of, documents and data.

A third broad problem is the compatibility of machine systems. The difficulties of arriving at standards and formats that can be used for the transfer of information between units of a cooperative system or network have been well demonstrated by the MARC project. Recent efforts to reach agreements and guidelines were reviewed by Overhage in his Annual Review chapter. A distinction should be drawn, I think, between flexibility in local record-keeping and conformity in the transfer of information among the units of a network.

Fourth is the problem of regulation. Existing communications networks are not well suited to information services, partly because of rate structures. High common-carrier tariffs and rigid controls over the use of communications utilities militate against information network development. The growing interdependence of computers and communications has further complicated the issues of policy and control.

Fifth is copyright, which is a familiar problem with new twists in the computer field. For example, is the copyright law violated when a document is put into a computer data base or when it is displayed? Even the old issues of fair use and office copying are still unresolved. How, then, should the process of modifying texts, manipulating and consolidating their content, and displaying them in new ways be interpreted under the law?

And finally, there is the problem--and it is a tremendous one--of educating librarians and information specialists, on the one hand, and the user public, on the other, in the nature, operations, and values of modern technological network extensions of familiar library and information services. What should the library and information science schools contribute? What sorts of continuing education programs should be offered? What is the role of in-service training by operating agencies that are engaged in network development? These considerations, again, are major reasons for building gradually upon alert, experimental, existing agencies that can do the necessary educational job.

In summary, then, some broad concerns in this area are:

17. Further development of communications and computing capabilities for large-scale document and data handling operations.
18. Further applications to operating information agencies, including experimentation with mixed, as well as pure, information networks.
19. The adoption of compatible machine systems, standard formats, languages, etc.
20. The regulation of communications utilities in such ways as to permit their use by information networks in flexible ways at reasonable cost.
21. Resolution of copyright restrictions, including those relating to manipulations of texts by computer.
22. The education of librarians, information specialists, and the user public in the nature, operation, and values of modern information networks.

Conclusion

I have tried in this paper to identify and describe the large areas of concern at this conference. I have dealt lightly with the technological problems and more heavily with the functional problems because I know less about the former and the engineers among us know less about the latter. We will all have to adjust our attitudes toward information services if the networks of the future are ever to be created.

Those among us, like myself, who have operated existing services will have to revise in fundamental ways our conception of the operative information agency. Our conception of institutional responsibility limited primarily to supportive segments of society will have to give way to that of broader social obligations. While each library, for example, must attend to the interests of its own clientele, it can minister fully to those interests only if it recognizes that their range and depth often extend far beyond the resources locally available. The educational, cultural, and technical interests of a local clientele will often be poorly served by protecting the user's access to inadequate local collections at the expense of access to larger, richer reservoirs of the information resource.

Cooperation, Communications, and Networks

The ideal of independent, locally self-sufficient programs must certainly give way to that of dependent participation in nationally sufficient programs. If national information networks were ever to be built, local libraries and information centers would have to be redefined as selective inlets to and outlets from those networks. The specifications, for example, of local acquisitional policy would need to be modified to reflect a new balance between resources that, on a cost-effectiveness basis, should be acquired at home and those that should be acquired only upon demand from various levels of network service. If the information networks could ever in fact deliver the goods efficiently and promptly at local service points, the effects upon the nature of local libraries and information agencies would be profound indeed.

I assume, of course, that somewhere higher up in the network hierarchy, the national resource would in fact be acquired and controlled. This is a precarious assumption. Librarians have often pointed out that the cooperative enrichment of local library resources is a condition to useful cooperative service. A poverty of resources can be shared without information networks.

The information and communications engineers among us might revise their conceptions of the nature and role of information networks by paying more attention to the substantive problems of information service. Information networks are not just a technological challenge. For every advance in technological power, there must follow, if not precede, a corresponding advance in the conception of the functions to be advanced. In the world of library and information services, these functions are, and always have been, the acquisition of information resources, with all the problems of selection, storage, and purging; the intellectual organization of those resources through catalogs, bibliographies, indexes, and, lately, computer-based retrieval systems; and the methods of physical delivery of copies of documents and data, all in the service of users whose needs should determine the goals of the service.

I hope that at this conference the engineers will listen to the practitioners who work with the information that networks will communicate, as I also hope that the practitioners will grasp the opportunity created by the engineers to pursue further their crucial social mission.

Our commodity, again, is not just documents and pieces of data; it is that growing part of our culture that is recorded, and therefore capable of being saved for recall as needed, our capacity to learn and remember having reached a human limit. The recorded information resource, when adequately organized and communicated, should become one of the greatest utilities of advanced societies.

References

1. Carl F. J. Overhage, "Information Networks," in American Society for Information Science, Annual Review of Information Science and Technology, v. 4. (Chicago: Encyclopedia Britannica, 1969), p. 339-44.
2. Ibid., p. 339.
3. Joseph Becker and Wallace C. Olsen, "Information Networks," in American Society of Information Science, Annual Review of Information Science and Technology, v. 3 (Chicago: Encyclopedia Britannica, 1968), p. 290-91.
4. Ibid.
5. Ibid.
6. Launor F. Carter, "What are the Major National Issues in the Development of Library Networks," News Notes of California Libraries 63:406-07 (Fall 1968).
7. R. C. Swank, Interlibrary Cooperation under Title III of the Library Services and Construction Act... (Sacramento: California State Library, 1967), p. 51.
8. R. C. Swank, "Partnerships in California: How Can Books and Information Be Mobilized for Every Californian," News Notes of California Libraries 63: 419-28 (Fall, 1968).
9. John G. Lorenz, "Networks for Knowledge," Mountain-Plains Library Quarterly 14: 3-6 (Spring, 1969).
10. A. G. Hoshovsky, "COSATI Information Studies--What Results," in American Society for Information Science, Proceedings, v. 6, Cooperating Information Societies ... 32nd Annual Meeting, San Francisco, California, Oct. 1-4, 1969 (Westport, Conn.: Greenwood Publishing Corp., 1969), p. 402.
11. Carter, "What Are the Major National Issues...," p. 415-16.
12. James A. Fava, "A Framework for Future Data Centers," in American Society for Information Science,

Cooperation, Communications, and Networks 151

Proceedings, v. 6, Cooperating Information Societies ... 32nd Annual Meeting, San Francisco, California, Oct. 1-4, 1969 (Westport, Conn.: Greenwood Publishing Corp., 1969), p. 417. The data, for example, of one ionospheric experiment is stored on 340,000 linear feet of microfilm.
13. Joseph Becker, "Tomorrow's Library Services Today," News Notes of California Libraries 63:430-31 (Fall, 1968).
14. System Development Corporation, National Document-Handling Systems for Science and Technology (New York: Wiley, 1967), p. 116-17, 296-98.
15. R. C. Swank, Interlibrary Cooperation under Title III..., p. 47.
16. Melvin Weinstock, "Network Concepts in Scientific and Technical Libraries," Special Libraries 58: 330 (May-June 1967).
17. For data on California see Swank, Interlibrary Cooperation under Title III..., pp. 7-17.
18. EDUNET; Summer Study in Information Networks, conducted by the Interuniversity Communications Council (EDUCOM) ... (New York: Wiley, 1967).
19. SDC, National Document-Handling Systems..., p. 102-12.
20. Carter, "What are the Major National Issues...," p. 408, 416; Joseph Becker, "The Future of Library Automation and Information Networks," in Library Automation; a State of the Art Review; Papers Presented at the Preconference Institute on Library Automation Held at San Francisco, Calif., June 22-24, 1967, under the sponsorship of the Information Science and Automation Division of the American Library Association (Chicago: A. L. A., 1969), p. 1-6.
21. Becker and Olsen, "Information Networks," p. 290.
22. Carter, "What are the Major National Issues...," p. 410-11.
23. Swank, Interlibrary Cooperation under Title III..., p. 61-68.
24. Hoshovsky, "COSATI Information Studies...," p. 403.
25. William G. Colman, "Federal and State Financial Interest in the Performance and Promise of Library Networks," in University of Chicago, Graduate Library School, Library Networks--Promise and Performance, the 33rd Conference ... July 29-31, 1968 (Chicago: University of Chicago Press, 1969), p. 99-108.

26. Carter, "What are the Major National Issues...," p. 416-17.
27. SDC, National Document-Handling Systems..., p. 129-89.
28. Ibid., p. 7-69.
29. E. g., G. Flint Purdy, "Interrelations among Public, School and Academic Libraries," in Univ. of Chicago, Graduate Library School, Library Networks..., p. 52-63; and William S. Budington, "Interrelations among Special Libraries," in ibid., p. 64-77.
30. Joseph Becker, "Telecommunications Primer," Journal of Library Automation 2: 48-56 (September 1969).
31. _____, "Tomorrow's Library Services Today," p. 429-36.
32. Overhage, "Information Networks."

Bibliography

Aines, Andrew A. "The Promise of National Information Systems," Library Trends 16:410-18 (Jan. 1968).

Becker, Joseph. "The Future of Library Automation and Information Networks," in Library Automation; a State of the Art Review; Papers Presented at the Preconference Institute on Library Automation Held at San Francisco, Calif., June 22-24, 1967, under the sponsorship of the Information Science and Automation Division of the American Library Association. Chicago: American Library Association, 1969. 175 p.

_____. "Telecommunications Primer," Journal of Library Automation 2:48-56 (September 1969).

_____. "Tomorrow's Library Services Today," News Notes of California Libraries 63:429-40 (Fall 1968).

Becker, Joseph, and Olsen, Wallace C. "Information Networks," in American Society of Information Science, Annual Review of Information Science and Technology, v. 3, p. 289-327. Chicago: Encyclopedia Britannica, 1968.

Bregzis, Ritvars. "The Bibliographic Information Network; Some Suggestions for a Different View of the Library Catalogue," in Anglo-American Conference on the Mechanization of Library Services ... 30 June-3 July 1966, p. 128- . Mansell Information/Publishing Ltd., 1967.

_____. "Library Networks of the Future," Drexel Library Quarterly 4:261-70 (October 1968).

Budington, William S. "Interrelations among Special Libraries," in University of Chicago, Graduate Library School, Library Networks--Promise and Performance, the 33rd Conference ... July 29-31, 1968, p. 64-77. Chicago: University of Chicago Press, 1969.

Carter, Launor F. "What are the Major National Issues in the Development of Library Networks," News Notes of California Libraries 63:405-17 (Fall 1968).

Colman, William G. "Federal and State Financial Interests in the Performance and Promise of Library Networks," in University of Chicago, Graduate Library School, Library Networks--Promise and Performance; the 33rd Conference ... July 29-31, 1968, p. 99-108. Chicago: University of Chicago Press, 1969.

Downie, Currie S. "Legal and Policy Impediments to Federal Technical Information Transfer," in American Society for Information Service, Proceedings, v. 6; Cooperating Information Societies...; 32d Annual Meeting, San Francisco, Calif., October 1-4, 1969, p. 411-15. Westport, Connecticut: Greenwood Publishing Corporation, 1969.

EDUNET; Summer Study on Information Networks, conducted by the Interuniversity Communications Council (EDUCOM) ... New York: Wiley, 1967.

Fava, James A. "A Framework for Future Data Centers," in American Society for Information Science, Proceedings, v. 6, Cooperating Information Societies...; 32d Annual Meeting, San Francisco, Calif., October 1-4, 1969, p. 417-29. Westport, Connecticut: Greenwood Publishing Corporation, 1969.

Hoshovsky, A. G. "COSATI Information Studies--What Results," in American Society for Information Science, Proceedings, v. 6; Cooperating Information Societies...; 32d Annual Meeting, San Francisco, Calif., October 1-4, 1969, p. 401-09. Westport, Connecticut: Greenwood Publishing Corporation, 1969.

Lorenz, John G. "Networks for Knowledge," Mountain-Plains Library Quarterly 14:3-6 (Spring 1969).

Mohrhardt, Foster E. "The Library Kaleidoscope: National Plans and Planning," in [Conference on] The Present Status and Future Prospects of Reference/Information Service; Proceedings..., School of Library Service, Columbia University, March 30-April 1, 1966, p. 83-92. Chicago: American Library Association, 1967.

Overhage, Carl F. J. "Information Networks," in American Society for Information Science, Annual Review of Information Science and Technology, v. 4, p. 339-77. Chicago: Encyclopedia Britannica, 1969.

Purdy, G. Flint. "Interrelations among Public, School, and Academic Libraries," in University of Chicago, Graduate Library School, Library Networks--Promise and Performance; the 33rd Conference..., July 29-31, 1968, p. 52-63. Chicago: University of Chicago Press, 1969.

System Development Corporation. National Document-Handling Systems for Science and Technology. New York: Wiley, 1967. 334 p.

Swank, R. C. Interlibrary Cooperation under Title III of the Library Services and Construction Act... Sacramento: California State Library, 1967. 78 p.

_____. "Partnerships in California: How Can Books and Information be Mobilized for Every Californian," News Notes of California Libraries 63:419-28 (Fall 1968).

Weinstock, Melvin. "Network Concepts in Scientific and Technical Libraries," Special Libraries 58:328-34 (May-June 1967).

11. Cataloging Cost Factors

When first invited to present this paper, I hesitated because I suspected that I could make no contribution. After reviewing the literature, I was sure. Perhaps in all library literature no other subject has been more fully and ably covered, although with less effect, than the cost of cataloging. I had made no new study and had no new information. Furthermore, in view of Felix Reichmann's excellent review of cataloging cost studies in Library Trends two years ago,[1] I did not feel justified in devoting this entire session to covering that ground again. That was not a good start for the preparation of a paper.

Two considerations, however, appeared to justify my effort and possibly the expenditure of your time. First, many of the studies and discussions of the cost of cataloging have not taken into account the full range of factors that do, or might, affect that cost, especially those factors that do not immediately pertain to the work of the main catalog department; and, second, many of us have not yet really faced up to certain signs of the future. We know there is trouble ahead--the red flags are already waving; but we are like the man who bumped into the door; we see it, we just do not realize it.

I would like, then, to attempt a rationalization of cataloging cost factors, an analysis of the variables, not with any expectation of contributing new ideas or information but with the hope that I might contribute something to the interpretation of things already known. The paper will deal, first, with cataloging as a part of its generic bibliographical func-

---

Reprinted from The Library Quarterly, 16 (October 1956), pp. 303-17, by permission of The University of Chicago Press. Copyright © 1956 by The University of Chicago Press.

tion and then with the factors that affect the cost of bibliographical services in general, with particular reference to cataloging. There will follow a brief account of cataloging cost studies and their limitations and, finally, a consideration of the future. The discussion will not be limited to the problems of author entry but will embrace all aspects of cataloging. I shall not argue the individual, detailed rules of practice but shall concentrate on generalities. Being a university librarian, I suppose anything I say will reflect the point of view of the research library, but I shall try to keep other types of libraries in mind.

In approaching the cost of cataloging, we need, I believe, to appreciate two things: first and foremost, the great significance of cataloging in modern library history and, second, the relationship of cataloging to other kinds of bibliography.

While I have never professed any scholarship in library history, it appears to me that, aside from the growth of library resources, the outstanding phenomenon of the last century has been the genius of librarians for making those resources available--for organizing them for use. Cataloging is the cornerstone of the modern library organization, the key to all its services. It is the most distinctive, the most uniquely professional, of all library work and the most indispensable. Circulation, reference, and even acquisition would be helpless without it. It is the bond that holds the scattered parts of our great libraries together. The most creative minds of the profession have been applied through the years to its perfection.

Cataloging is a great tradition; we need to remember that when we worry about costs. If you have ever seen a large library, as I have, that has tried to operate without it, you would recommend, as I did, that no expense be spared to correct the deficiency as fast as possible, with no quibbling about details. Indeed, I am dismayed at the manner in which head librarians have sometimes attacked cataloging and catalogers, at their lack of understanding of the very nerve center of their organizations; and I am equally dismayed at the defensiveness of many catalogers, who respond as though they had learned their job by rote and understood it no better than do their supervisors. I am further dismayed at the almost universal attitude of normal, promising graduates of our library schools--graduates who will accept any job but cataloging. Cataloging *is* a great tradition, but something is going wrong. What is it? I think we know.

Cataloging is still as indispensable as ever, but it has become through the years so formalized, so isolated as a technical process, that neither the administrator nor the cataloger can quite see it in full perspective, as Dewey, Cutter, Martel, and Hanson did in its simpler, formative years. Having been created, it grew according to the desired pattern, and the pattern became fixed, in the interest of economy and consistency. This was necessary and good, as long as the conditions of library growth and use were being met. Our uneasiness in recent years has arisen, perhaps, from the realization that this pattern, now grown to gargantuan proportions, is no long so vital and responsive to new conditions as it used to be. The catalogers, having been born and bred to the pattern, cannot easily climb out of it; and the administrators, having taken it for granted, cannot easily climb in. Hence the fruitless bickering back and forth across the fence. The crux may well be that the time has come, or soon will come, when again the best minds of the profession will be required to breach that fence, to draw the catalogers out or push the administrators in, and to shape a new pattern that will be as vital and responsive to the future as the great tradition has been to the past.

About thirteen years ago I wrote, here at Chicago, an article that is still sometimes cited in the literature: "Subject Catalogs, Classifications, or Bibliographies? A Review of Critical Discussions, 1876-1942."[2] That article is significant to me today, not for any reason that I suspected at the time, but because it illustrates the tendency of librarians, during the formative years of modern cataloging, to think of cataloging as something apart from, in opposition to, and better than bibliography for library purposes. In that frame of reference cataloging was chosen and evolved as a more or less self-sufficient instrument for the exploitation of our rapidly growing collections. Important exceptions soon appeared, such as the use of periodical indexes, and a great deal of deference has since been paid to published bibliographies of one sort or another as they have proved their usefulness; but the original pattern remains, and the habit of thought persists. The dictionary catalog is still conceived as something essentially different from other types of bibliography. This fact is clearly evinced by the frequent references to cataloging as a separate library function, by its evolution as a separate department of the library organization, and by the specialization of librarians in cataloging as such. The great tradition began and still continues in a context that promotes isolation from, not integration with, other forms of bibliographical activity.

In approaching the factors that affect the cost of cataloging, we need, then, to appreciate not only the significance of cataloging as such but also its relationship to other kinds of bibliography. These other kinds have become increasingly important since the conception of cataloging as a separate library function. Let us consider for a moment the nature of bibliography in general--the broader function of which cataloging is a very important part.

In the broadest sense, bibliography (and I mean enumerative bibliography) is the organization of books for use-- all books for any use. It includes published lists, in the more limited sense of the term, as well as card files and all other forms of arrangement. Acquisition is the selection and accumulation of books; circulation is their physical control--their preservation, lending, location, and the like; and reference is professional assistance to readers in their use. Bibliography, including cataloging, is their substantive organization.

Bibliography is exceedingly complex. It defies logical analysis and offers little satisfaction to the system-seeker. Its many parts cover book production, the analysis of serials and other special forms of materials, and the literature of the various disciplines, languages, and periods, in addition to library and other collections. It includes the work of scholars, booksellers, catalogers, reference and special librarians, and all others who select and arrange books. Although few systematic patterns occur within this complex-- certainly few as systematic as the dictionary catalog--its varied parts have been evolved through much experience and intelligent application. They are the best work of scholars and librarians alike, and, taken together, they do an extraordinary job.

This vast complex of bibliography has been characterized sometimes as the pathfinder, or the road-guide, to the world of books. To me, a better characterization is a series of sieves, a large collection of different sieves, that sift and resift the books of the world, first coarsely and then more finely, until the desired books are separated out. There are different sieves for different purposes, and each

Cataloging Cost Factors

may be likened to a principle of classification--author, language, subject, period, or what you will. Similarly, each set may be likened to a pattern of reader interests. If only we could analyze these patterns of interest and translate them into principles of classification, into sets of bibliographical sieves, we would have taken the first real step toward a science of bibliography.

Meanwhile, bibliography is largely an art; it is the artful combination of whatever sieves may be available or devised to separate out the desired books. On the one hand, the reader is confronted with all the books in the world, as though they were heaped for burning; on the other hand, after using all the sieves he can muster, he is still confronted with a residue of books that he must sort for himself. And here is one of the greatest practical problems of bibliography: how much of this sifting should be done for the reader, and how much should he be left to do for himself? How finely should the sieves sift?

The dictionary catalog is one of these sieves, a very important one; but it does not stand alone. As we all know, there is abundant evidence that many scholars seldom use the catalog at all, except to find the call numbers of books they have already selected. Consider, for example, our own habits as librarians. When we survey the library literature, do we use the subject catalog? I doubt it. Certainly we do not use it alone. So, in discussing the costs and values of the catalog, we must try to extend our minds, stretch our imaginations, to embrace not just cataloging as a separately conceived and organized function, but all bibliography, conceived as an integrated whole. We must always remember that, as the acquisition department shares the selection of books with the reader and as the reference department shares the use of books with the reader, so does the catalog department share a broader bibliographical function, again with the reader.

In this broader frame of reference, then, let us consider some of the factors that affect the cost of cataloging-- indeed, the cost of bibliographical services in general. These factors are the variables, the ways in which more or less money might be spent.

The first factor, or variable, and the least tangible is the extent to which bibliography is designed to satisfy the varied and specialized needs of the reader. I have likened bibliography to a variety of sieves that sift progressively from coarse to fine. The question is: how varied and how fine?

One of the most significant changes in scholarship since the formative years of library cataloging has been the bewildering proliferation of specialties. The range and variety of reading interests have become vastly more complicated than they were in Dewey's or Cutter's day. When our present classifications and catalogs were conceived, it did not seem unreasonable to divide up knowledge into a linear sequence of more or less exclusive compartments, among which the reader could move back and forth as his needs might require. The interrelationships among the disciplines were still fairly simple. But in recent years these interrelationships have begun to overtax that conception of organization. Increasingly we have had to think in terms of more specialized patterns of organization. Every specialty, it might be argued, represents a different focus of interest, a different slant, on the whole of knowledge. Around this central interest the whole of knowledge is arranged peripherally, according to its relevance to the central interest. Thus the tree of knowledge is approached differently by the artist, the botanist, and the builder. It is the same tree, the same objective reality, but for each specialty the parts are classified differently. Taken together, the various specialties are like a field of overlapping circles, each with a different center, but all circumscribing the rest of the field to a greater or less extent.

The difference between this multi-dimensional conception and the traditional linear conception is not so much one of kind as of degree. There have always been overlapping disciplines, and measures have always been taken in the library catalog and elsewhere to accommodate them. There are special catalogs for special purposes, and there are bibliographies, indexes, and abstract journals. The present point is that the degree of fineness with which books are sorted and resorted for an ever increasingly specialized scholarship is one of the major factors in the cost of bibliography; and in this process the role that is assigned to library cataloging, as against other forms of bibliography, is a major factor in the cost of cataloging. This cost may be held down by resisting specialization and enforcing uniformity, or it may be allowed to increase by responding to numerous individualized demands; or other instruments may be created to satisfy the new, the unusual, and the particular. But satisfy them we must, by one means or another.

Cataloging Cost Factors

The second factor, or variable, is the degree of bibliographical coverage of the world's books. The growing complexity of scholarly specialization is rivaled only by the multiplication, in both numbers and varieties, of books and other library materials. It is commonly assumed that the unit cost of cataloging or of any bibliographical service increases as ever sharper distinctions must be drawn among ever larger quantities of materials. The "no conflict" principle is increasingly more difficult to apply, and the definition of the relationships among books becomes more and more subtle. But this is familiar ground. There are two other variables in this area that I should like to emphasize. The first is the extensiveness of the coverage in any bibliography, and the other is the intensiveness of the coverage.

Regarding the former, it may be said that the cost of any bibliographical endeavor will vary with the completeness with which the desired field of books is covered. This variable is easily recognizable in union catalog projects and in national bibliography; but it is also recognizable in library cataloging. Through the years, in an effort to control costs, more and more categories of materials in the library have sometimes been omitted from the catalog--whole blocks of materials, such as government documents, technical reports, audio-visual materials, and pamphlets. The self-arranging materials, the specially indexed materials, all those that are "uncataloged but organized for use," are growing in significance. The contents of special and departmental libraries may be omitted from the subject catalog. At Stanford these omissions have become so numerous that a special pamphlet --What's in the Card Catalog?--is revised and reissued each year, primarily for the information of the library staff. Libraries may differ widely in the coverage of the catalog, and the total cost is by no means represented by the catalog.

The cost of any bibliography may vary not only with the extensiveness but also with the intensiveness of its coverage. One manifestation of this variable is the amount of analytical work that is undertaken. Another, somewhat less obvious, is the degree to which a bibliography gathers to each subject not merely the books about it--that is, the secondary sources--but every kind of book that would be useful to the student of that subject--the primary sources, the background materials, and the books on related subjects. There is a big difference between the subject catalog, which is limited to specific entry for books that deal explicitly with a subject, and some of our great analytical bibliographies;

and there is even considerable difference among our catalogs. By and large, our catalogs have tended to become less and less intensive through the years. The intensive coverage of the literature of many fields has been delegated to special indexes and bibliographies, the cost of which also needs to be reckoned, along with cataloging.

These factors relating to readers and books may all have an important effect on the cost of bibliographical services. The next factor relates to the degree of co-ordination among the various tools that comprise the bibliographical system--the amount of duplication, for example. Outright duplication in a poorly co-ordinated system is, of course, uneconomical. However, not all overlapping is duplication. Let us keep in mind, as we consider this factor, that the deliberate organization and reorganization of the same books for different purposes may be altogether desirable, even at extra cost. Our methods can hardly be less diverse than the scholarship we serve.

With regard to the catalog, much has been done to insure that it does not unnecessarily duplicate information that is readily available in the published bibliographies. Although variations in practice still exist, the record is a pretty good one. But another kind of overlapping or duplication occurs in greater degree than may be commonly recognized. This happens in large libraries between central cataloging and the special indexing that is done locally in the service departments. A great deal of such indexing has evolved in some libraries. In one public library system that I have studied, one hundred and eleven special indexes and catalogs, some of substantial proportions, were being made in the service departments of the main library alone.[3] I should not be surprised if, in that instance, the service departments were spending more on the subject organization and analysis of library materials than the main catalog department. Call them by whatever name you will, these special projects are bibliographical charges against the library budget, over and above the cost of cataloging. They may supplement, replace, or duplicate the catalog; they may even arise in protest to the catalog, to its lack of responsiveness to specialized needs, but they are part and parcel of the bibliographical system. It would be very revealing and useful to know just what proportion of the total bibliographical service in a library system is borne by cataloging, in the traditional acknowledged sense, and what proportion by other instruments and to learn how the respective costs add up.

Moving on, now, to another dimension of the problem, we may note that variations in cost arise from the degree to which bibliographies and catalogs are produced centrally or co-operatively. It has long been recognized that if a bibliography is generally useful and can be published for wide distribution, the benefit is economically shared by all; the job need not be done locally over and over again. In many libraries local indexing jobs are still being done, which, if they could be perfected and published, would be useful the country over.

Library cataloging does, of course, benefit from centralized and co-operative effort. L. C. cards have been published for half a century. Yet the degree to which libraries take advantage of this benefit varies greatly. One library may use L. C. cards or copy merely as an aid to its local brand of cataloging, as information for the catalogers; another may practice blind acceptance of the cards, with no local review or alterations whatever. The effect on local cost may be considerable.

There are good reasons why many libraries benefit little from centralized cataloging. First a library may feel compelled to abide by local practices that are at variance with L. C. practice. Uniformity at the local level may seem to be more important than conformity at the national level. It is not easy to depart from local practices that have become intrenched through many decades, even though one might prefer to change them. On the other hand, many library situations may legitimately require a degree of specialization that is incompatible with a practice designed for universal acceptance. The value of specialization may frankly outweigh the economy of standardization.

There is reason to suspect, however, that some libraries take less advantage of centralized cataloging than they might. Ralph Ellsworth at Iowa, in his characteristically thorough and imaginative way, has cut the bonds of the past in order that he might accept L. C. cards, everything on them, without question or change. A report on his costs would be revealing. But most librarians have not been so bold; they buy L. C. cards or take copy from the printed catalogs but work the cards over locally to such an extent that only limited value is realized from centralized processing.

The centralized publication of special indexes and bibliographies does not appear to raise as many problems as

centralized library cataloging. The bibliography is not so
bound to the past and it need not conform to any standard
practice beyond that of the specialty served. Whereas library cataloging strives for a kind of universality that embraces all libraries and subject fields, the special bibliography does not. It is easier to generalize the need of a
single group of specialists the world over than that of all
specialists, in all disciplines, in the clientele of a single
library.

The degree to which the many parts of the bibliographical system can be economically produced and distributed centrally is closely related to the forms into which
the parts are cast, and this is the next factor that affects
cost. We have long been familiar with such forms as the
list, the sheaf, and the card. More recently we have become acquainted with microforms and punched cards, and
now the possibilities of electronic devices are being explored.

Although form is a basic factor in the cost of bibliographical services, little variation in practice has occurred
in this area for many decades. Cards have been uniformly
used for library catalogs and many other locally compiled
indexes; the printed list has been generally employed for
bibliographies and indexes intended for wide distribution.
Yet important variations in the form of library catalogs may
well occur in the near future, through the photo-offset reproduction of card files in cumulative book form. The Library
of Congress has paced this movement with the publication of
its author and subject catalogs. The Harvard library staff
is contemplating the publication of segments of the main catalog, particularly the voluminous authors. The New York
State Library has just published experimentally a title-a-line
catalog of its holdings in the social sciences. These developments portend significant future changes in the form and usefulness of the catalog and will introduce a new variable into
the computation and interpretation of cost.

The last general cost factor is the efficiency of the
process by which a bibliography or catalog is compiled.
This includes the quality of the personnel--their training,
experience, and morale--the organization of the work, and
the like. In the catalog department more or less attention
may be paid to revision, to the smooth flow of books and
cards, and to the co-ordination of cataloging with other library processes. Although most catalog departments may
be reasonably efficient, considering the complex nature of the

Cataloging Cost Factors

job, the economy of their performance may still vary appreciably not only from library to library but also from year to year in the same library.

In view of all these factors any evaluation of the cost of cataloging is exceedingly difficult. The catalog is still the basic instrument for the organization of library materials, but it must be increasingly regarded as part of a larger, interrelated complex--the bibliographical system as a whole. The total cost of a library's bibliographical service may be shared in varying degrees by the catalog, by other locally compiled tools, and by published indexes and bibliographies. Generally speaking, any or all of these tools may vary in cost according to the degree to which (1) they undertake to satisfy the highly specialized, overlapping interests of modern scholarship, (2) they provide both extensive and intensive coverage of the pertinent resources, (3) they are well coordinated with one another, (4) they benefit from centralized or co-operative processing, (5) they are cast in the most economical forms, and (6) they are made by an efficient organization and staff. Those are the factors, then, that affect cost.

Now let us consider the studies of the cost of cataloging, of which, by now, there are many. As already noted, Felix Reichmann has recently reviewed these studies chronologically from 1876 to the present. In order not to duplicate his review, we shall merely identify the several types of studies that have been undertaken.

Most studies of the cost of cataloging have treated of unit costs in one way or another--the cost per volume, title, or other unit. The simplest and most familiar consists of dividing the number of units cataloged into the total budget of the catalog department. Most administrators and head catalogers have probably made this calculation over and over again, and occasionally this kind of data has been published.

This simple calculation is especially useful when made before and after some known variation in cataloging policy or procedure. Assuming that all other variables remain constant, the effect of a known variable may be readily determined. Thus Jerrold Orne reported decreases in cataloging costs over a three-year period that resulted from clarifying the distinction between clerical and professional work, from fuller acceptance of L. C. cards, and from the formulation of clearer instructions;[4] and Helen Jones reported decreases due to improved co-ordination of the acquisition and catalog departments.[5] These are studies of changing costs in a single library.

Another type of study that involves a single library is work measurement. Instead of computing unit costs by dividing output into budget, the work itself is analyzed and measured; the time spent on each step of the process is determined, and costs are then derived from those data. Robert Miller's dissertation is an early example.[6] Later examples are to be found in the survey of the New York Public Library[7] and in the Public Library Inquiry.[8] Studies of this type are especially useful in spotting inefficient steps in the process and in devising better ways of doing some jobs, especially the more mechanical jobs.

Still another type of study within a single library is based on production per cataloger, with costs inferred from the production figures. The number of titles or volumes processed by a department may be divided by the number of staff members to obtain a gross average; or statistics of the output of individual staff members may be compared, depending upon the purpose of the study.

Then there are the comparative studies, which may be based on any of the three types of data mentioned above. Information on unit cost per title or volume may be collected from a number of libraries, with more or less effort to account for irregularities of policy and organization among those libraries. Reichmann's own study, which is reported in his article in Library Trends, is based on production data in order to side-step the effects of salary differentials. While Reichmann could not account for differences among the libraries "as regards definitions, structures, and material processed," he did undertake to include the cost of cataloging done outside the main catalog department.

As one reviews these studies, several general impressions are inescapable. First, the studies of individual libraries can be extremely useful if they show the effects of specified changes of policy or procedure, with other variables held constant. Data of this kind are useful not only to the library studied but to other libraries as well. They are, however, useful only in regard to the known variable; they provide no basis for evaluating the general cost of cataloging in that or any other library. It is the change in cost that is significant, not the total cost.

Second, the comparative studies are uniformly hopeless, if not downright misleading. The tremendous differences reported in the unit costs among libraries cannot be explained by any known variable, such as size or type of library, ratio of clerical to professional staff, or acceptance of L. C. cards. Cataloging is not standardized, and the wide range of factors that determine cost has not even begun to be controlled.

Third, none of the studies has attempted to relate costs to values or results, except in regard to selected variables in a single library. By and large, they provide no basis for concluding that cataloging of any kind or in any library costs too much or too little or that any catalog department is more or less efficient than another. To appreciate the complexity of the problem and the inadequacy of the existing studies, let us examine them in the light of each of the general cost factors that were described above.

The first factor--the degree of fineness with which the increasingly specialized and overlapping interests of modern scholarship are accommodated--plays little part in the studies, although it may be reflected in certain distinctions between simplified, standard, and bibliographical cataloging. The number and kind of subject and other added entries and the nature of the descriptive detail, for example, may bear upon this factor. Variations from standard practice that are intended to satisfy unusual needs may also be related to it. The most explicit consideration of this factor has probably taken the form of discussions about the effect of omissions or simplifications upon the reader or reference librarian-- that is, the cost to the reader of saving money in the catalog. Again, how much should be done for the reader in the catalog, and how much should be left for him to do for himself? It may be further pointed out that no studies have related the role of the catalog to that of other bibliographical means of serving the more specialized needs of the reader. The whole area is a great maze which will never be untangled until (a) adequate studies of readers' needs have been made, (b) the most economical bibliographical means of satisfying those needs have been determined, and (c) the role of the catalog as one of those means has been established. This is a big order, perhaps an impossible one.

In regard to the second factor, which is the coverage of library resources, it has been reasoned that the more extensive the coverage or the larger the library, the greater the unit cost of cataloging. The comparative studies, however, appear to indicate that, if this is true, the evidence is canceled out by other factors. The cost data do not correlate positively with over-all size of library. Differences among libraries in types of materials cataloged, moreover, could affect unit costs, in that some materials are more difficult to process than others. The inclusion or omission of large blocks of materials, such as government documents and the holdings of departmental libraries, would probably affect total cost more significantly than unit cost. In any event, this factor has not yet been controlled in the studies. Neither has variation in the intensiveness of the coverage been controlled--the amount of analytical work, for example, done in the catalog as against the amount left to published bibliographies and indexes.

Similarly, in regard to the third factor, the degree of co-ordination between the catalog and other tools, particularly the special indexes and catalogs that may also be compiled locally by the service departments, has been left undefined. Reichmann obtained data on work done by staff members outside the main catalog department, but there is doubt that these data could have been interpreted as including anything other than conventional cataloging. It would be difficult to evaluate any data on cataloging unless these other costs were also known.

The fourth factor--the degree of centralization or co-operation--has received attention in the cost studies, in that cataloging with and without L. C. cards and in some cases the degree of acceptance of L. C. cards have been differentiated. The gross comparative studies, however, either have not accounted for this variable at all or have not been able to isolate its effect. Like so many other factors, it remains one of the imponderabilia.

The form of the catalog, which is the fifth factor, does appear to be so well standardized that we need not look here for any explanation of the differences in cataloging costs. Minor differences might conceivably arise between the dictionary and the divided catalog, for example, but I doubt that they could even be detected in the total budget.

It is the last factor--the efficiency of the cataloging process--to which attention has been directed most frequently in the cost studies. Emphasis has been placed on streamlining the procedures, on work simplification, and the like.

Within a single library, it is relatively easy to measure changes in cost due to changes in the process, provided that no important changes in the other, more imponderable, factors occur during the period of study. But when the gross costs from several libraries are treated comparatively, the differences in cost that are due to this factor are lost among those that are due to other factors. Nothing is controlled.

The studies in general, then, offer little help in the evaluation of cataloging costs. Most of them are incapable of interpretation, in that variations in cost cannot be related to variations in the basic factors which determine cost and which, if related to library objectives, might form some basis for judgment. None of the studies, moreover, treats of cataloging as part of the broader bibliographical complex, a knowledge of the total cost and function of which would be important to the evaluation of cataloging.

Before leaving this subject in such a hopeless state, it might be well to consider what possible kinds of studies would really be helpful. I should certainly conclude, first, that no gross comparative study of a statistical nature is likely to cope with the entire range of factors that I have outlined, at least without many preliminary studies of a more specific and limited nature--specific with regard to individual cost factors and limited to individual libraries. The existing studies of changes in cost due to changes in particular factors point the way. We need many more such studies, and they should treat of a wider range of factors, not just the efficiency of the process and the use of L. C. cards but also the provision of specialized subject services, the alternative use of bibliographies and indexes for analytical and other purposes, and the compilation of special subject indexes in the service departments as against their incorporation into the general catalog. These additional factors are more difficult to get hold of, but they are every bit as important.

For purposes of evaluation, studies of the use of the catalog would be helpful if related to costs. If we could know, for example, the utility of various added entries and could tell the difference in cost if they were or were not made, we might be able to pass reasonable judgment. But even studies of the use and cost of the catalog would leave much to the imagination, because they would still fail to inform us about the relations of the catalog to other kinds of bibliography. Even though it were demonstrated that a job needs to be done and could be done at reasonable cost in the catalog, there would still be the possibility that the same job might be done better at less cost in some other way.

The most valuable single kind of study that could be made at this time, I believe, would be case studies of the experience of readers in using the entire range of a library's bibliographical services--studies that could then be related to analyses of the costs of the entire range of services. I am thinking of studies that would reveal the context in which the catalog is used and would relate its use to that of special indexes, abstract journals, even the bibliographies in textbooks and encyclopedias. By such means we might be helped to see the problem whole. The studies would, of course, have no statistical validity, but they might reveal new patterns and relationships that could be used later for statistical analyses. In any case, I am certain that such studies would preclude any future effort to interpret the cost of the catalog alone. Only by means of such studies could the variables pertaining to readers' interests, to coverage of services, and to the co-ordination of bibliographical services be assessed.

So, as we look toward the future, there is little to depend upon except insight and common sense. Any really helpful study of costs must either isolate the effects of individual variables by means of controlled experiments or probe deeply into the entire complex of variables in individual situations by means of case studies. Meanwhile, a simple appreciation of the full range of variables is probably more important than all the cost data now at hand. The potentialities of each factor are most significant, and the signs of the future with regard to some of them are fairly clear.

Take the first factor again. There seems to me no doubt whatever that, by one bibliographical means or another, our libraries must continue to respond to the increasing complexities of scholarly specialization. The general library catalog, by its very nature, resists specialization and tends toward standardization. It tries to do a uniform job for all readers in all disciplines the country over, and its massive inertia to change is impressive. A rudimentary job of this nature may always be basic to the bibliographical system, but the relative significance of the catalog, especially the subject catalog, seems bound to diminish as other more flexible means of specialized services are evolved. We can have only one general card catalog, but we can have as many overlapping, inconsistent bibliographies as there are specialties to be served. As I read the signs, we are still concentrating too much upon the economies of standardization, as applied to the general card catalog, while neglecting the values of specialization, as applied to other kinds of bibliographical service. I would venture to predict that, in due course, the large library will spend more on its total bibliographical service than has yet been dreamed of in connection with the main catalog department alone.

Take the second factor. As the sheer quantity of material increases, how long can we cover it in a single alphabet? How large can the catalog grow? In this I do share Fremont Rider's alarm. Does anyone really believe that we can go on indefinitely adding cards to a general catalog? The American library is still very young; it might last for centuries. Somewhere along the way it seems to me inevitable that we shall have to break it down, divide it up into more manageable parts; and this means, in a sense, that sooner or later we shall have to specialize even the general catalog. To a certain extent this is already being done; large blocks of materials are being handled separately, without even author entries in the general catalog, and the subject approach to still other materials is delegated to special catalogs and bibliographies. In the future there could evolve a decentralization of the catalog on several bases: forms, such as periodicals and documents; subjects, such as the humanities and social sciences; or historical periods. Ultimately, some historical division will certainly be necessary. Sometime we shall have to draw a line, to stop the cumulations, and to start over again with a new organization that is appropriate for the times, leaving the past to stand alone for what it was. Bibliographies, incidentally, do this; it is only library cataloging that is still believed to be everlasting, forever capable of fusing the past with the future. We have really known better for a generation.

Then the third factor. I have pointed out that an increasing amount of special cataloging and indexing is being done in the service departments and that this activity, like central cataloging, is a part of the total bibliographical system. I have also indicated that cataloging has evolved historically as a separate library function; the catalog department in the library organization is widely separated from other aspects of bibliography. If cataloging is to be integrated more closely with other kinds of bibliography, I believe it will become increasingly necessary in the future to break down this functional and organizational isolation of the catalog department, to reorganize in some way that will express the unity of the broader bibliographical function. There are signs already that responsibility for both subject cataloging and subject bibliography, including special indexing, may be gravitating slowly toward the subject departments of the large library. This tendency is, on the one hand, toward decentralization of subject cataloging but, on the other hand, toward integration of the entire bibliography of a subject. The possibility is highly significant.

And then the fourth factor. While it appears in one respect that our catalog departments do not take the fullest advantage of L. C. cards, it appears in other respects that maybe they should not. Where the standardization that goes with centralization is desirable, the fullest possible acceptance of L. C. cards is also desirable; but where standardization is undesirable, so also are the cards. Generally speaking, I think it would be agreed that standardization and therefore centralization are altogether desirable in author entry and descriptive cataloging, and I see no reason why L. C. cards should not be fully accepted for these purposes. As our great collections continue to grow, their uniform author control and description will continue to be essential. It is likely that in due course even the author catalog will have to be broken down into more manageable parts; but the more diversified our library systems become, the more necessary that the author catalog be preserved and further developed in some standard form as a central finding list.

For the subject control of these collections, however, it is not at all clear how the universal acceptance of L. C. practice, as applied to general cataloging, can cope with the future. Indeed, it cannot cope with the present. If subject control should gradually become decentralized, I should expect that new and varying standards would evolve in each of the major subject fields, according to the peculiar nature of each field, its type of literature, and the availability of other kinds of bibliography. This line of reasoning suggests that, even though our efforts to centralize author cataloging should be redoubled, we should exercise caution in requiring the centralization of subject cataloging. If deviations from centralized subject cataloging should be permitted, however, we should be certain that they arise from the legitimate needs of scholarly specialization, not from the local cataloging tradition or from the personal preferences of the catalogers.

The fifth factor is form. If the signs portend increasing specialization through decentralization or if, in any case, the general card catalog must sometime be divided historically, the advent of new and economical methods of publishing the catalogs in book form is most opportune. The possibility of publishing the catalog in cumulative form through substantial periods of time and of maintaining only the current supplements in card form looks very much like a pattern for the future. With the termination of any cumulation, the rules could be changed, even the shelf classification. The subject catalogs could be separately published in as many sections as needed and according to as many different sets of rules. The flexibility of such a pattern, in both the historical and the subject dimensions, would offer great hope for the future. If, in addition, the evolution of electronic forms of bibliography should offer further help in the more specialized areas, so much the better.

Whatever else happens, we may assume, in regard to the sixth factor, that efforts to improve the efficiency of catalogers and catalog departments will continue. But let us remember that the other factors are fundamental to the very nature of the bibliographical system and therefore to its cost.

Cataloging is indeed a great tradition, but we are crossing a watershed. There is no cause for alarm. No catalogs are likely to collapse in our lifetime, and no bibliographical wands are about to be waved. The change will be slow and orderly, but the intimations of the future are already with us, together with the vestiges of the past. Our task is to tell the difference, if we can, to read the signs, and to plan accordingly.

This conference is directed "Toward a Better Cataloging Code"--that is, toward a better code of author entry. After all this discussion of cataloging cost factors, the least I could do, I suppose, would be to try to show some relevance to the topic at hand. Most of what I have said is probably more relevant to subject than to author cataloging. Yet there are implications for the author code, and these implications are placed in a broad frame of reference.

First, and most important, in this broad frame of reference, the usual haggling over the details of author entry, as far as cost is concerned, seems rather unimportant. One thing that the cost studies do show is that cataloging--all phases of cataloging--is really a modest part of the total cost of library service. Far more is spent on public service. And only a small part of the cost of cataloging derives from author entry. To me this means that, in framing a new code, attention should be directed primarily toward devising the best possible code, without undue regard to cost. The author catalog will continue to be absolutely basic to library service; its job will continue to grow more and more complex. We would be penny-wise and pound-foolish to single out the author code as a target for our parsimonious guns.

Aside from cost, the code can be improved. Mr. Lubetzky has demonstrated that. The organization, the principles, and the rationalization of the function of the code are the important things. In due course the author catalog may have to be divided, but even the parts of it will be larger in the future than the whole of it today. We need a code that will be certain to distinguish authors and to collect an author's works and that will be as helpful as possible to the reader, who, God knows, will in any case have trouble enough in using the library. And we need a code that will do all this in the most lucid possible manner--and let us not confuse lucidity with simplicity; they are not the same thing.

We pay for author entry, description, and subject cataloging. We pay for classification. We pay for published bibliographies, indexes, and abstract journals. We pay for serial records and document check lists. We pay for the arrangement of all materials that are "uncataloged but organized for use," and we pay for a large variety of special catalogs and indexes that are compiled locally in the service departments. Indeed, we pay for reference librarians, who try to plug the gap between what we do accomplish and what we might, and the price of the reference librarians may surpass all the rest. Beyond that, the reader pays. Meanwhile, the convolutions of modern scholarship become ever more involved, and the numbers and varieties of books multiply. Of all things, let us not skimp on the author code. It is the very heart of the library service.

References

1. "Costs of Cataloging," Library Trends, II (1953), 290-317.
2. Library Quarterly, XIV (1944), 316-32.

3. Los Angeles, Bureau of Budget and Efficiency, Organization, Administration, and Management of the Los Angeles Public Library, Vol. VII: Technical Services (Los Angeles, 1950).
4. "We Have Cut Our Cataloging Costs!" Library Journal, LXXIII (1948), 1475-78.
5. "Cataloging Short-Cuts in the Pasadena Public Library," Journal of Cataloging and Classification, VIII (1952), 173-74.
6. "Cost Accounting for Libraries: A Technique for Determining the Labor Costs of Acquisition and Cataloging Work," (unpublished Ph.D. thesis, University of Chicago Graduate Library School, 1936).
7. Cresap, McCormick, and Paget, The New York Public Library: Survey of Preparations: Reference Department (New York, 1951).
8. W. O'D. Pierce, Work Measurement in Public Libraries (New York: Social Science Research Council, 1949).

12. Subject Cataloging in the Subject-Departmentalized Library

This paper is written to explore the case for decentralization of subject cataloging and classification, together with subject bibliography, in university libraries organized along subject-departmental lines. For the sake of argument, decentralization is favored. Nothing is immediately urged or recommended, however, except that each of us flex his imagination and apply himself to a major cataloging problem.

My interest in this problem has a fourfold origin.

First, three years ago I wrote a paper called "The Catalog Department in the Library Organization."[1] After acknowledging the close relationship between order work and cataloging, I said that the relationship between cataloging and bibliography is still more close and that their functional unity might be expressed administratively by creation of a combined catalog and bibliography department. I then described how such a department might function in a centralized library with a general reference service of the traditional kind. But I begged a question rather badly by devoting only one paragraph at the end of the paper to the status of a central bibliography department in the subject-departmentalized library. The present paper is intended to finish that paragraph.

Second, I find no clear evidence that the implications of subject-departmentalization for cataloging have ever been squarely faced. Our present system of subject cataloging is a logical complement to centralized service, as exemplified by the general reference department. As long as the spot-

---

Reprinted from Bibliographic Organization by Shera and Egan, pp. 187-99, by permission of The University of Chicago Press. Copyright © 1951 by The University of Chicago Press.

light shines on general reference and circulation, with the
departmental libraries remaining in the background, the general
subject catalog, supported by its departmental offspring,
is appropriately cast in the lead role. But when the light
shifts to the departments and the emphasis is placed on their
special subject interests, the general subject catalog slips
into shadow. The light has already shifted insofar as the
grouping of library services under broad subject divisions
constitutes an acceptable compromise between centralization
and decentralization. General reference is already vestigial
in a few university libraries, and departmental libraries are
being consolidated or coordinated into larger units. The
emphasis is on specialization in these larger units, yet cataloging
is still aimed primarily at general service. It may
be time to see whether subject cataloging can be adapted to
meet the needs of decentralized service through subject-divisional
organization.

Third, the old cry is still heard that subject cataloging
is poorly integrated with published bibliographies, that
much subject cataloging unnecessarily duplicates the bibliographies,
and that the bibliographies are not being fully exploited.
To the extent that this is true, I have an abiding
interest in effecting whatever reconciliation is necessary to
release for other purposes some of the big money now spent
on cataloging. Progress is being made, but no change in
the essential structure of the catalog has yet occurred.
There seems to be no really practical way of reconciling the
nature and methods of general library cataloging with those
of specialized subject bibliography. Sometimes I think that
only a basic reorganization of library services could effect
that reconciliation. It might be that specialization through
subject divisions will provide the necessary upheaval and
that the opportunity for integrating cataloging with bibliography
will occur at the divisional level instead of the general
level. If a general subject catalog cannot be synchronized
with subject bibliographies, which are decentralized as a
matter of course in the subject-divisional scheme, perhaps
special subject catalogs could be.

The fourth reason for this paper is the appearance in
book form of the Library of Congress Subject Catalog. In
past years there has been much speculation about the possibility
of delegating some of the functions of the general subject
catalog to the Cumulative Book Index, the Cambridge
Bibliography of English Literature, and other fairly general
bibliographies. These schemes have never come off, even

Subject-Departmentalized Library 179

experimentally. Now we have this new tool which clearly duplicates a large part of the subject catalog. Can it be put to work in place of that part of the subject catalog which it duplicates? If local subject catalogs were decentralized, perhaps the LC Subject Catalog could satisfy any vestigial need for a general subject list. In any case it is important that the potentialities of the new LC Subject Catalog be conscientiously investigated.

As a basis for discussion let me describe a proposition--an imaginary scheme for decentralization of subject cataloging and classification in a university library organized into subject divisions.

This hypothetical library has four subject divisions for upperclass, graduate, and faculty use: a humanities division, a social science division, a biological science division, and a physical science and engineering division. Each division has a central reading room (not necessarily in the main library building) with a well developed reference service and an open-shelf collection of frequently used books and journals. The smaller departmental libraries in each of these subject areas operate as branches of the related division and are administered by the division chief and his staff of subject specialists.

There is no general reference department, periodical room, or reserved book room, these services being allocated to the subject divisions. For lower class students, however, there is a general education division consisting of an open-shelf library of the books, journals, reference works, etc. used in connection with freshman and sophomore courses.

In addition to the four subject divisions and the general education division there is an acquisition division of the conventional sort, with purchase, gift and exchange, serial, and binding departments. There is a bibliography division which includes the catalog department and a central bibliographic service. The bibliography and acquisition divisions could, if desired, be consolidated into one division. 2

A circulation division controls the physical disposition of books throughout the system and maintains and lends books from the central stack, which serves as storage for seldom used books. A division of special collections handles rare books and manuscripts.

Within this subject-divisional library bibliographies and catalogs are disposed as follows:

The heart of the bibliographic system is the central bibliographic service, administered by the chief bibliographer. This service employs a union author-title catalog of the resources of all parts of the system. No general shelflist is used. The subject card catalog is separate from the author-title catalog and contains only books published to 1950. No general subject catalog is maintained for books published after 1950. Beginning with 1950 the LC Subject Catalog is used for general purposes, together with the CBI and other general subject lists. The service also employs the LC Author Catalog, other library catalogs (such as the British Museum catalog), the trade and national bibliographies, the general periodical indexes, etc. With this equipment and a card index to bibliographies located in the subject divisions, the service functions as a clearing house for bibliographic information and for the referral of inquiries to the appropriate subject divisions.

In each subject division an author-title catalog and a shelflist are maintained. These cover all books, including those stored in the main stack, which fall within the relevant subject areas. Author lists only are kept in the smaller branches, and these are limited to the books actually located in the branches. The divisions and branches are equipped with as good a collection of subject bibliographies, indexes, annual reviews, and abstract journals as is needed or available.

To the extent that the published tools leave significant gaps to be filled, special subject catalogs and indexes are compiled locally by the divisions. These special catalogs are made only when necessary, only as long as necessary, and are designed to satisfy the specific needs of specific readers. The extent and nature of local subject cataloging varies from division to division according to the adequacy of the published bibliographies. In some areas (for example, geology) no subject catalog is compiled. In others (for example, business) full subject catalogs are compiled. Between these extremes is a wide variety of practice. All such catalogs and indexes are special in purpose and design and are supplementary in the sense that they are discontinued as soon as the special need passes or is satisfied by a new bibliography.

Subject-Departmentalized Library

In this bibliographic system it is a function of the central bibliography division, which includes the catalog department, to prepare the unit cards for the author-title catalogs, both main and divisional, for the divisional shelflists, and for the central card list of bibliographies. For books published after 1950 the bibliography division sends all copies of these cards without classification numbers or subject headings with the books to the service divisions. For books published before 1950 subject headings are assigned and subject cards included, but classification numbers are still omitted.

The subject specialists in the divisions then classify the books within exclusive blocks of numbers assigned to the divisions and decide where the books go--to the divisional reading room, a branch, or the main stack. The cards for the main author-title catalog and the main subject catalog for books published through 1950 are returned with call numbers and location symbols to the bibliography division for filing. The divisions file their own cards and prepare the entries, if any, for the special subject catalogs and indexes needed in the divisions.

The coordinating authority is the chief bibliographer, who approves the plans for all subject cataloging and classification done in the divisions and reviews the work from time to time. The subject cataloging of the divisions, however, need not be uniform, since the cards are not interfiled in a general catalog. Within the blocks of numbers assigned to the divisions, the classification schedules are applied without possibility of conflict and the call numbers identify the divisions to which the books belong.

That is briefly the hypothetical organization. Now let us see what elements in the present situation tend toward that kind of organization and then consider some of the angles. The decentralization of the subject approach to books may not be as alien to present practice as at first it might appear.

First, to the extent that subject divisions and branches now exist, subject bibliography and reference service are already decentralized. It has been taken for granted that the bibliographic apparatus in special subjects belongs in the subject departments, whether duplicated elsewhere or not. The general reference service may be entirely gone, as at the University of Nebraska; it may be vestigial, as at the

University of Colorado; or as at Stanford, it may be fragmentary. At Stanford half of all library use, including nearly all service in the physical and biological sciences, occurs in the departmental libraries; and the so-called general service is actually specialized in the humanities and certain social sciences.

Second, the hypothetical organization is already approximated to the extent that subject catalog cards are now made for the general catalog without being supplied to the subject departments, or for the subject departments without being filed in the general catalog. At Stanford, out of 28 departmental and special libraries, subject cards for 9 are now made only for the departmental catalogs, and subject cards for 15 are made only for the general catalog. For only 4 are duplicate sets of cards now filed in both the general and departmental catalogs, where service is concentrated. These situations qualify or cast doubt upon the theory of the general subject catalog.

Third, the hypothetical organization is further approximated to the extent that analytics and other entries for serials (especially periodicals), government publications, and other materials are omitted from the general subject catalog in deference to published indexes and bibliographies. The approach to periodical literature is almost entirely through special indexes. The significance of this fact to the research worker ought not to be underestimated. Herman Fussler, in his study of the literature used by chemists and physicists, showed that over 90 per cent of the references cited by research workers in these fields are from serial publications. [3]

Fourth, to the extent that subject departments now perform special cataloging or indexing activities, our hypothetical organization is again approximated. It is fairly common practice for a central catalog department, in processing books for departmental libraries, to prepare subject cards for the general catalog but to supply only author cards with tracings to the departments. The departments then make for themselves whatever subject catalogs or indexes are needed to supplement the published bibliographies. Seventy-seven departments at the University of California operate on this basis. A few maintain full subject catalogs; most probably do not. Some may engage upon special indexing or abstracting projects in place of, or in addition to, straight subject cataloging. At the Los Angeles Public Library, in which all departments are supplied with subject catalogs by the central catalog department, the subject specialists in the departments were recently found to be compiling a total of 111 special indexes and catalogs, large and small. At Stanford, a good example is the biological science division, which regularly operates without a subject catalog but carries on a variety of special indexing and abstracting activities.

Fifth, while centralized cataloging is clearly the vogue in university libraries, there has always been the exception of a few departmental libraries, usually autonomous or located at a distance from the main library, which have done all their own cataloging. These exceptions may or may not be important to this discussion, but they may be kept in mind as a further tendency toward our hypothetical organization.

These present conditions, the extent of which I am not able to measure, should at least remind us that the elements of our hypothetical organization do now exist in one form or another. How would the reader be affected if these elements were combined and elaborated into the kind of decentralized pattern which has been outlined?

The crux of any argument about decentralization of subject cataloging is probably the ability of the reader to get along satisfactorily without the general subject catalog. Special catalogs and indexes made in the departments would obviously be useful, as the bibliographies are now. But is the general subject catalog dispensable? No reliable answer can be given, although a little information and a lot of argument are available.

It appears at present that the advanced student, graduate or faculty, is less dependent upon the general subject catalog than the undergraduate student, but that he still uses the subject catalog to an extent that must be reckoned with. At the University of California, according to data recently compiled by LeRoy Merritt,[4] graduate students, who comprised 18.3 per cent of the university population during the period of study, borrowed from the main loan desk 16.2 per cent of all books derived from the subject catalog, 21 per cent of those derived from the author catalog, but 46.3 per cent of those borrowed without reference to either author or subject catalog. Faculty members, who comprised 4.7 per cent of the population, borrowed 2.1 per cent of the books derived from the subject catalog, 3.4 per cent of those derived from the author catalog, but 10.1 per cent of those obtained without reference to either catalog.

Unfortunately, we cannot say whether this use of the subject catalog is large or small, important or unimportant, in relation to the use of other subject tools. No data are available on the extent to which these same readers depend upon subject bibliographies, indexes, abstracts, etc. in quest of books obtained not only from the main loan desk but also from the departmental libraries--data that would enable us to see the facts of subject catalog use in broader perspective. The existence of the bibliographies, their acceptance as part of the scholarly equipment of special fields, and the interest of the scholarly world in perfecting them are presumptive evidence that they are extensively and necessarily used. It could still be that the general subject catalog plays a minor part in the scholars' subject approach to the literature of many fields. It was possible for the authors of the recent study on "Bibliographical Services in the Social Sciences" to report on present services and make recommendations without discussion of any role that the subject catalog might play. [5] My own study of "The Organization of Library Materials for Research in English Literature" indicated that the bibliographies in that field are more useful than the subject catalog. [6] Before it can be concluded that the general subject catalog is indispensable to the advanced student, it will have to be shown that the present use of the subject catalog is important and desirable and that the same job cannot be done better by other and cheaper methods. In our hypothetical organization, it is assumed that for the most part the job can be done better by other methods and that the advanced student can and should be taught to use the special apparatus of his field, supplemented only when necessary by locally compiled catalogs or indexes.

With respect to the beginning student, the logic of our hypothetical organization is more clear. At the University of California undergraduate students, who comprised 70.8 per cent of the population, borrowed 72.8 per cent of the books derived from the subject catalog, 63.7 per cent of those derived from the author catalog, but only 17.6 per cent of those derived from no catalog. The bulk of subject catalog use was therefore undergraduate. This fact may have either of two meanings: the extent of a good thing or the extent of a bad thing. Is heavy undergraduate use of the general subject catalog of a large research library a good thing?

The underclassman is typically engaged with the acquisition of a general education. It has been variously estimated that he needs for that purpose a library of several thousand, 50,000, or even 100,000 books, depending upon the nature of the curriculum. But patently he does not need a large research library and is not equipped to use one. A million-volume research library without stack access is an obstacle to his finding the comparatively few books he really needs. He gets in the way of the advanced students who do need a research library. The small, select, open-shelf library of the liberal arts college is better suited to his purpose. It follows that if his use of the research collection is inappropriate, so also is his use of the subject catalog of that collection.

Our hypothetical organization provides a separate general education division--a special library which would contain the books which freshmen and sophomores are expected to consult. Since there is no standard bibliography for such a literature, the divisional staff would be obliged to make some kind of subject catalog. Whatever kind is made, it should be sufficient for the collection and for the users of the collection and should be more direct and helpful than the general subject catalog. The staff of the division, moreover, being responsible for the orientation of new students, could teach the use of this smaller collection with some hope of success. When the student begins to specialize during his junior and senior years, he would be graduated to the subject divisions, where from the beginning he would be taught the bibliography of his chosen fields.

There is, then, the possibility that the general subject catalog is dispensable, that the advanced student could be served better through published bibliographies, supplemented by catalogs made in the divisions, and that the beginning student could be served better by the catalog of a select, general education library. But let us suppose that there is still left a significant residual need of a general subject catalog. To what extent could the new <u>Library of Congress Subject Catalog</u> fill that need? Any number of copies could, of course, be supplied, and we could hope for some fat cumulations in future years.

We know that university libraries now use LC printed cards for about 50 to 70 per cent of the books cataloged and therefore added to the subject catalog. In 1948-49 Stanford cataloged 60.5 per cent of its books with LC cards, the Uni-

versity of California about 67 per cent. That leaves 30 or
40 per cent not covered by LC. LeRoy Merritt, in connection with his "Subject Catalog Inquiry" at the University of
California, recently analyzed a small sample of 1,784 books
actually loaned through use of the subject catalog to determine the incidence of LC cards. 67.9 per cent had been
originally cataloged with LC cards. But since LC cards
had been subsequently printed for another 12.6 per cent,
cards were available at the time the books were used for
80.5 per cent. If these proportions were to continue, that
would leave 19.5 per cent not covered by the LC Subject
Catalog. With an 80 per cent display in this one list, with
such other general lists as CBI available, and with well developed subject approaches in the subject divisions, there is
reasonable doubt that the general subject catalog would be
worth while.

Let us examine more closely now the relationship
which our hypothetical organization would establish between
subject cataloging and bibliography. As already noted, our
heart has been willing but our hands unable to arrange any
really effective coordination between local subject cataloging
and published bibliography. Two reasons may be suggested.

First, cataloging is a distributive or book-to-subject
process, while bibliography is a collective or subject-to-book
process. The cataloger takes books in hand and distributes
them among subjects in a prearranged schedule. The bibliographer takes a subject in hand and collects books around
it. There is no way for the cataloger to avoid duplication
of the bibliographies, and yet provide full coverage, without
searching the bibliographies for the titles being cataloged.
Second, because of the existence of the general subject catalog, the pressure for uniformity and consistency of practice
is not between cataloging and bibliography in any field, but
between cataloging in different fields. Cataloging for chemistry is coordinated with cataloging for economics, history,
and romance languages, not with chemical bibliography.

To some extent the decentralization of subject cataloging would get around both of these difficulties. The subject
specialist in a division would take stock of the adequacy of
the bibliographies in his field and define the areas not covered or the functions not performed. With a knowledge of
the field, its bibliography and its readers, he could take the
necessary subjects in hand and list only the relevant books
which the division acquired. He could reason that this book

treats of an area which is already covered, but that one does not. By defining his work in terms of subjects a larger degree of coordination should be possible.

Regarding the other difficulty, lack of a general subject catalog would release at once the bond of uniformity around cataloging in different fields. Whereas the pressure is now toward coordination of all subjects by one bibliographic method, the pressure would then be toward coordination of all methods for each subject. The cataloger would join the bibliographer in serving the community of scholars in each field, wherever they may be. The institutional inter-departmental dimension would be superseded by the departmental inter-institutional dimension.

If subject cataloging were coordinated with bibliography and oriented to the more specialized services of the subject divisions, several changes might be expected in the nature of the cataloging still to be done. These changes are inherent in the idea of specialization.

First, in our hypothetical organization subject cataloging would become less extensive but more intensive. The scope of the work would be narrowed as large subject areas are relinquished to bibliography; but in those specific areas in which local work is done, the subject specialist would be inclined to do a more thorough job--a job more nearly approximating the best work found in the best bibliographies, for lack of which he would be trying to compensate. He might indulge more freely in analytics for both journals and books, seek out the more ephemeral and peripheral materials, and dig into the primary sources. With any given potential it is possible to do much with few subjects or little with many subjects. We can have a shallow lake across a wide plain or a deep pool in a narrow valley. To the extent that breadth is no longer needed we can have depth.

Second, a change might be expected in the nature of the subject headings or classifications used. The approach of the central catalog department to the organization of knowledge is panoramic, that of the subject specialist is focal. The cataloger stands on a hill, views the world all around him, then makes a picture which is unrolled scene by scene before the spectator. The specialist goes down into the fields, selects a particular scene, then makes pictures of that scene from every angle--close-ups to which all the rest is background. He has a slant on the world, and

all he sees is oriented to his particular interest. In the
background he does see other specialties, but the whole is
arranged and interpreted from his point of view. So with
books, his arrangement or interpretation is different from
those of specialists in other fields; and none is like the cataloger's, except possibly the philosopher's. To the extent
that we can do without the panoramic, as far as subject
headings are concerned, we can develop the focal approach.
We can try to see the literature through the specialist's
eyes, use his language, and arrange things for his convenience.

Third, a more selective and discriminating treatment
of books might be expected. A general catalog department
tends to handle books uncritically, and with good reason.
Lacking the focal approach, it has no specific orientation
and therefore no criteria for evaluating them. The panoramic
method is by nature undiscriminating, since discrimination
involves reference to special purposes or needs. Those
needs would be more keenly felt and more readily defined in
the subject divisions, where every new book, journal, and
pamphlet could be examined with an eye for research in
progress, the requirements of the curriculum, and the interests of a known clientele.

And fourth, one further change--toward change itself.
The more intensive, focal, and discriminating a job becomes,
the more quickly it becomes obsolete. Again, there is a
price to pay for the value received. The price is temporal-
ity; the value is adaptability. The ideal of the stable, om-
nifarious catalog would be gone; that of the ephemeral and
individual would take its place.

Since decentralization might change the nature of subject cataloging, a corresponding change might be desirable
in the qualifications of those who do the work. Let us end
this discussion with a quick look at the manner in which the
library staff might be affected.

We have come to think of two general qualifications
of a good cataloger: a knowledge of catalog techniques and
subject or language competence. For the present objective,
which is the construction of a general catalog, we are probably right in assigning the greater value to techniques. A
good cataloger can get along in our present system without
unusual subject background, but a subject specialist can get
nowhere without a knowledge of cataloging. If there were,

however, no general subject catalog and if that part of cataloging were delegated to the subject divisions, the balance might tip in the other direction. A knowledge of cataloging techniques would still be important, but subject background would be indispensable. For the new objective, which would be intensive, focal, selective cataloging closely coordinated with bibliography, the emphasis would be reversed.

Catalogers would not be out of a job, however. They are already subject specialists to some degree and could pursue those interests further with profit and pleasure. As a group they are still one of the most able in the library profession, and they have long since been ready for change. If they are on the defensive now, it is only because they are afraid of being shelved. Our hypothetical organization would bring them out into the open and make their presence felt throughout the library system.

One of the attractive aspects of the decentralized plan is the possible redistribution of staff. We now have a heavy concentration of staff in the so-called technical departments, while in the service departments, especially the departmental libraries, the staff is thinly spread. Important service units are often left with no professional supervision at all. A very large part of our real professional know-how never reaches the reader in a direct personal way. In our hypothetical organization, some of the catalogers could be transferred to the subject divisions, where their cataloging abilities would be welcomed and where they could vary their work with service responsibilities. The central catalog staff would then be reduced to the size required for descriptive cataloging only.

Another shift, however, would probably occur from the general reference department, which would be discontinued, to the central bibliographic service, which would be combined with the catalog department into a new bibliography division. Some reference workers might become general bibliographers, others might be allocated to the subject divisions. The new bibliography division, then, might be almost as large as the original catalog department, although its functions would be quite different. This difference would be important to the professional outlook of the staff.

The functions of the new bibliography division would be narrower in one way and broader in others than those of the present catalog department. The delegation of subject cataloging and classification to the subject divisions might be regarded as a loss by some who stay on with the bibliography division, but the central catalogers or bibliographers would still have authority over the subject cataloging activities of the subject divisions. Also their sphere of interest would be extended to embrace the entire field of bibliography, and they would have specific responsibility for the operation of a service department. This service would bring them into direct contact with the reader. All in all, their opportunity would be substantially greater than now to make a distinguished contribution to the library program; and those who transferred to the subject divisions would have an equally good opportunity to extend their bibliographic horizons and to work directly with the reader.

References

1. Library Quarterly, XVIII (January, 1948), 24-32.
2. Cf. John J. Lund, "The Cataloging Process in the University Library: A Proposal for Reorganization," College and Research Libraries, III (1942), 212-18.
3. "Characteristics of the Research Literature Used by Chemists and Physicists in the United States. II," Library Quarterly, XIX (April, 1949), 126-27.
4. His "Subject Catalog Inquiry," as yet unpublished.
5. Library Quarterly, XX (April, 1950), 79-100.
6. Library Quarterly, XV (January, 1945), 49-74.

13. The Pacific Northwest Bibliographic Center

The Pacific Northwest Bibliographic Center[1] was founded in 1940 with a grant from the Carnegie Corporation; since the expiration of the grant it has been supported by the libraries of the region. It is owned by the Pacific Northwest Library Association and has always been located in the University of Washington Library at Seattle. The region served by the Center includes Washington, Oregon, Idaho, Montana, British Columbia, and Alaska.

At the time of its inception, the Center was conceived broadly as an agency of regional library cooperation, both to facilitate the exploitation of the existing resources of the region and to foster their future growth. This broad objective was pursued with vigor and imagination during the early years of the Center. Not only were the Union Catalog and the interlibrary loan services instituted but, concurrently, experiments with other devices of cooperation were undertaken: the surveyal and description of regional resources, bibliographic information services, joint purchasing, prevention of last copy discards, and specialization of fields of acquisition. Gradually, however, these other devices failed or receded into the background; only the Union Catalog and interlibrary lending flourished. Whereas in the beginning these services absorbed only part of the energy of the staff, in due course they absorbed nearly the whole of it. By 1957 the Center had become almost exclusively a clearinghouse for interlibrary loans.

While many librarians of the region are satisfied that the Center should continue to concentrate on the Union Cata-

---

Reprinted by permission from Libraries and Librarians of the Pacific Northwest, ed. Kroll. University of Washington Press, 1960, pp. 220-239.

log and interlibrary lending, there are those who regret that other significant parts of the original program have not also prospered. The conviction persists that the Center could, and should, contribute more profoundly in a wider variety of ways to the exploitation and enrichment of regional resources. Many have watched, for example, the growth of the Midwest Inter-Library Center, which is dedicated primarily to the enrichment of regional resources for research through programs of cooperative acquisition. The Midwest Inter-Library Center has no union catalog at all, but supports instead the National Union Catalog for the location of research materials. Some have noted that the emphasis since World War II on library cooperation has tended away from regional union catalogs and toward such acquisitional projects as the Farmington Plan. They have speculated about the implications of the expansion of the Library of Congress printed author catalog into a current printed National Union Catalog and about the eventual publication of the entire National Union Catalog, which might possibly render the regional union catalog obsolete.

In presenting an analysis of the Center's program, this report will consider its contribution, both present and potential, (a) toward the exploitation of existing resources and (b) toward the augmentation of those resources. It will conclude with a consideration of the organization, administration, and financial support of the Center.

The Exploitation of Resources

The Center, as noted above, now devotes itself almost exclusively to the exploitation of existing resources by means of interlibrary loans based on the Union Catalog.

Use of the Center for Interlibrary Loans

Use of the Center for the location and negotiation of interlibrary loans was analyzed for the calendar year 1956. Table 1 indicates that the libraries of Washington were responsible for about 65 per cent of the borrowing and lending through the Center. Oregon, with three-fifths the population of Washington, was responsible for about 15 per cent. Montana requested 8.5 per cent of the loans but supplied only 1.7 per cent of the books. Activity in Idaho, British Columbia, and Alaska was relatively small.

TABLE 1
INTERLIBRARY LOANS BY STATES AND PROVINCES, 1956

	Libraries Borrowing or Lending		Requests for Loans		Volumes Loaned	
	No.	Per Cent	No.	Per Cent	No.	Per Cent
Washington	114	37.6	7,670	64.7	6,480	66.5
Oregon	43	14.2	1,822	15.4	1,460	15.0
Montana	33	10.9	1,005	8.5	170	1.7
Idaho	10	3.3	465	3.9	360	3.7
British Columbia	12	4.0	406	3.4	300	3.1
Alaska	5	1.6	37	.3		
Other*	86	28.4	452	3.8	970	10.0
Total	303	100.0	11,857	100.0	9,740	100.0

*Includes 75 libraries within the region that used the Center infrequently

The public libraries of the entire region, as indicated by Table 2, requested 68.9 per cent of the loans and supplied 50.4 per cent of the books, while the academic libraries

TABLE 2
INTERLIBRARY LOANS BY TYPE OF LIBRARY, 1956

	Libraries Borrowing or Lending		Requests for Loans		Volumes Loaned	
	No.	Per Cent	No.	Per Cent	No.	Per Cent
Public	154	50.8	8,173	68.9	4,910	50.4
Academic	49	16.2	2,269	19.1	3,860	39.6
Special	14	4.6	963	8.1		
Other	86	28.4	452	3.8	970	10.0
Total	303	100.0	11,857	99.9	9,740	100.0

requested 19.1 per cent and loaned 39.6 per cent. Generally speaking, the academic libraries loaned nearly twice as many books as they borrowed, while the public libraries borrowed nearly twice as many as they loaned.

The larger academic libraries, however--those that are significantly engaged with research--borrowed heavily through other sources of interlibrary loans. In 1955-56 the University of Washington Library, for example, borrowed 1,759 books from libraries outside the region as compared with 599 borrowed from within. In 1956-57 the University of Oregon Library borrowed 431 from outside the region as compared with 480 from within, but of the latter only 257 were borrowed through the Center, the other 223 having been borrowed directly from other Oregon libraries. This phenomenon probably reflects a general deficiency in the resources of the region for research and the tendency of research libraries to operate on a national instead of a regional basis. The smaller academic libraries of the Pacific Northwest, on the other hand, do appear to rely almost wholly upon the Center for these services. The librarians of the State University of Montana, the University of Idaho, Idaho State College, and the College of Puget Sound, for example, reported that 90 per cent or more of their requests are handled by the Center.

A further breakdown of the data on use indicated that, while the academic libraries of Oregon requested almost as many loans (6.9 per cent) as those of Washington (7.1 per cent), the public libraries of Oregon requested only about one-seventh as many (7.3 per cent) as those of Washington (51.2 per cent). This difference in public library use appears to reflect the difference not only in population but also in the degree to which the state libraries satisfy the needs of the smaller public libraries within their jurisdictions. By general agreement the smaller libraries of both states send their requests for loans to their state libraries instead of directly to the Center, and the state libraries fill them if they can. In practice the Oregon State Library, which has a large and well developed collection, fills 90 per cent of the smaller public library requests of that state and refers only 10 per cent to the Center; the Washington State Library fills 60 per cent and refers 40 per cent to the Center. The larger public libraries of the region, such as Spokane, Portland, and Tacoma, send their requests directly to the Center, since their own resources are comparable to, or better than, those of the state libraries.

An analysis of use by income class also reflects the extent to which the requests of the smaller public libraries are diverted from the Center. The 102 participating public libraries with incomes of $25,000 or less, taken together, accounted for only 21 per cent of the requests handled by the Center. The fifty-two public libraries with incomes of more than $25,000 accounted for 48 per cent.

The practice of diverting the requests of the smaller public libraries to the state libraries and of transmitting them to the Center only when the state libraries cannot fill them is sound and should be extended. The Center can and should handle requests from any place in the region when its services are really needed, but the ordinary backstopping of the new, small, but growing public libraries that form the vanguard of the popular library movement is properly a state library function. It is the peculiar function of the Center to take over when other agencies, operating within their own jurisdictions, need interjurisdictional help. Also, in the long view, the most significant functions of the Center are likely to relate to the exploitation of the more unusual or unique resources of the region.

Recommendation: That interlibrary loan services to the smaller public libraries continue to be diverted as much as possible from the Center to state library or other local agencies, and that the Pacific Northwest Library Association encourage the further development of such agencies in the states and provinces of the region.

Certain generalizations about who uses the Center seem plausible on the basis of the 1956 data. The Center does not serve primarily either the small public libraries or the large research libraries. The former rely heavily upon the state libraries or other local agencies and send only their exceptional requests to the Center; the latter rely heavily upon other research libraries of the nation. The Center serves primarily the in-between group of both public and college libraries, to which the resources of the region are reasonably adequate for the supplementation of their own substantial collections.

The Negotiation of Interlibrary Loans

The Center not only supplies the location of books needed for interlibrary loan but also negotiates the loans. Once the librarian of any requesting library has submitted his request to the Center, he can forget about it until the book is delivered. The Center locates a copy or copies of the book and arranges for one of the holding libraries to send it to the requesting library. If a search outside the region is desired, the Center conducts that also. The Center takes care of all correspondence with the holding libraries and all reports to the requesting library up to the point at which the book is delivered. From there on the transaction becomes a normal interlibrary loan relationship between the holding and the requesting library.

Although the negotiation of loans by the Center is useful to and appreciated by the librarians of the region, there is reasonable doubt that it is worth the cost. The major part of the cost of any interlibrary loan is still borne directly by the two participating libraries, which must still keep their records complete, mail and return the books, and so on. The Center saves them mainly the writing of the requests to the holding libraries. On the other hand, the negotiation of these requests by the Center causes the Center to duplicate in large part the records of both participating libraries and to operate a complex system of reporting among them and between them and itself. The Center, in effect, becomes a third party to every negotiation. What would be a small additional burden to the requesting library therefore becomes a heavy burden to the Center. It is believed that the negotiation of loans is a job that could be efficiently done by the individual libraries of the region, just as it is done by most other libraries of the nation, and that the total cost to the region would be less if the Center, as a third party, were not involved.

It is also believed that the use of a multiple request form (possibly four-part) would facilitate the loan procedures. With such a form the Center could handle each request only once, yet report the locations to the requesting library, indicate the order in which the holding libraries should be approached, and pass on a copy of the request to the first holding library. Follow-up data and correspondence would not be processed by the Center. The requesting library would follow up, when necessary, directly with the holding libraries.

As a general principle, the Center ought not to provide services that the individual libraries can perform as well or as cheaply for themselves. The Center should concentrate its efforts upon services that the individual libraries cannot handle. The peculiar functions of the Center, in regard to interlibrary loans, are the locating of copies of the book and the equitable distribution of the lending burden among the holding libraries.

Recommendation: That the Center continue to supply locations for interlibrary loan, propose the order in which the holding libraries are to be approached, and transmit the requests to the first holding libraries, but that it discontinue all subsequent negotiations, correspondence, and record-keeping; and that it adopt a multiple request form for regional loans.

The Union Catalog

The Regional Union Catalog lists by author the holdings of forty libraries in the Pacific Northwest, the Library of Congress, and the John Crerar Library of Chicago. It consists of (a) a main catalog of 2,800,000 Library of Congress cards coded to show regional locations, (b) a main supplement of 1,200,000 uncoded cards (at the back of the trays in the main catalog) representing regional holdings for which no Library of Congress cards have yet been found in the main catalog, (c) a regional supplement of 263,800 uncoded, prefiled cards from the forty libraries and the John Crerar Library, and (d) a Library of Congress supplement of 236,250 prefiled Library of Congress depository cards. The main catalog is, in effect, a catalog of the Library of Congress that shows which titles are also held in the Pacific Northwest. The main supplement is a catalog of titles held in the region but which are not also held by the Library of Congress, or for which the Library of Congress has not yet supplied cards, or which simply have not yet been coded. The regional supplement is a catalog of titles held in the region but which have not yet been coded in the main catalog or, lacking Library of Congress cards, set aside in the main supplement. The search for a location of any title in the region may involve the checking of all three of these files.

The forty Pacific Northwest libraries whose holdings are recorded in the Union Catalog include public, academic, and special libraries. An analysis of the number of cards contributed by these libraries in relation to the number of volumes supplied for interlibrary loan as a result of those contributions suggests that a review of the selection of contributing libraries is needed. Certain libraries, such as a historical society library, should be covered even though their collections are entirely noncirculating, but others might be dropped which are infrequently called upon to lend books through the Center, either because they contain few uncommon items, are disadvantageously located, or both.

The pillars of the Union Catalog should continue to be the large public and academic libraries (a) with resources that are unique to the entire region, (b) with good basic collections for general service to their immediate localities, and (c) with organizations that can efficiently administer the lending procedures. Next in importance should be the special libraries that, because of their uniqueness, are significant regionally even though they may not be heavily used locally. All other libraries, regardless of type, should be excluded unless (a) their general collections help to fill a geographic gap in the lending system or (b) they own special collections of significance to the region. In the latter case, they could be asked to report to the Union Catalog only their acquisitions in these specialties. No library that merely duplicates in part a larger collection in the same locality should be included. Briefly, the objective should be twofold: to record all unique holdings regardless of location and to record duplicated holdings only in the degree necessary to distribute geographically the general burden of interlibrary lending.

Recommendation: That the selection of libraries that report holdings to the Union Catalog be revised, and that selective reporting of special collections in some libraries be adopted.

While the intelligible, systematic, and economical construction of the Union Catalog requires a consistent policy in the treatment of special types of materials, it was found that the contributing libraries report, for the most part, whatever is locally cataloged. Some libraries, for example, catalog government documents and report them; others do not. Some catalog and report serials; others do not. Some catalog microfilm, audio-visual materials, or manuscripts; others not. There is no consistency in the representation of special materials in the Union Catalog.

A consistent policy would require, first, decisions about the kinds of special materials that can best be covered by the Union Catalog, in view of both the nature of their use and the cataloging practices of the contributing libraries; and second, the adoption of programs for the coverage of other kinds of special materials by union lists or descriptions of collections. These decisions should then be adhered to by all contributing libraries. If they are not, the result will be extra work for the Center staff, incomplete utilization of regional resources, and unequal distribution of the interlibrary loan burden.

Recommendation: That a consistent policy be applied to the kinds of special materials that are recorded in the Union Catalog and to the kinds that are to be recorded or described by other methods.

Pacific Northwest Bibliographic Center

Although a major part of the entire effort of the Center is devoted to the maintenance of the Union Catalog, this work is far from current. The Library of Congress supplement and the regional supplement each contains over 230,000 cards, whereas 50,000 would probably be optimum for the purposes of prefiling. The entire main supplement of some 1,200,000 cards, which still await editing and coding, comprises 40 per cent of all the cards submitted on a current basis by the contributing libraries since the original catalog was constructed. At the present rate of editing and coding, it would take the Center staff forty to fifty years to catch up.

The continuing presence of this backlog is significant to the economy of the Center for several reasons. First, the unedited and uncoded titles, whether in the regional or the main supplements, exist frequently in as many as six or more cards per title, all but one of which would be discarded if the coding were completed. Arrearages in coding therefore inflate artificially the size of the Union Catalog. Second, since the unit cost of most processes connected with the Union Catalog, such as filing and searching for locations, increases with its size, the backlog also increases the cost of operating the Center. And third, the additional size of the catalog is costly of space and equipment, which are already at a premium. So, the larger the backlog the less able is the Center to eradicate it, because of the constant additional drain it places upon the Center's financial, physical, and human resources.

It is believed that this backlog might be brought under control if the use of the Library of Congress depository card catalog as the foundation of the Union Catalog were discontinued. The Library of Congress depository catalog was wisely adopted for this purpose when the Union Catalog was established, but since that time LC has published its cards in book form. For all general bibliographic purposes, and for the location of books at the Library of Congress, the book catalogs can now be used in place of the depository catalog. The coding process, moreover, would be facilitated by abandoning the policy of withholding regional cards in the main supplement until matching LC cards are found. Many of these cards have remained in the main supplement and have been searched and re-searched repeatedly ever since the Union Catalog was established. The elimination of the depository cards would require the direct use of the best regional cards in the main catalog without waiting for the depository cards.

It may be further noted that one and one-half staff members are now required just to file the depository cards, yet about one half of all cards in the main catalog are LC cards that show no regional locations. If these cards were withdrawn, both filing and searching costs would be reduced without detracting from the usefulness of the catalog for regional location purposes. The total bulk of the Union Catalog, including the LC supplement, would be reduced by about 1,600,000 cards, or about 36 per cent, with important savings in space and equipment. This, together with the elimination of the coding backlog, if that could also be achieved, would reduce the entire catalog possibly to about 2,000,000 cards, as contrasted with the present 4,500,000.

Opposed to the discontinuance of the LC depository catalog is the argument that the book catalogs are more difficult and costly to consult. Whereas the depository catalog presents all the data in a single alphabet in good-size type, the book catalogs scatter the data among several alphabets in type of suboptimum legibility. Also, the task of identifying titles and establishing new forms of author entry would be complicated, and the Union Catalog would gradually deteriorate in quality. There is substance to these arguments, yet almost all of the libraries in the country that once maintained current, complete depository catalogs have found it desirable to discontinue or curtail them because of the net savings in filing, space and furniture.[2]

Recommendation: That the LC depository card catalog be discontinued.

The recent expansion of the published LC author catalog into a National Union Catalog that shows selected locations in other libraries throughout the country raises questions about the future of the regional Union Catalog. If it becomes possible to locate current books in the Pacific Northwest by means of the National Union Catalog, and especially if the entire National Union Catalog, as it now exists in card form at Washington, D.C., were published, would the regional Union Catalog still be needed?

The answer appears to be yes, but within certain limits. The National Union Catalog is designed to serve primarily the interests of research, not the extension of the popular library movement. The Pacific Northwest Union Catalog serves both, but particularly the latter. The several regional locations in the National Union Catalog would not satisfy the general library needs of the Pacific Northwest for any but the older and less frequently used books.

An analysis of the interlibrary loans negotiated by the Center in 1956 showed that about 53 per cent were imprints dated 1940 or later and about 70 per cent 1930 or later. Thus, all but 30 per cent of the loans were of books published in the last twenty-six years. This means, for example, that if the regional Union Catalog were divided, like the National Union Catalog, between pre-1956 and later imprints, and if the entire National Union Catalog were eventually published, the pre-1956 regional catalog might be discarded by 1982. The 30 per cent burden of locating pre-1956 imprints might then be handled by the National Union Catalog, the 70 per cent burden of locating post-1956 imprints by the post-1956 regional catalog. If this hypothesis is correct, the regional Union Catalog need not be permanently cumulative; it would need only be a current catalog, to be replaced at intervals by cumulations of the National Union Catalog.

Recommendation: That consideration be given to the possibility of dividing the Union Catalog between pre-1956 (or other current date) and later imprints in order that the future of the Union Catalog might be coordinated with that of the National Union Catalog.

The Union Catalog and the interlibrary loan services are the principal methods now employed by the Center to exploit the existing resources of the region. In the earlier years of the Center additional methods were tried--ways of telling what materials are at hand, who has them, and where there is strength or weakness. John Van Male's Resources of Pacific Northwest Libraries: A Survey of Facilities for Study and Research (1943) is still a landmark in the Center's history.[3] It is believed that, if time and funds were available, the Center could again usefully supplement its Union Catalog services by engaging in the description of regional resources by collections, subjects, or forms of materials.

It is quite possible, for example, that the government document collections of the region could be treated more effectively by means of general description than in the Union Catalog. Manuscripts and archives are particularly well suited to general description. Separate union lists of serials and newspapers might be worth while. A number of librarians of the region have frequently proposed that the Center compile, or sponsor the compilation of, bibliographies based on regional resources and that it extend its bibliographic reference services.

Recommendation: That, as time and means become available, the Center resume and expand its earlier efforts to exploit the resources of the region by means not only of the Union Catalog and the interlibrary loan service but also of surveys and descriptions of resources, union lists, bibliographies, and bibliographic information services.

The Augmentation of Resources

Fostering the growth of the resources of the region, along with the preservation of existing resources, is the second broad objective of the Center, and in the long run this objective might well prove to be more important than the exploitation of existing resources, to which the Center has been devoted almost exclusively in recent years.

The present resources of the region are far from adequate for research; and insofar as the Center has failed to enrich those resources it has also failed to serve the best interests of research. The Center should be the spearhead of a major cooperative effort to enable the Pacific Northwest to take its proper place among the research centers in the country.

In the early days of the Center, the founders and directors did perceive in the region a peculiarly favorable opportunity for the orderly and economical development of the resources of the entire region by cooperative means. This perception found expression in a number of projects, some of which have long since been abandoned and none of which has borne important fruit. Concurrently, cooperative efforts in other parts of the country tended increasingly toward acquisitional programs, both national and regional. The Farmington Plan, the foreign newspaper microfilming, and other projects of the Association of Research Libraries and the establishment of the Midwest Inter-Library Center are notable examples. The example of other libraries of the country, together with the reasoning of the founders of the Center and the continuing clear need of regional library development, is cause to re-examine carefully this aspect of the Center's program.

In 1943, long before the Farmington Plan was instituted, the libraries of the Pacific Northwest, under the leadership of the Center, entered into a bold, imaginative, though perhaps too idealistic "Agreement for Regional Library Specialization."[4] The pact failed, although the objective and general method are still eminently sensible. Now that a number of years have passed, it is quite possible that a new pact, conceived along more modest and realistic lines, might succeed. Certainly it should be tried. Although the new pact should not be expected to accomplish too much, it should be designed to accomplish something, and it should bind no librarian to more than he is likely to be able to deliver.

Recommendation: That a new agreement for specialization of acquisitions in selected fields be negotiated.

More successful has been the program to prevent the discard of the last copies of titles owned in the region.[5] Early in the 1940's the librarians of the region agreed that, upon withdrawing their last copies of books, they would send lists or canceled catalog cards to the Center for checking in the Union Catalog. If the books proved to be the only copies in the region, they would be sent to specified libraries that had agreed to preserve those in selected fields. Many libraries still submit their lists, but others protest that they are merely asked to store trash. Among the fifty or so participating libraries are many small public and college libraries to which the goal of preserving infrequently used materials for research is more or less alien.

The project is basically sound, but it is suggested that the responsibility for preserving these discards be reassigned to only a few research libraries instead of being widely distributed among a large number of libraries of various sizes and types. It is also suggested that the possibility be explored of submitting the lists directly to the appropriate research libraries, instead of first to the Center. The research libraries might then make their selections on the basis of their own holdings and might save the Center a substantial checking job. This procedure would sometimes result in the preservation of more than one "last" copy, but there could be no harm in that.

Recommendation: That responsibility for the preservation of last copies be reassigned to a small number of research libraries, and that these libraries agree upon an objective set of rules about the kinds of materials that need not be preserved; also, that the possibility be studied of having the discarding libraries submit their lists directly to the appropriate research libraries without having the lists checked in the Union Catalog.

A recent report of the Pacific Northwest Library Association Committee on Bibliography concluded that a cooperative storage library in the Pacific Northwest would not be needed for possibly twenty or twenty-five years.[6] This conclusion, however, does not necessarily imply that the Center should not own and hold selected bibliographic or research materials on behalf of the region if, for any reason, they are not being acquired by one of the individual libraries or could be made more generally useful at the Center. The Midwest Inter-Library Center, for example, is acquiring on microfilm such materials as foreign newspapers, early American imprints (Evans), and large collections of early literary works. It is not suggested that the Center should ever acquire anything that any of the individual libraries does acquire and makes generally available, but it is pointed out that a firm policy of nonacquisition by the Center could result in failure to take advantage of certain kinds of acquisitional opportunities that are essentially cooperative in both origin and utility.

It is also pointed out that, whether or not these special materials are housed at the Center, the staff should ideally be in a position to keep up with all important cooperative developments in the acquisitional field, to evaluate them for regional purposes, to take the initiative in assuring that needed materials are acquired, one way or another, and to share with other regional and national agencies the responsibility for proposing and promoting new acquisitional projects. One of the most valuable services that the Center could perform would be to serve as a clearinghouse for information, negotiation, decision, and action about every broad kind of acquisitional opportunity.

Recommendation: That the Center serve as a clearinghouse for information, negotiation, and decision about all kinds of acquisitional opportunities of regional import, and that present policy be revised to enable the Center to acquire and house special materials for the region when such action would clearly advance the interests of the region.

Pacific Northwest Bibliographic Center

Organization, Administration, and Finance

According to Article VII of the bylaws of the Pacific Northwest Library Association:

> The responsibility for the administration of the Pacific Northwest Bibliographic Center shall be vested in a Board of Managers consisting of elected members, one from each state and province actively represented in this Association; and the director of the library housing the Pacific Northwest Bibliographic Center, and the President of this Association, who shall be ex officio member of the Board of Managers with full voting rights. [7]

The managers from all states and provinces are therefore elected by the PNLA membership at large. The term of office is three years, with terms staggered for continuity. The board elects its own chairman annually and reports annually to the association. The director of the Center serves ex officio as secretary to the board but has no vote. The director is employed by the board.

While this pattern is in accord with the democratic spirit of the PNLA, it does not assure the best choice of managers inasmuch as the members of one state or province may not be informed about the best qualified persons from another. Election by the membership at large places responsibility for the Center not only upon the libraries that participate in and finance its services but also and equally upon those that do not. The libraries that do support the Center are not represented, as institutions, in the administration of the Center. The present board, being small, does not provide for wide participation in policy making for the Center and, as presently constituted geographically, is unable to maintain close working relationships with the Center.

Recommendation: That the board of managers be replaced by a large council to consist of representatives of the libraries that subscribe to the support of the Center and by an executive committee elected by and from the council.

The entire council could meet annually to transact its business and review the program of the Center. The executive committee could meet quarterly or even monthly in order to provide closer, more continuous leadership. Such leadership is urgently needed. The Center staff, being largely absorbed by routine responsibilities and working under the handicap of overwhelming arrearages, cannot be expected to attend adequately to the solution of many internal problems, to develop new ideas, to keep pace with recent developments in library cooperation, or to survey continuously the bibliographic needs of the region.

Recommendation: That the proposed council, through its executive committee and other working committees, participate actively in the formulation of policy and the solution of specific problems, and assume a position of leadership in program development and promotion.

The Center staff is not only inadequate in size but also suffers too much turnover, especially in the clerical ranks. Of the four file clerks, all paid at the minimum annual rate of $2,660, two had been with the Center only a few months.

Recommendation: That at least two of the positions of file clerk be upgraded in order to attract and keep able assistants and to provide for the advancement of beginning assistants.

If possible, the size of the staff should be increased. Savings in the housekeeping activities of the Center--savings that might arise from the discontinuance of the LC depository catalog and of the negotiation of interlibrary loans--could enable the staff to catch up in due course with its present backlog. But a larger staff will be needed if the Center is again to expand its program into other areas of library cooperation.

An examination of the present formula for support of the Center and of the present subscriptions in relation to the use of the Center suggests that several methods might be used to increase its financial resources. In 1956, for example, the libraries of Washington provided a little more than half of the entire support of the Center but requested 64.7 per cent of all loans, the subscription per request being $1.17. Those of Oregon provided 26.3 per cent of the support, but requested only 15.4 per cent of the loans, at $2.51 per request. British Columbia and Alaska paid $3.01 and $6.39 per request, respectively. The mean was $1.47 per request. The librarians of Washington could, and probably would be willing to, pay a larger subscription. This might take the form of weighting the formula by states or of

Pacific Northwest Bibliographic Center

negotiating a special subscription by the Washington State Library on behalf of the public libraries of the state.

The public libraries of the region, which provided 66.4 per cent of the support, requested 68.9 per cent of the loans at $1.42 per request. The academic libraries subscribed 31.6 per cent of the support at $2.43 per request. The special libraries had practically a free ride at $.36 per request. The public libraries could well be asked to pay more in relation to the academic libraries, and the special libraries should certainly be required to cover the full cost of their own requests.

By income class, the large libraries (over $25,000 income) subscribed 85.8 per cent of the support, requested 63.2 per cent of the loans at $2.00 per request. The medium-sized libraries ($5,000 to $25,000 income) subscribed 10.7 per cent at $.88 per request, and the small libraries (under $5,000 income) paid only $.48 per request. There is the possibility that the medium-sized libraries in particular could justifiably pay more in order to narrow the wide gap between them and the large libraries.

It is believed, therefore, that the income of the Center could be very appreciably and equitably increased. An immediate goal of $25,000 per year as contrasted with $17,000 in 1956, would seem altogether reasonable. And if the Center could re-embark upon new and imaginative programs for the exploitation and augmentation of resources, it is further possible that foundation support might again be obtained. The new Council on Library Resources, for example, might well be receptive to any promising experiments in the regional organization of library resources and services.

Recommendation: That the income of the Center be increased and that attention be given to the following possible methods: (1) weighting the public library formula by states and provinces in order to reflect local differences in demands upon the Center, or negotiating a special subscription from the Washington State Library; (2) raising the public library rates in relation to those of the academic; (3) revising upward the rates applied to Class B (income $5,000 to $25,000) libraries; (4) promoting additional paying memberships from all types of libraries, including special libraries; and (5) soliciting foundation grants.

The Center has always been hospitably housed in the University of Washington Library, to the mutual benefit of the university and the Center, but additional space is a prime need. When the university is able to expand its library, it is to be hoped that more adequate quarters can be provided. The new quarters should be separate but not distant from the main circulation rotunda; they should give the Center a place of its own without inconveniencing the staffs of either the Center or the library.

In a very real sense the library's hospitality and generosity have made the Center's existence possible. The library has always provided free quarters for the Center, together with all necessary equipment and supplies. The Center owns nothing--no desks, typewriters, chairs, or catalog cases--except the cards in the Union Catalog itself. It depends entirely upon the library's bibliographic equipment, including the Library of Congress book catalogs. The subsidy even includes a full-time clerk.[8]

Yet this extraordinary dependence may not be altogether desirable. The Center should be an independent regional enterprise, wherever it may be housed. And the budget of the Center should reflect all costs--space, utilities, equipment and supplies, janitorial services, and so on--in order that the library's subsidy may be fully known and credited.

Recommendation: That the University of Washington Library plan separate quarters for the Center as part of its building program, and that the Center's budget express all costs, including all the subsidies now provided by the library.

Conclusion

The Center is a valuable service to the region, but it would be still more valuable if it could again embark upon a broader, more imaginative program for the exploitation and enrichment of the regional resources. To do so it would need to reduce certain housekeeping activities to the minimum consistent with the purposes of the Center and, in addition, to expand its income in order to catch up on routine work and leave time for additional creative projects. While the present program of the Center serves well the interlibrary loan needs of the public and college libraries, the research interests of the region require, in particular, that new programs of cooperative acquisition be developed. To this end

Pacific Northwest Bibliographic Center

more active participation of the subscribing libraries in policy formulation and the administration of the Center is urgently needed. Leadership should be vested in a working executive committee elected by and from a large council of representatives of the libraries that actually subscribe to the support of the Center.

References

1. A summary of the full survey report, "The Pacific Northwest Bibliographic Center; a Survey," July, 1957 (mimeographed). Sponsored jointly by the board of managers of the Center and the Library Development Project. The consultant visited the Center July 8 to 19, 1957, examined its operations, looked at its records, talked with the staff, and interviewed twenty-five prominent librarians of Oregon, Washington, Idaho, Montana, and British Columbia. He also reviewed in large part the literature pertaining to the Center and to other such centers in the United States and abroad. Special assistance was received from Ralph Esterquest, a former director of the Center and recently director of the Midwest Inter-Library Center in Chicago, and from George Schwegmann, Jr., chief of the Union Catalog Division of the Library of Congress.
2. George Piternick, "Library of Congress Depository Catalog Questionnaire; a Summary of Answers" (University of California General Library, Catalog Department, Berkeley, May 31, 1957; mineographed).
3. John Van Male, Resources of Pacific Northwest Libraries: A Survey of Facilities for Study and Research (Seattle: Pacific Northwest Library Association, 1943).
4. "Proceedings of the Conference on Library Specialization," PNLA Quarterly, VIII (January, 1944), 57.
5. "Standing Committee Reports: Bibliography," PNLA Quarterly, XI (October, 1946), 35.
6. PNLA Committee on Bibliography, "A Library Storage Center for the Pacific Northwest" (Seattle, 1952; dittoed).
7. "Constitution of the Pacific Northwest Library Association: Article VII, Pacific Northwest Bibliographic Center," PNLA Quarterly, XVII (October, 1952), 64.
8. Prior to October, 1956, the University of Washington Library provided the Center with the services of one

full-time and one half-time clerk; this was reduced to one full-time clerk in October, 1956. In September, 1957, following this survey, another full-time clerk was assigned to the Center, making a total of two full-time clerks provided by the library. As of January, 1958, the university provided the services of one full-time and one half-time clerk.

14. A Dream in Action: The California Library Network Plan

I was much pleased with the invitation to join you today.[1] I could not have refused even if I had had a good reason, because I view the evolution of Black Gold, as a cooperative public library system, into TIE, as a booming multitype of library system, to be one of the most promising recent developments in California librarianship. What you have done is fully consistent with, and exemplary of, the California Library Network master plan. You are a model for the entire state. I wanted to join you today if only to congratulate you and to wish you well.

The growth of TIE since 1969, and that was only four years ago, has been remarkable. Especially remarkable has been the wide range of types of libraries that have joined you, from special and institutional libraries, through school and community college libraries, and public and private four-year college libraries, to the University of California at Santa Barbara. Whatever problems you might have, I'm sure you must feel a great deal of pride in what has been accomplished. I hope you will also stop to think once in a while--when, possibly, the drudgery of interlibrary loan forms, or lost books, or unanswerable reference questions gets you down--that you are in the vanguard of the evolution of new concepts and institutional forms of library service. There is behind what you are doing a set of ideas that need to be kept in mind and reaffirmed from time to time.

This set of ideas is synthesized in the California Library Network plan,[2] especially in the statement of "basic concepts and goals." These are very long-term, almost dream-like goals. When a draft of the master plan was

---

Reprinted by permission from the California Librarian, January 1974, pp. 18-25.

first considered, I wrote to the CLA Council: "I tend to think of it as a sort of wide-angle picture in the mind, a picture that hopefully might become widely shared by California librarians and that might fix our eyes on the same horizon. The goals themselves are highly idealistic.... They are probably not capable of ever being fully achieved. But the practical obstacles to full achievement do not invalidate the goals. Our success is still to be measured by the distance we have traveled down the road, even if the road has no end."

O. K., you have started down that road. What I say to you today is that, whether you fully realize it or not, those ideas are very practical, down-to-earth, everyday concerns of TIE.

One of these ideas is that the total library collections of the state--or the country, or even the world--should be viewed as a public resource. Here is the language of the California Library Network plan.

> The tremendous growth and diversification of recorded information has far outreached the capacity of any man or all men to learn and remember. The more advanced the society and the greater the totality of learning, the greater is man's dependence upon records for access to that learning. The ability of man to save written words, sounds, and pictures, and other symbols for future recall upon demand is one of his greatest achievements. In both the arts and the sciences, the cumulated product of that achievement has now become a general cultural asset of the greatest significance. Unlike oil, water, forests, or other natural resources, the record of man's learning is a high refinement of civilization itself--a refinement that is crucial to the continuing growth of advanced peoples.... <u>The Master Plan aims to strengthen, organize, and exploit the total recorded information resource in the universal public interest.</u>

Those are highfalutin words, but I think they are for real, and I hope you do too; and I want to see the connection between them and what you are doing right here in TIE. Your stock-in-trade <u>is</u> the general cultural asset, this late high refinement of civilization. Within your geographical boundaries, and reaching beyond when needed, you <u>are</u>

A Dream in Action

viewing your separate libraries as a collective resource to be used by anybody and everybody; and you're working hard at it. There is nothing in the master plan, by the way, that even suggests a physical centralization of library resources in some kind of "library supermarket." Not at all. But there is the suggestion, which you are observing, that libraries are no longer for the exclusive use of single clienteles. The physical book--the artifact--is indeed the property of some institution, private or public; but its content is to be shared. Once any book has been published, its content is public; and it is our job as librarians to see to it that, within reasonable contraints, that part of the content that is of interest to anybody is made available to him.

The second idea in the master plan is two-pronged. It says,

> All people have the right to have access to the total library resource, according to their individual needs. Yet, at present, there is immense unevenness in the quality, quantity, and availability of library resources and services throughout the state, because of varying constraints--geographical, social, economic and educational--on local library development.

These inequalities are dramatic. I totted them up in 1967 when I was doing a study for the State Library,[3] and I found that the greater Los Angeles region of the state had 43 percent of all books in California libraries (all types of libraries, except elementary school) and that the East and South Bay region had 31 percent, totaling 74 percent in those two areas. In sharp contrast, the North Mountain region had one percent, the lower San Joaquin Valley region had three percent, and the Santa Barbara Coast area had 4.5 percent. This is your region, and it includes the University of California at Santa Barbara. What you do with this 4.5 percent is another story--and a splendid one. But my emphasis here is on the _individual_ anywhere and his access to to the _100 percent._ I have asserted on a number of occasions, and I now reaffirm, my conviction that the individual in Santa Barbara, whether student, businessman, prisoner, engineer, lawyer, or child--or the reader in Chico, Etna, Modoc, or Railroad Flat--has, as an individual, the same full range of library needs as his counterpart who lives in San Francisco or Los Angeles. And I believe that this whole business about "books per capita" is an outrageous fallacy in the perception of the peoples' need for library resources and in the allocation of library funds.

In TIE you at least ameliorate this outrage. So you have only 4.5 percent of California's library resources, but you at least try to make sure that you share that percentage among individuals in all walks of life; and you have created an institutional structure by means of which you can call upon the resources of the San Francisco and Los Angeles areas.

This is a good beginning. It is the beginning of times when anybody in the Santa Barbara Coast region can get reasonable equity of access to the totality of the recorded, public information resource, regardless of where it is located. The master plan generalizes this notion by saying: the plan "aims to insure that, insofar as possible, all people have free, realistic, and convenient access to all library resources and services that might enrich their lives, regardless of the accident of their residences or the economic conditions of their local governments."

Correlatively, the master plan also says that, "by extending the resources available to local libraries," it "aims to help libraries respond more sensitively to the special needs of all sectors of the communities they serve." This is a cut into the tradition of libraries that are attuned to service mainly to the middle class, educated, white, Christian elite. We know now that there are other people, and that these people are important. They have library and information needs too, even if they don't recognize the library as a place to satisfy them. There are the non-readers, who might be reached by other media, or by other kinds of information that our libraries do not provide. There are the prisoners, the blind, the infirm, and all down the line of people in our society who do not share the privileges of it, and haven't the least interest in what we, as librarians, might view as proper and uplifting, or scholarly, or patriotic, or artistic, or perhaps just consistent with a self-serving theory of book selection. These people--all people--need to be reached, and they need to be reached on their own terms and in ways for which they are ready, and to which they can respond--emotionally, socially, and educationally.

So, the individual's right to access to that part of the total library resource that is potentially useful to him, and

A Dream in Action

the library's responsibility for providing appropriate, or relevant, styles of service to individuals in all walks of life, are central, long-term goals. This is really a tough one, but I can see that TIE and Black Gold are making progress here too. There is, for example, the Black Gold's outreach program, to which TIE contributes, for persons in prisons and jails, detention homes, hospitals and rest homes, and for Spanish speaking children and adults.

The doing of these things--control of the total information resource in the general public interest, provision of equal access to that resource by individuals of all kinds everywhere, and sensitivity in the styles of service to different social groups--requires the evolution of cooperative forms of library organization and service. I will add, parenthetically, that the powers of modern computing and telecommunications technologies require absolutely cooperative forms of library organization and service for their utilization. But that's another story. My point now is simply that none of the goals I have described can conceivably be reached without cooperative library systems and networks. Again, you are in the vanguard.

But you, as do other librarians the country over, operate under a system in which libraries are conceived as local institutions, serving specialized clienteles and supported by local funds. The urge toward local self-sufficiency and autonomy is still compelling; and the sharing of resources and services--that is, of combined resources and services to all kinds of people--is still marginal to our traditional system. We are still legally and institutionally locked into a political pattern that militates against universal access to the total library resource. If you don't believe this, consider the present public policy of both our state and federal governments toward library support.

What we're really looking for is a legal and institutional form of library service that breaks out of the constraints of local political jurisdictions. The idea of independent, locally self-sufficient programs should gradually give way to that of more dependent participation in regionally, or nationally, sufficient programs. If state and national information networks were ever to become fully effective, local libraries and information centers would have to be redesigned as selective inlets to and outlets from those networks. The specifications, for example, of local acquisitional policy would need to be modified to reflect a new balance between resources that should be acquired at home and those that should be acquired only upon demand from other levels of network service. If the networks ever should in fact deliver the goods promptly at local service points, the long-term effects on the nature of local libraries and information agencies would be profound indeed.

Now, we have assumed that networking requires state and/or federal funding as well as local funding. The California Library Network plan says that "state and federal funds are especially needed, and appropriate, for the development and operation of the system and network centers and the resource and research libraries, whose services cross local and type of library boundaries in order to extend and equalize library services to all people." There is no mention here of state or federal aid for the operation of local libraries themselves within their own jurisdictions. Only aid for system and network operations. This doctrine was confirmed by the State Library, the University of California, the State University and College, the Community College, and the School systems of California in a report to the State Senate as requested by Senate Resolution 226.[4] It was also incorporated last year into the aborted Senate Bill 530, which was to have become the California Library Network Act of 1972.

So, we have had a strong commitment, and we still have, to government support for system and network operations.

But now state and federal funds are both being withdrawn. The basic, local tax support for public libraries has been limited in California by SB 90, and revenue sharing is still a big question mark as far as libraries are concerned. Academic and other types of libraries are also hurting badly.

What do we do? Keep trying, I guess, while hunting for new angles, new approaches to library funding. The CLA/CIL Government Relations Committee is now working on new state legislation, and the ALA Committee on Legislation is restudying the concepts of federal aid in relation to state and local funding. The National Commission on Libraries and Information Science has requested proposals for a basic analysis of alternative patterns for financing public libraries.

A Dream in Action

My vote is certainly for not throwing in the sponge, or letting any of the existing library systems die. Automation will in many cases be delayed. Some services will have to be curtailed. But let's carry on with whatever tools are available. And in doing so, let's remember that, while the full flowering of a California Library Network will indeed require state funding, the whole structure must rest upon the strength of the cooperative spirit at the grass roots level--the level of TIE--, and this is something that cannot be bought with state or federal funds.

The grass roots creation of cooperative library systems is the foundation of network development. Nothing could ever come out of a state or national information network without the educated experience and willingness of librarians at the local level. How else could the goods ever be delivered to the businessman in Petaluma, the teacher in Placerville, the mechanic in Barstow, or the patient in Vacaville? Let's not let go of any of our cooperative library systems. They are the basic institutional forms upon which the California Library Network is being built and will continue to be built, with or without extra-local funds.

There are two final goals of the California Library Network plan that should also be reaffirmed in troubled times. These have to do with institutional and professional opportunities and responsibilities.

The first of these says, "Libraries of all types and their parent institutions, private as well as public, are indebted in large degree to the society that sustains them. In recent years[5] federal and state funds have become widely available to school, college and university, and institutional libraries, as well as public libraries, and to special libraries through research and development contracts with business and industrial firms. Beyond these and other considerations of public aid is the elemental obligation of all institutions in a free society to justify their privileges and share their assets with the people of that society. <u>The Master Plan aims to give all types of libraries, private as well as public, a means of discharging through voluntary cooperative action their obligations to the larger communities from which they derive their existence.</u>"

There might be a tendency in hard times for libraries, or their parent institutions, to retreat from this position--to withdraw into themselves and again to seek self-sufficient

services to an exclusive clientele. In some instances such
a retreat might be necessary; but if so, it should not be
done as a matter of principle. By forsaking their broader
obligations to society, libraries could do double harm--first,
to others who would benefit from their resources and, second, to their own clienteles who would lose access to larger
and richer resources elsewhere. I'm proud that the University of California, for all its budgetary traumas, is not
closing its library doors to the people of the state, but
keeps them open and continues to search for realistic ways
to open them more widely.   U. C. Santa Barbara is an excellent example. Perhaps more in hard times than in any
other, it is essential to keep the principle clearly in mind--
that no library can go it alone--any type or size of library--, the principle that there is an obligation to readers
to keep the pipe lines open, and that there is a broad social
purpose in doing so. The pipe lines might get rusty, the
flow of information sluggish, and the information itself muddied; but keep the lines open.

  Let me put the point this way. If we really believe
that there is a body of recorded knowledge that is, in its
totality, a public resource; if we really believe that people
everywhere, regardless of their bank accounts or places of
residence, should have equitable access to that resource; if
we really believe that such access should be tailored to their
individual needs; if we really believe that our locally supported, more or less autonomous libraries cannot on their
own give to their clienteles such access to the total resource, and that only by means of cooperative systems and
networks could such access be given; if we really believe
that local libraries, and their parent institutions, do in fact
have a broad responsibility for service to the society from
which they derive their existence; and if we really believe
that librarians, as professionals, have responsibilities not
only to the institutions for which they work but also to the
whole society; then there could be no question about the future directions of our professional mission.

  TIE is going strong, and again I congratulate you.
You have broken down old barriers, old habits of thought
about what you were doing, why, and for whom. Please do
hang in there, regardless of the paucity of federal or state
funding. Such funding would help, of course; but the lack
of it should not compromise the social and professional goals
you exemplify. You are the best argument in the whole
state for the renewal of state and federal funding for library

services in California. Try to remember this while smudging forms, crawling over catalogs and bibliographies, pushing book trucks around, or bungling telephone calls. Try to remember that all such things are being done for purposes that might sometime bring to fulfillment a dream--a dream that is realistic, socially responsive, and professionally responsible, and that might lead to a new alignment of library service structures.

The really big game here is the establishment of public policy about the significance of the total, recorded information resource to all sectors of society and about the role of libraries in the organization and dissemination of that resource. We lost the last round in California last year, but the ideas are not lost; and if these ideas should become compelling in the future, the reason will be the example set all over the country by such systems as Black Gold and TIE.

The final goal of the master plan has to do, not with libraries as institutions, but with librarians. It says, "librarians and information specialists must extend their professional loyalties beyond their own institutional clienteles to society at large. It is essential that each librarian's primary responsibility be to his own clientele, but it is also recognized that the pursuit of total library services through cooperative action requires a realistic commitment to the broader social goals of the library profession. <u>The Master Plan aims to provide channels through which librarians can meet their professional obligations to the whole society.</u>"

This means that librarians, if they are truly members of a profession, are not just employees of a particular institution to which their loyalties are exclusively devoted. My library right or wrong? Not at all! If librarianship is a profession with a broad social mission, then these local institutional loyalties must be compromised in the general social interest. I have long suspected that one of the greatest of all obstacles to interlibrary service to the whole society is the excessive, parochial commitment of librarians to the institutions for which they work. Documentalists and information scientists have never shared this disability. They do take a broader look at society's needs for information and at the processes by which that information can be supplied. I wish we could come someday to say, in all of our cooperative agreements, not that each library must first of all preserve its autonomy but that the interests of its clientele require primary dedication to cooperative library systems, only by means of which that clientele can in fact be fully served.

References

1. This is an edited version of a speech that was taped at the Annual Workshop of the Total Interlibrary Exchange (TIE) at Santa Barbara, May 18, 1973. Its purpose was to show how TIE exemplifies the goals of the California Library Network master plan. Since most of what was said there is also applicable to other cooperative library systems in California, the speaker was urged to prepare a version for publication.
2. CLA Newsletter, December 1971.
3. Interlibrary Cooperation under Title III of the Library Services and Construction Act.... (Sacramento, Ca: The State Library, 1967).
4. CLA Newsletter, Nov. 1972.
5. This is sounding out-of-date already.